Introduction to Aboriginal Health and Health Care in Canada

Vasiliki Douglas, PhD, MA, BA, BSN, is an instructor at the College of New Caledonia, Prince George, British Columbia, in the School of Health Sciences. Dr. Douglas holds a PhD in History of Nursing and Anthropology (University of Alberta, Edmonton, Alberta), a BA and MA in Ancient History/Classics (McGill University, Montreal, Quebec) and a BSN (University of British Columbia, Vancouver, British Columbia). She is a member of the International Network for Circumpolar Health Research. She was a Natural Sciences and Engineering Research Council of Canada (NSERC) ArcticNet Postdoctoral Fellow (UNBC/2009–2011); and has won multiple research grants to study and present on Indigenous Health Research (Canada and Norway). Dr. Douglas has publications focusing on Inuvialuit and Inuit traditional medical care: midwifery, food/cultural security, reconciling traditional knowledge, and climate change (*International Journal of Circumpolar Health, Nursing Inquiry, Alaska Medicine*). She is the principal investigator on a current research project: "Food Security, Ice, Climate and Community Health: Climate Change Impact on Traditional Food Security in Canadian Inuit Communities." Dr. Douglas speaks three languages including French and Greek and has studied Latin and Inuktitut.

Introduction to Aboriginal Health and Health Care in Canada

Bridging Health and Healing

Vasiliki Douglas, PhD, MA, BA, BSN

SPRINGER PUBLISHING COMPANY
NEW YORK

Springer Publishing Company, LLC
11 West 42nd Street
New York, NY 10036
www.springerpub.com

Acquisitions Editor: Margaret Zuccarini
Production Editor: Michael O'Connor
Composition: Newgen Imaging

ISBN: 978-0-8261-1797-7
e-book ISBN: 978-0-8261-1799-1

13 14 15 16 17 / 5 4 3 2 1

Library of Congress Cataloging-in-Publication Data
Douglas, Vasiliki Kravariotis.
  Introduction to aboriginal health and health care in Canada : bridging health and healing / Vasiliki Douglas.
    p. ; cm.
  Includes bibliographical references and index.
  ISBN 978-0-8261-1797-7 — ISBN 978-0-8261-1799-1 (e-book)
  I. Title.
  [DNLM: 1. Minority Health—Canada. 2. Ethnic Groups—ethnology—Canada. 3. Health Services, Indigenous—Canada. 4. Minority Groups—Canada. 5. Transcultural Nursing—methods—Canada. WA 300 DC2]
  RA563.M56
  362.1089'00971—dc23   2013011533

Special discounts on bulk quantities of our books are available to corporations, professional associations, pharmaceutical companies, health care organizations, and other qualifying groups. If you are interested in a custom book, including chapters from more than one of our titles, we can provide that service as well.

For details, please contact:
Special Sales Department, Springer Publishing Company, LLC
11 West 42nd Street, 15th Floor, New York, NY 10036–8002
Phone: 877–687-7476 or 212–431-4370; Fax: 212–941-7842
E-mail: sales@springerpub.com

Printed in the United States of America by Bang Printing.

Contents

Preface

ORIGINS OF THIS TEXT

Pedagogical Gap

This book has its origins in my experience teaching Aboriginal health to nursing students. When I began I was aware that there was a large and rapidly growing body of research on Aboriginal health. I was, however, surprised to find that there was no textbook specifically written to introduce nursing students to this important field. The pedagogical gap this presented was one that I found hard to fill, and in conversation with others in the field, found that my experience was common among my fellow instructors.

There is broad agreement that nursing students need a dedicated textbook on Aboriginal health in Canada. As schools of nursing increasingly adopt the Canadian Nursing Association's recommendations to fully integrate Aboriginal health into their curricula, the lacuna left without such a text becomes only more obvious.

SUGGESTIONS BY STUDENTS

I have now taught Aboriginal Health to nursing students for half a decade and the structure of this book reflects both my experience teaching and the suggestions of many students for improvements in course structure and content. They have been my proofreaders and editors from well before this project was no more than a vague idea through its development into a reality. I am extremely grateful to them for their support and encouragement and the excellent feedback they offered when I ran many of the concepts I developed past them.

Personal Experiences of Aboriginal Health Issues
and Perspectives on Health and Wellness

My doctoral research concerned the development of community midwifery programs in the Canadian Arctic. My fieldwork there, and the hospitality and assistance I experienced from Inuit, nurses, administrators and physicians, did much to nurture my interest in Canadian Aboriginal health. More importantly, my observations of how Inuit residents and midwives interacted with each other led me to develop the concept of epistemological accommodation, which is the theoretical core of this book.

PURPOSE OF THIS TEXT

Nursing Students and Instructors

This text is intended primarily to provide nursing students with an accessible guide to the health of Canadian First Nations, Métis and Inuit—the Aboriginal peoples of Canada. Most nurses practising in Canada will encounter Aboriginal patients in the course of their careers, indeed for some the majority of their patients will be Aboriginal. It is important for these and future professionals to understand the range of cultural expression that comprises Aboriginal culture and society in Canada today. It is important to be mindful that some Aboriginal patients may participate in traditional culture, while some may not. However, most Aboriginal people in Canada do share certain cultural tropes that may differ from those of the general population, and it is important for health care professionals to be aware of these differences. Not only is it important for the professionals to be aware that they may exist for their patients but it is also important to understand that it is incumbent upon them to provide appropriate, culturally safe care without losing sight of their own professional standards.

For the increasing number of nursing students and future professionals who are Aboriginal, this textbook provides an explanation of how their values and worldview may differ from those of their colleagues but can still be accommodated within the profession. This text also, I hope, gives a sense that Aboriginal health is a concern in Canada, that both governments and individuals, including many nurses, are working to improve the health and well-being of Canada's native peoples. This is important, as health and wellness are areas of primary concern for individuals and for communities. This concern is particularly poignant for Aboriginal communities, given the disruptive consequences of the progression of events contributing to the effects of acculturation and for the relationship of health to physical, emotional, mental and spiritual well-being. More acute than the concern for health among the dominant (non-Aboriginal) population, the centrality of it within the Aboriginal population is reflective of its potential for healing. It is recognized ultimately as a contingent to the very survival of Aboriginal culture in Canada.

The health of a population is determined by the value ascribed to it by society. Community health does not merely hinge on the absence of disease, though history has illustrated how epidemics and disease patterns are responsible for the downfall of communities, peoples and empires from many parts of the world, old and new. In the immediate context of our modern Canadian health care system, the delivery of health care to our Aboriginal peoples is important simply because vast resources are dedicated to a relatively small population without the benefit of a relatively good improvement in the health outcomes of the same people relative to the general Canadian population. In other words, the study of health and well-being of the Aboriginal population in Canada merits an analytical and heterodox approach to reconfiguring the societal, historical, institutional and professional interests involved in producing improved health outcomes for this vulnerable population.

Questioning the status of health and the delivery of health care to Aboriginal populations is synonymous with challenging our ideas and approach to contributing to and interfacing with the recipients of nursing care to produce improved health. Questions about the role of nursing in the evolving Canadian health care system are increasingly made to favor open and innovative approaches to redefining and reinterpreting health care policy and programs. Such questions can open new approaches to more personal interpretations of the relationship among health, health care and Aboriginal peoples and to a more macro and health system focus. The nursing profession's ideas and concerns about Aboriginal health care have undergone changes and are reflective of widespread questioning by individual practitioners who consider the degree to which, and the ways in which, health care can be approached to actually produce improved health.

Vasiliki Douglas

Acknowledgments

This project succeeded due in large part to the support and assistance of the First Nations, Inuit and Métis who have guided me through the forbidding maze of materials on aboriginal health in Canada, beginning with the Inuit midwives and staff of the Inuulitsivik Maternities and the Rankin Inlet Birthing Centre many years ago.

Marlene Erickson and Darlene Macintosh of the Aboriginal Resource Centre at the College of New Caledonia have given me guidance and shared their own knowledge, expertise and insight into the Northern British Columbia First Nations experience with me. I am also deeply indebted to the Inuit and Dene of the Inuvialuit Settlement Region, NT and the Vuntut Gwitchin of Old Crow, YK for their hospitality and support during my research into health and food security in the Canadian Arctic.

I also owe a debt of gratitude to my Aboriginal patients in the Complex Care and Acute Care hospital settings and to my undergraduate nursing students of the Northern Baccalaureate Nursing Programme. Both my patients and the aboriginal and non-aboriginal students in my Introduction to First Nations Health course at the College of New Caledonia contributed to my ever-growing understanding of the continuing impact of colonisation on Aboriginal peoples in the Canadian health care system. In particular, my students have been questioning, challenging and providing me with feedback while I have been field-testing the material that went into this book for the past 6 years. They, and the numerous guest speakers from the First Nations and Métis communities of the region, have helped to shape this manuscript into its final form. All are continuing to encourage on-going dialogue on the development of a new nursing curriculum framework to address the health needs of Canadian Aboriginal peoples.

Guidelines for Faculty

WHO SHOULD USE THIS BOOK

Instructors teaching courses focusing on Aboriginal health in Canada, along with their respective students, are the primary audiences for this book. Although the book's focus on cultural safety has its genesis in the Canadian nursing context, this concept has wide applicability across the Health and Social Sciences as it has been taken up by other professions in different fields. I have considered that this text could be applied to courses in fields as diverse as Education, Native Studies, Anthropology, Social Work, Medicine, Sociology, and History, as well as Nursing, and as a result, I have written it with this broad context in mind. Altogether, I have tried to avoid a dry and narrow focus on a single instructional model. Rather, I have tried to:

- Stimulate the critical thought processes of those involved in teaching and learning about Aboriginal health by considering both the contemporary and historical context of the critical issues in the field.
- Encourage readers to engage in self-reflective action grounded in understanding the context of Aboriginal health that constitutes the theoretical core of cultural safety.
- Motivate readers to go beyond the limited, and limiting, static approach to Aboriginal health that is embodied in cultural competency, and instead consider both members of the Canadian Aboriginal community and their health as individual, fluid and evolving entities.

WHAT THIS BOOK IS ABOUT

This book is about Aboriginal health in Canada during an era of changing rights and responsibilities. Aboriginal health is neither unremarkable nor static, as even its history is rapidly evolving as new facts are uncovered and old interpretations are overturned. In essence, I have attempted to reflect the following aspects of teaching and learning in Aboriginal health:

▪ Aboriginal approaches to health and healing are as valid and important as the bio-medical model of health.

▪ The biomedical model is also valid and important, but too often it is treated as a belief system, rather than a tool, as all sciences are.

▪ The vast majority of Aboriginal people want the benefits of modern health care, but they do not necessarily want to accept it as more than a tool to facilitate their healing.

▪ Each person's health is individual, as are his or her beliefs. Canadian First Nations, Métis, and Inuit are distinct peoples with much in common, but each of these peoples are also made up of individuals with individual needs, desires, and beliefs. Understanding this is fundamental to understanding both Aboriginal Health in Canada and working towards improving it.

HOW THIS BOOK IS ORGANIZED

This book is intended to serve as a practical means of introducing Aboriginal health to undergraduate students. It is neither comprehensive, nor is it intended to serve as a reference manual. The emphasis is on practical utility. Each chapter is, so far as it is possible, meant to be self-contained, while also being strongly supported by the material in the other chapters.

Chapter Organization

Each chapter begins with a clear set of objectives. These function as the themes and questions that the chapter will answer. The chapter body strives to provide proof and context for these objectives. In all cases I have included as much primary source material, including photographs, charts, historical text documents, and artwork as possible. These provide both a means of giving context to the issues discussed in each chapter and may be used to stimulate discussion in class as well.

All the chapters also include critical thinking exercises and discussion questions that may either be assigned to students in the classroom, given as take-home exercises or used as the basis for student activities. They have been designed to be flexible enough to meet the needs of a broad range of instructors and their individual requirements.

Each chapter concludes with a reference section that includes various Internet sources relevant to the chapter topics. This is not intended to be exhaustive—that would be an entire book on its own—but will provide students with a guide to extending their knowledge of the subjects discussed in the chapter.

Narrative Structure

This book is broadly organized into two sections, the first on theory and the second on practice. This order represents my own approach to Aboriginal health, in which the history and theory prepare the students to receive the "facts on the ground"; thus, infusing them with meaning. However, pedagogical preferences vary, as do the exigencies of scheduling, and all the chapters in this book have been written in such a way as to permit their order to be varied as the course and instructor require. If necessary, both the major divisions between theory and practice and the order of individual chapters may be rearranged to suit particular situations.

Part I

Part I includes both a philosophical discussion of the differences between Aboriginal and non-Aboriginal epistemologies and the historical context of Aboriginal health. I believe firmly that current issues only have meaning within these contexts. Although not vital to learning the facts of Aboriginal health today, they are important nevertheless in understanding why the Canadian Aboriginal population faces the challenges to its collective health that it does—in essence the historical context gives meaning to these issues.

Similarly, I have incorporated the three major theoretical concepts that have informed both Aboriginal nursing and transcultural nursing in general into a separate chapter, where I define and evaluate them. While cultural sensitivity, cultural competency, and cultural safety are grounded in nursing, all have been widely used in nonnursing contexts and have important applications. The individualized and patient-centered approach inherent to cultural safety is the one framework that I have found the most pedagogically and practically useful. I have applied it with vigor throughout this book, but in such as way that it does not, I hope, stand between the instructor and the contents. Instructors who wish to avoid this aspect of theory may do so by neglecting this chapter altogether without loss of meaning in the rest of the book.

Part II

By practice, I mean the current state of Aboriginal health in Canada. In Part II, these are sorted into areas of health that students, health professionals, and fellow academics have identified as being of special concern. I have used the internationally recognized determinants of health as a secondary structural framework to provide a way of placing disease rates in their socioeconomic context in Canada today. The determinants provide a means of relating the health of individuals to the health of the population in ways that most students can understand and the introduction to them forms the first chapter in Part II.

The remainder of Part II focuses on specific health issues that have been identified as currently important. The chapters on diabetes, chronic and infectious diseases, women and children's health and mental health reflect this current consensus, but their order is arbitrary. Instructors may use them in any order they see fit.

The relative importance of various issues today determines their prominence. In the historical context, tuberculosis is arguably the most important health issue for Canadian Aboriginal peoples. Today, however, diabetes is far more prevalent and constitutes a more pressing epidemiological threat. Consequently, diabetes has an entire chapter devoted to it, while tuberculosis is folded into the chapter dealing with the other chronic and infectious diseases. Similarly, women and children's health issues are distinct within the Aboriginal population, leading to a special chapter devoted to them.

Concluding Chapter

This book concludes with my reflections on the epistemological importance of emerging hybrid health systems. These are organizations that incorporate both Aboriginal and non-Aboriginal approaches to health. In doing so, they embody the best attributes of cultural safety. In many ways this chapter ties together the previous nine, by giving a sense of how Aboriginal health in Canada may be understood as an epistemological whole, but also by how it can be approached as a practical undertaking, both in the classroom and in the field.

HOW TO USE THIS BOOK

This is neither a cookbook nor a repair manual. The book does not prescribe any one way of "doing" Aboriginal health or demand that instructors follow it step by step. And although I have attempted to create an integrated "way of knowing" about Aboriginal health and healing, the different parts of the book can be used creatively in ways that suit individual instructors in their particular pedagogical contexts. To do otherwise would, I believe, denigrate both the complexity of Aboriginal health in Canada and the abilities and diversity of those of us who are teaching and learning about it.

The statistical data in this book derives from the most recent sources available. However, research is ongoing on Aboriginal peoples and new data is constantly being collected and released. I realize that faculty do need to teach prospective health care professionals to stay abreast of current information about Aboriginal peoples in Canada. Statistics Canada is the major source of information on Aboriginal health in Canada and updated statistics on Canadian Aboriginal peoples can be found at the following link: http://www12.statcan.gc.ca/nhs-enm/2011/as-sa/99-011-x/99-011-x2011001-eng.cfm#a7

Aboriginal Culture and Health

1

Introduction: First Nations, Métis, and Inuit in Canada: Understanding the Issues

Chapter Objectives

- To explain multiculturalism policy and the nature of Canadian society.
- To introduce the three Aboriginal peoples of Canada.
- To explain their demographics and how they compare with the demographics of the Canadian population.
- To survey the significant milestones in governmental response to Aboriginal concerns over the last four decades.
- To provide the background to the growth of Aboriginal health as a discrete subject in Canada and to indicate why knowledge of Aboriginal health is important to nurses and other health care providers.

Key Concepts

Affordability
Cost of Care
Social Justice
Population Growth
Multiculturalism

Aboriginal Health
Nation
Health Promotion
Population Health

Key Terms

Romanow Report (Royal
  Commission on the
  Future of Health Care in
  Canada)
Royal Commission on
  Aboriginal Peoples
Multiculturalism
Demographics
Ottawa Charter
Status Indian
Non-Status Indian
Treaty Indian

Métis
Inuit
Aboriginal People
Band
Customs
First Nations
Reserve
Treaty
Self-Government
Canadian Charter of Rights
  and Freedoms

MULTICULTURALISM

The Government of Canada declared its commitment to multiculturalism in 1971 and explicitly incorporated multiculturalism into the Charter of Rights and Freedoms when the Constitution was repatriated in 1981. This was partly in response to concerns expressed by Aboriginal groups that the focus on English and French cultures excluded both them and other ethnic groups from equal participation in the Canadian cultural mosaic.

A PART OF THE CANADIAN CULTURAL MOSAIC

Canada is an immigrant nation, where the original population has been overwhelmed by successive waves of other peoples who have migrated here. Nursing historian John Murray Gibbon recognized that, unlike the "melting pot" model of cultural integration practised in the United States, in Canada different immigrant groups retained substantial elements of their cultural identity, while still participating in Canadian civil society and sharing common values. He called this the Canadian cultural mosaic in his influential book, *The Canadian Mosaic*, published in 1938. Gibbon explicitly contrasted the mosaic to the American melting pot.

When the Canadian government developed an official multiculturalism policy in 1971, Gibbon was referenced and his concept was used as the model for intercultural relations in Canada. This provided an alternative model of Canadian society to both assimilation and English–French biculturalism. Over time the concept has evolved, but multiculturalism and the cultural mosaic is still the basis for Canadian concepts of their national social organization. This was affirmed by Section 27 of the Charter of Rights and Freedoms and was enshrined in law in the Canadian Multiculturalism Act in 1985.

Multiculturalism Policy of Canada

3. (1) It is hereby declared to be the policy of the Government of Canada to

(a) recognize and promote the understanding that multiculturalism reflects the cultural and racial diversity of Canadian society and acknowledges the freedom of all members of Canadian society to preserve, enhance, and share their cultural heritage;

(b) recognize and promote the understanding that multiculturalism is a fundamental characteristic of the Canadian heritage and identity and that it provides an invaluable resource in the shaping of Canada's future;

(c) promote the full and equitable participation of individuals and communities of all origins in the continuing evolution

---

(continued)

Multiculturalism Policy of Canada   *(continued)*

and shaping of all aspects of Canadian society and assist them in the elimination of any barrier to that participation;

(d) recognize the existence of communities whose members share a common origin and their historic contribution to Canadian society, and enhance their development;

(e) ensure that all individuals receive equal treatment and equal protection under the law, while respecting and valuing their diversity;

(f) encourage and assist the social, cultural, economic, and political institutions of Canada to be both respectful and inclusive of Canada's multicultural character;

(g) promote the understanding and creativity that arise from the interaction between individuals and communities of different origins;

(h) foster the recognition and appreciation of the diverse cultures of Canadian society and promote the reflection and the evolving expressions of those cultures;

(i) preserve and enhance the use of languages other than English and French, while strengthening the status and use of the official languages of Canada; and

(j) advance multiculturalism throughout Canada in harmony with the national commitment to the official languages of Canada.

(2) It is further declared to be the policy of the Government of Canada that all federal institutions shall

(a) ensure that Canadians of all origins have an equal opportunity to obtain employment and advancement in those institutions;

(b) promote policies, programs, and practices that enhance the ability of individuals and communities of all origins to contribute to the continuing evolution of Canada;

(c) promote policies, programs, and practices that enhance the understanding of and respect for the diversity of the members of Canadian society;

(d) collect statistical data in order to enable the development of policies, programs, and practices that are sensitive and responsive to the multicultural reality of Canada;

(e) make use, as appropriate, of the language skills and cultural understanding of individuals of all origins; and

(f) generally, carry on their activities in a manner that is sensitive and responsive to the multicultural reality of Canada.

(Canadian Multiculturalism Act, 1985)

> **Section 27 of the Canadian Charter of Rights and Freedoms**
> **Is Somewhat Less Verbose. It States:**
>
> This Charter shall be interpreted in a manner consistent with the preservation and enhancement of the multicultural heritage of Canadians. (Charter of Rights and Freedoms, 1982)

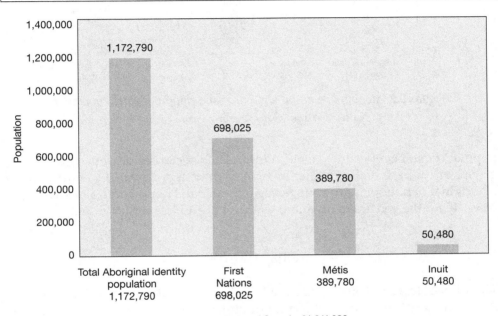

Note: Total Population of Canada: 31,241,030.

Figure 1.1 *Aboriginal Demographics According to Statistics Canada 2006*

Source: Statistics Canada, Census of Population, 2006.

A FOUNDING NATION OF CANADA

Beyond the place Aboriginal peoples hold in Canada's cultural mosaic, they have been recognized, along with the English and French, as one of Canada's three founding nations. Although Canada recognizes the place of all ethnic groups in the cultural mosaic, these three groups are considered founders of the nation due to their roles in the creation of Canada. The First Nations, Métis, and Inuit are recognized as having a special place because they were here first, and they played a key role in the creation of Canada.

DEMOGRAPHICS OF CANADA'S NATIVE POPULATION

Canada's Aboriginal population is diverse and widespread (Figure 1.1). Although many Aboriginal peoples share common cultural characteristics, many do not. In addition, government policy has created divisions within the Aboriginal

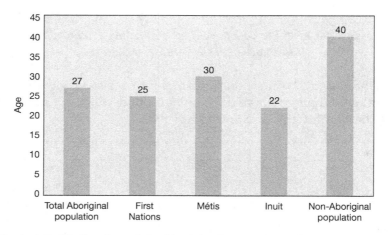

Figure 1.2 *Median Age of the Aboriginal and Non-Aboriginal Population*
Source: Statistics Canada, Census of Population, 2006.

population, some reflecting existing cultural and social divides, others redefining groups on the basis of their eligibility for government programs. Overall Canadian Aboriginal populations are younger than the general population (a median age of 20 vs. 40 for the general population) (Figure 1.2) and less well educated.

FIRST NATIONS

The Canadian First Nations are the Aboriginal peoples who reside below the Arctic Circle and who are part of a continuum of Aboriginal peoples who, despite enormous social, linguistic, and cultural diversity, stretch from boreal Canada to South America. In Canada, they are divided into two groups, Status Indians and Non-Status Indians.

Status Indians

Status Indians are those First Nations who are officially recognized by the Department of Aboriginal Affairs as legally members of an existing First Nations band. There are approximately 565,000 Status Indians in Canada, making them the largest Aboriginal group by population (see Figure 1.1). Their communities and reserves stretch from coast to coast, and many also live in urban areas as well.

Status means eligibility for certain government programs, some of which might be specific to the treaty rights of that band. Each Status Indian receives a band number and identity card to provide access to services. Indian Status provides some privileges, including income tax exemption, but only for Status Indians residing on their reserves. Status Indians living and working off reserve have much the same rights and responsibilities as any other Canadian.

Eligibility for Indian status is determined through ancestry, but not through blood. It is gained through inheritance of status itself. The children of Status

Indians and Non-Status individuals are eligible for registration, but they must marry someone else with status for their children to inherit it. If they marry someone without status, whether a Non-Status Indian or a non-Indian, then their children lose status. Since the majority of Status Indians form relationships with non-status partners, this provision has serious implications for the long-term viability of Indian Status in Canada.

Historically, Indian Status brought far more restrictions than privileges. Status Indians were required to live on their reserves, were subject to movement controls in some regions (particularly the Prairies), were barred from voting, were not allowed to drink alcohol, and were closely supervised by Indian Agents resident on their reserves. In effect, Status Indians were wards of the state, with a status similar to that of children. These restrictions could only be evaded by an individual giving up status, leaving the reserve, and entering the general population: effectively ceasing to be Aboriginal. While some Aboriginal individuals were willing to do this, most were not. Those who gave up their status, and their descendants, either merged into the general population, or became Non-Status Indians.

Non-Status Indians

Non-Status Indians number approximately 130,000 (see Figure 1.1). They are people of Aboriginal ancestry who self-identify as First Nations, but cannot claim status for various reasons. These reasons may include their ancestors voluntarily giving up their status, female ancestors losing their status by marrying a non-First Nations man, or other equivocal factors (such as the lack of documentation). These leave Non-Status Indians either unable or unwilling to qualify for Indian Status. Non-Status Indians are not eligible for government programs or services provided to Status Indians and, therefore, do not have the right to reside on First Nations reserves.

However, government recognition has no bearing on their participation in Aboriginal culture and society. Non-Status Indians may be as intimately involved in the culture of their community as Status Indians, even if Canadian governments do not recognize this fact. The existence of status and the right of Canadian governments to decide who, in effect, is Aboriginal and who is not is a very contentious one. Recently, Canadian governments, at the federal, provincial, and municipal levels, have extended various cultural services to Non-Status Indians, without actually granting them Status or access to federal services for Status Indians. Concomitantly, this is now the fastest growing Aboriginal group in Canada as people of First Nations ancestry are publicly reclaiming their heritage and identity, even without the benefits of status.

INUIT

The Inuit are a separate, non-First Nation indigenous people inhabiting Canada's high Arctic. They are closely related to other indigenous peoples in the circumpolar north, including those of Greenland, Alaska, and the Russian Arctic. According to the 2006 Census, the Inuit population of Canada is approximately

Traditional Dance in an Arctic Community

Source: V. K. Douglas.

50,000 in number (see Figure 1.1). The Inuit comprise the majority of the population in Canada's newest territory, Nunavut, and have a substantial presence in the Northwest Territories, Northern Québec, and Northern Labrador, the region they refer to as Inuit Nunangat.

MÉTIS

Canada's Métis population is close to 400,000 (see Figure 1.1). The Métis are the descendants of marriages between Aboriginal women and fur traders and explorers. Traditionally, the origin of the Métis is the Red River Settlement of the Hudson's Bay Company and it was also the largest Métis settlement. However, Métis settlements spread across Canada, springing up wherever a fur trading post was established along the trading routes. A hybrid culture, the Métis evolved from their mixed ancestry into a unique indig-

The Métis Flag

enous people, neither First Nations nor European, but combining aspects of each into a separate whole. The Métis were recognized as a separate people by both of the fur trading companies active in the Northwest Territories, the Northwest Company, and the Hudson's Bay Company. When Western Canada was incorporated into the Confederation in 1867, the Canadian government was also forced to recognize the existence of the Métis as a distinct people. Despite dispersal across the west after the Red River and Northwest Rebellions in 1869 and 1885, and a subsequent history of marginalization, the Métis have survived and now claim a place among Canada's other indigenous peoples.

The Métis flag in predates all other contemporary Canadian flags except for the Royal Ensign. The Métis flag was flown by the Métis as early as 1816, although the infinity symbol can also be set upon a red background. The flag symbolizes the union of two people and the belief that the Métis culture shall live forever.

URBAN ABORIGINALS

This is not a formal grouping, but a geographic one. The increasing urbanization of Canada following the Second World War has also affected the Aboriginal population. Thus, Canadian cities host substantial Aboriginal populations that have migrated there in search of employment, education, and socioeconomic opportunities. Often these peoples moved to urban centres at government urging in the 1960s and 1970s, with the belief that there would be better services and employment opportunities than in the remote communities they came from. On the government's part, this was both an attempt to improve the economic situation of remote, impoverished citizens, and part of the ongoing program of assimilation of Aboriginal peoples by encouraging them to blend into existing urban populations.

This population movement blends groups from widely differing geographic and cultural regions, leading to significant migration of cultural practices. For instance, the Medicine Wheel, a traditional Prairie First Nations concept of health, is now used in urban Aboriginal populations in British Columbia, even though it is not traditionally used by the indigenous First Nations population there. Urban Aboriginal populations may include Status Indians, Non-Status Indians, Métis, and some Inuit. Health status varies widely among individuals across the urban Aboriginal population, but their experiences are characterized by high levels of poverty and poor access to health care despite their proximity to urban health care facilities and services.

ABORGINAL PEOPLES IN CANADA

The Canadian Aboriginal population (Figure 1.3) is substantial and growing rapidly, especially the Non-Status Indian and Métis populations, which are benefiting from increased willingness of people of Aboriginal ancestry to self-identify as Aboriginal. However, even smaller populations may be regionally significant. The Inuit form a majority in Nunavut, whereas western and northern Canada have significant Aboriginal populations, often regional majorities. Thus, the Northwest Territories have a majority Aboriginal population (combined First Nations and Inuit), as does Nunavut, and Northern Québec and Northern Labrador.

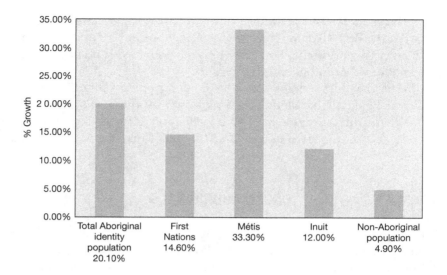

Figure 1.3 *Growth of the Aboriginal Population, 2001–2006*
Source: Statistics Canada, Census of Population, 2006.

Not only is the Aboriginal population growing much faster than the general population, but their family characteristics also differ. A high proportion of Aboriginal children live in single-parent families, yet also paradoxically benefit from active large multigenerational families. However, these families typically reside in more crowded, less prosperous conditions than families in the general population. Other socioeconomic indicators are also lower: Unemployment rates are high in the Aboriginal population, while high school and postsecondary education rates are lower than those of the general population.

OTTAWA CHARTER

The World Health Organization (WHO) held the first International Conference on Health Promotion in 1986. Although not specifically concerned with Aboriginal health, the conference marked a significant shift in focus for public health policy from prevention of disease to identifying and improving the determinants of health. The conference concluded with the Ottawa Charter on Health Promotion (1986), which identified the social and environmental prerequisites of health as: peace, shelter, education, food, income, a stable ecosystem, sustainable resources, social justice, and equity. In essence, the Ottawa Charter recognized that health is a byproduct of a healthy environment. In pursuit of this goal, the Charter envisaged a variety of actors, including government, nurses, physicians and other public and private bodies, cooperating to improve all of these factors as a means of improving the health of the entire population.

The Ottawa Charter was officially adopted by the WHO after the conference. Its prerequisites for health have evolved into the modern basis for public health in Canada—the determinants of health. This approach has informed the Canadian approach to public health ever since, and indeed forms the basis for attempts to improve the health of Canada's Aboriginal peoples. The Charter's principles recognize that as long as one segment of the Canadian population remains in ill health, the health of the entire population will inevitably suffer. The Ottawa Charter did not lead to any immediate changes in the structure of health care and health promotion in Canada. However, it recognized that the focus should change from reacting to specific health crises, such as outbreaks of infectious disease, to promoting the health of the general population before it could become endangered.

ROYAL COMMISSION ON ABORIGINAL PEOPLES AND THE ROMANOW REPORT

The Royal Commission on Aboriginal Peoples was founded in the wake of the Oka Crisis, when public and international awareness of the poor socioeconomic conditions that Canada's Aboriginal peoples laboured under was at its height. Its Commissioners included some of the most eminent Aboriginal scholars and politicians in Canada. The Commission produced a lengthy report in 1996 that made some key recommendations.

The Report suggested that Parliament pass legislation, including a Royal Proclamation, committing Canada to a new relationship with its Aboriginal peoples. As well, the Commission recommended that Canada create a national Aboriginal parliament, create legislation to initiate a new treaty process and also recognize Aboriginal nations and governments as integral parts of the Canadian order of government. The Commission also called for the Department of Indian and Northern Affairs to be abolished and replaced with two departments, one dealing with self-governing Aboriginal groups, the other dealing with non–self-governing groups. The Commissioners also recommended that the Aboriginal land and resource base be expanded and that Métis be granted self-government and full Aboriginal rights (equal to Indian status). Finally, the Commission recommended that 10,000 health professionals be trained to improve Aboriginal health and that Aboriginal authority over education and child welfare be recognized.

Coincidentally, the Commission's report arrived when a new government had taken power, one primarily concerned with reducing the Federal budget deficit through stringent spending controls. Thus, most of the Commission's recommendations were ignored, although its recommendations did lead to the gradual devolution of powers from the Department of Indian and Northern Affairs to local Aboriginal authorities.

This development served two purposes, however, as it placed the responsibility for health on First Nations themselves, which handily removed direct federal responsibility for health outcomes. The devolution of powers also satisfied some of the demands of Aboriginal activists for greater control of their own affairs.

Much more tellingly, other more far-reaching proposals of the Commission were not implemented. Aboriginal self-government was an inexpensive, cost-saving measure, which resonated with the government of the day.

Text From the Preamble of the Royal Commission on Aboriginal Peoples

Canada is a test case for a grand notion—the notion that dissimilar peoples can share lands, resources, power and dreams while respecting and sustaining their differences. The story of Canada is the story of many such peoples, trying and failing and trying again, to live together in peace and harmony.

The Oka Crisis

The Oka Crisis erupted in 1990 and led to a tense stand-off between the Canadian army and armed Mohawk activists on the Kanesatake reserve near the village of Oka, Québec. The crisis originated in a land dispute. The village of Oka planned to expand its municipal golf course onto a plot of land that was claimed by the Mohawk as a traditional burying ground. The intransigence of the municipal government led to rapid escalation and the involvement of the provincial police, the Surété du Québec. After a police officer was shot and killed during an ill-advised attempt to rush a Mohawk road blockade, the Québec government requested assistance from the Federal Government under the National Defence Act and sent in the Canadian Army. The result was to galvanize Aboriginal activists across Canada. Protests took place and road blockages were erected in support of the Mohawk across the country, most notably in Québec, where the major freeway bridge across the Saint Lawrence River was blocked by Mohawks from the Kahnawake reserve, effectively cutting off the city of Montréal from its suburbs on the South Shore.

Fortunately there were no further fatalities, and after a prolonged siege the activists surrendered in return for some consideration of their grievances. Oka, however, has left two legacies. First, it actually increased Canadian public awareness and sympathy for the plight of Canadian Aboriginal peoples, and second, it exposed to international gaze the poor socioeconomic conditions many Aboriginals laboured under. The Federal Government was highly embarrassed, as it had

(continued)

The Oka Crisis (continued)

previously shown impressive leadership on international issues such as apartheid in South Africa, only to be accused of more covert racism toward its own Aboriginal population at home. The Oka Crisis also increased Aboriginal militancy, as the violence at Oka seemed to work better than the quiet diplomacy pursued by advocacy groups such as the Assembly of First Nations. The Oka Crisis was soon to be succeeded by armed confrontations at Gustafsen Lake in British Columbia, Ipperwash Provincial Park in Ontario, and Burnt Church in New Brunswick.

Indirectly, the threat of further confrontations may have encouraged both provincial and federal governments into greater attempts to resolve Aboriginal issues. Following these conflicts the federal government created the Royal Commission on Aboriginal Peoples, while the British Columbia provincial government finally began the process of dealing with its own long-standing land claims issues after over a century of colonization and denial.

Romanow Report

While the Royal Commission on Aboriginal Peoples saw much of its report relegated to the archives in 1996, by the end of the century health care had become an urgent issue in Canada and led to the creation of the Royal Commission on the Future of Health Care in Canada, led by the former Premier of Saskatchewan, Roy Romanow. The Romanow Report was released in 2002 and, like its predecessor, found serious shortcomings in the health experience of Canada's Aboriginal peoples. In the Report's words:

> In fundamental terms, there is a "disconnect" between Aboriginal peoples and the rest of Canadian society, particularly when it comes to sharing many of the benefits of Canada's health care system. There are at least five underlying reasons for this disconnect:
>
> ▪ Competing constitutional assumptions
> ▪ Fragmented funding for health services
> ▪ Inadequate access to health care services
> ▪ Poorer health outcomes
> ▪ Different cultural and political influences
>
> (Romanow Report, 2002, p. 212)

Unlike its predecessor, the Romanow Report concluded that adequate funds were available to improve Aboriginal health care, but most of them were wasted in mismanagement and in the fragmentation of resources. Romanow's recommendations were to:

- Consolidate fragmented funding for Aboriginal health to take the best advantage of the total potential funds available in order to improve health and health care for Aboriginal peoples;

- Create new models to co-ordinate and deliver health care services and ensure that Aboriginal health care needs are addressed;

- Adapt health programs and services to the cultural, social, economic, and political circumstances unique to different Aboriginal groups; and

- Give Aboriginal peoples a direct voice in how health care services are designed and delivered.

(Romanow Report, 2002, p. 212)

While not all of the Romanow Report's recommendations have been followed to date, some action has been taken, including the creation of an Aboriginal health authority, the First Nations Health Authority, in British Columbia in 2011. There are also ongoing attempts to adapt and create health programs that are tailored to the needs of Aboriginal communities.

EASING DEMANDS ON RESOURCES

Perhaps more importantly, Romanow identified serious systemic problems with the Canadian health care system in general. He found that, despite the recommendations of the Ottawa Charter, the system still focused its resources on the treatment and prevention of disease and ill health. He recommended that a serious focus on the determinants of health would be more effective and economical in maintaining the health of the general population. The dual focus on saving money and improving service delivery has made Romanow's recommendations more attractive to economy-minded Canadian governments than the far-reaching conclusions of the Royal Commission. In those cases where he recommended increased expenditures (such as pharmaceutical expenses), his report has proved less influential and thus, little has changed.

However, because Romanow's recommendations focused at the level of population health, they also apply to the Aboriginal population. The result has been some improvements in health care delivery and on developing programs focused on population health among the Aboriginal community as part of the overall change in focus stemming from the Report.

The Romanow Report clearly laid out the advantages to improving the determinants of health for the Aboriginal population. Its conclusions can be simplified as in Figure 1.4.

The Canadian Aboriginal population has a high birth rate and is growing rapidly. The general population is not, although immigration is continuing to contribute to overall population growth. Health issues in the Aboriginal population have serious implications for Canadian economic, social, and physical well-being, given these trends. If a large proportion of the population lives in poverty and misery, it will drag the rest of the population down, through cost to the health care system, contagion, and social problems.

Regional statistics are also only part of the story. Within each province are regions that have much larger Aboriginal populations than the provincial totals indicate. The northern regions of both Ontario and Québec comprise over half of their total geographic area, and the Aboriginal populations of both provinces are concentrated in these regions, while the non-Aboriginal population is concentrated in the south (Figure 1.5).

Figure 1.4 *Summarizing the Main Conclusions of the Romanow Report*

Source: V. K. Douglas.

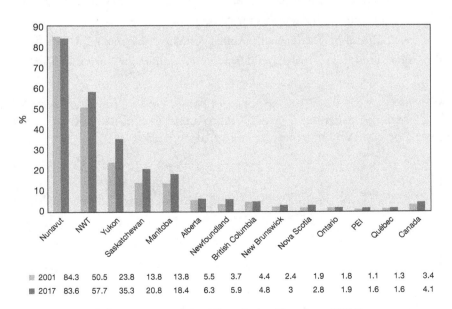

	Nunavut	NWT	Yukon	Saskatchewan	Manitoba	Alberta	Newfoundland	British Columbia	New Brunswick	Nova Scotia	Ontario	PEI	Québec	Canada
2001	84.3	50.5	23.8	13.8	13.8	5.5	3.7	4.4	2.4	1.9	1.8	1.1	1.3	3.4
2017	83.6	57.7	35.3	20.8	18.4	6.3	5.9	4.8	3	2.8	1.9	1.6	1.6	4.1

Figure 1.5 *Aboriginal Population Trends to 2017*

Proportion of the Aboriginal population in the total population by province andterritory, 2001 and 2017 (projected)
Source: Statistics Canada 2005.

CRITICAL THINKING EXERCISE—THINKING ABOUT DIFFERENCE

Valuing and identifying cultural differences exercises are common. This is a hybrid of several exercises designed to help bring to light one's membership in the dominant cultural group in Canada.

This exercise can be performed alone, but is better when done as a group exercise, comparing your results with others' results.

First ask yourself this series of questions. Give yourself one point for "Yes" and subtract one point for "No."

1. You are female.
2. You are under 25 years of age.
3. You have brown eyes.
4. You are of non-Caucasian ancestry.
5. You have ever been afraid to walk in your neighborhood at night.
6. You attend church or temple regularly (not necessarily every week).
7. You have ever participated in a sweat.
8. You have used herbs for health purposes.
9. You have gone to elementary or high school away from your family.
10. You have not been allowed to speak your language of birth.
11. You have been followed by security personnel while shopping in a store.
12. You have been refused any service due to your age, ethnicity, or gender.
13. You know of community services for Aboriginal peoples.
14. You have cultural practices other families you know may not.
15. You understand the socioeconomic factors that influence Aboriginal health.

Add up your results. A high score indicates you are marginalized. A low or negative score indicates the degree you are a member of the dominant group in Canadian society. Which group do you think this is?

Discussion Questions

1. Why were the recommendations of the Royal Commission on Aboriginal Peoples largely ignored?

2. The Federal Government did devolve power to Aboriginal governments in the 1990s and after. What are two interpretations of why this happened?

3. Who has the largest population among the Aboriginal peoples of Canada?

4. What was the impact of the Oka Crisis on Canadian governments?

5. What was the impact of the Oka Crisis on Aboriginal activism?

6. What is the fastest growing group among the Aboriginal peoples of Canada? Why?

7. What does the Métis flag symbolize?

8. Why is Aboriginal population growth significant for even overwhelmingly non-Aboriginal provinces, such as Ontario or British Columbia?

REFERENCES AND FURTHER READING

An Act for the preservation and enhancement of multiculturalism in Canada (Canadian Multiculturalism Act). R.S.C., 1985, c. 24 (4th Supp.).

Canadian Charter of Rights and Freedoms, s 2, Part I of the Constitution Act, 1982, being Schedule B to the Canada Act 1982 (UK), 1982, c 11.

Esses, V. M., & Gardner, R. C. (1996). Multiculturalism in Canada: context and current status. *Canadian Journal of Behavioural Science/Revue canadienne des sciences du comportement, 28*(3), 145.

Frideres, R. (2008). Aboriginal identity in the Canadian context. *Canadian Journal of Native Studies, XXVIII*(2), 313–342.

Gibbon, J. (1938). *The Canadian mosaic: the making of a northern nation.* Toronto, ON: McClelland & Stewart.

Kymlicka, W. (2003). Canadian multiculturalism in historical and comparative perspective: is Canada unique. *Constitutional Forum, 13,* 1–8.

Légaré, E. I. (1995). Canadian multiculturalism and Aboriginal people: Negotiating a place in the nation. *Identities: Global Studies in Culture and Power, 1*(4), 347–366.

Porter, J. (1965). *The vertical mosaic: An analysis of social class and power in Canada.* Toronto, ON: University of Toronto Press.

Statistics Canada. (2005). Projections of the Aboriginal populations, Canada, provinces and territories (2001 to 2017). Ottawa, ON: Statistics Canada.

Woodcock, G. (1990). *A social history of Canada.* Toronto, ON: Penguin Books.

Recommended Websites

First Nations Health Authority: www.fnhc.ca/index.php/iFNHA/

Ottawa Charter Emblem: www.who.int/healthpromotion/conferences/previous/ottawa/en/index4.html

Ottawa Charter on Health Promotion: www.who.int/healthpromotion/conferences/previous/ottawa/en/index.html

Report of the Royal Commission on Aboriginal Peoples: www.parl.gc.ca/Content/LOP/ResearchPublications/prb9924-e.htm

Report of the Royal Commission on the Future of Health Care in Canada (Romanow Report). http://publications.gc.ca/site/eng/237274/publication.html

2

Western and Aboriginal
Ways of Knowing

Chapter Objectives

1. To explain the philosophical concepts of epistemology and ontology.

2. To explain how different people have different ways of understanding the world.

3. To explain traditional Aboriginal epistemology.

4. To explain the philosophical underpinnings of modern health care.

5. To introduce the concept of epistemological accommodation.

6. To explain how nurses can mediate between the biomedical system and patients who have other ways of knowing.

7. To define the differences between Aboriginal and Western world views and ways of life and to place these in their historical context. To provide a theoretical framework for understanding Aboriginal health issues and how practitioners can relate to them.

Key Concepts

Epistemology

Ontology

Health

Healing

World View

Philosophy

Society

Culture

Nature

Key Terms

Ways of Knowing

Modern

Premodern

Authority

Health Care

Epistemological
  Accommodation

Medicine Wheel

Biomedicine

ABORIGINAL WAYS OF KNOWING

The Canadian health care system often has problems with Aboriginal patients and communities. Aboriginal patients may refuse to participate in the system in important ways: by adopting a position of passive resistance, or by refusing to conform to societal and professional expectations of how patients should behave. Behaviour may range from not following directions, to actively evading the directions of health care providers. Although individuals all have their own motivations for their personal behaviours, it is important to remember that Aboriginal patients may not think about health in ways that precisely correspond to the ways mainstream Canadian society does. They may also have personal experiences, or have shared in family experiences, of unpleasant confrontations with the health care system.

Even though First Nations, Inuit and Métis may not look different than other Canadians, their cultural values and life experiences may be quite different than those of the majority. This may include different ways of understanding diseases, or simply a different understanding of the importance of ill health, one that places it within the context of the family and community. Thus, the greatest challenge for nurses may be communicating with their patients in a way that bridges this cultural divide. Conversely, many people who seem to be identifiably Aboriginal may be completely assimilated culturally, and become highly offended at the assumption that they do not share dominant Canadian cultural values. Nurses must learn to recognize differences as well as to overcome them in order to provide appropriate care and promote health.

Aboriginal patients may see their health in traditional terms, biomedical terms or a mixture of both. The Aboriginal approach to knowledge tends to see the world as a unified whole, a concept that will be further discussed in the chapter, and often have specific reactions that may express this and other cultural tropes that health care providers should recognize. These have been tabulated by Dumont (1993; Tables 2.1 and 2.2) and serve as a useful guide when approaching Aboriginal patients. However, it is still important to remember that not all Aboriginal patients will react the same way, or according to the same belief systems.

EXAMPLE

Saik'uz elder Sophie Thomas, who died in 2010, lived near Stoney Creek, BC. She was a member of the Dakelh Nation, also known as the Carrier. Their population of over 10,000 people is concentrated in communities in Central British Columbia. As well as a politician and activist for Aboriginal rights and women's well-being, she was well known for her ability as a traditional healer and for her extensive knowledge of her people's traditional healing plants. Over the course of her life, she spoke at major international naturopathic and traditional healing conferences as well as serving as the elected Chief of her band. Her treatments

Table 2.1 *Aboriginal and Non-Aboriginal Values*

Aboriginal Values	Non-Aboriginal Values
Form consensus with the group (harmony)	Get ahead and pass by others
Go forward for the benefit of the group	Go forward for one's own benefit
Importance of the present	Importance of the future
Stoic in the face of adversity; is aware of the Creator; spirituality is the bond that exists between individuals and natural laws, thus defining a way of life	Does not always remain stoic when confronting adversity; spirituality is left in the background of modern life, or as a tool that helps to escape from the suffering in life, according to a system of beliefs
Religious acts are spontaneous and may occur anywhere	Religion is compartmentalized (religious acts are delegated to certain days of the week)
Great respect for elders	Quasi indifference to elders
Indifference to ideas of different social classes	Great importance for professions vs. trades
Little or no importance for external appearance of person	Great importance associated with clothing

Source: Dumont (1993).

for cancer were particularly noted, as was her belief that spirituality and a strong connection to the land were essential to a healer.

"The Creator does the healing, I am only a servant."

"If we look after our earth, it will look after us. If we destroy it, we'll destroy ourselves."

— Sophie Thomas, www.sophiethomas.org/

She spoke widely on traditional medicine, naturopathy and Aboriginal culture and health. Her cancer treatments were well known in her community and among other Aboriginal communities in British Columbia and across Canada.

Although there have been attempts by scientists to isolate the active medicinal ingredients in her medications, Sophie's patients and supporters strongly believe that her abilities as a healer were based on more than biologically active medicines: They were based on her capacity for caring:

"My name is Mabel. I had cervical cancer. They told me I had to have radiation. I was three months pregnant. My unborn child would have to be aborted. I was scared. Sophie looked after me. She gave me her medicine. Today my boy is 17 years old" (www.sophiethomas.org/).

OTHER WAYS OF KNOWING

This is by no means restricted to the Aboriginal population. Immigrants from traditional societies, members of very traditional cultural groups, and many older Canadians may also possess conceptions of health that differ from the

Table 2.2 *Aboriginal Values and Health*

Concepts	Traditional Aboriginal Values	Non-Aboriginal Values
Health	The global sum of all vital functions and the harmony established among them	Absence of disease
Sickness	Often the result of an imbalance in the person's life, which may be psychological, spiritual, emotional or physical	Very often associated with physical or biological deficiency
Treatment	If a plant has been praised in the oral tradition, treatment using traditional methods might very well be sufficient	Must successfully pass scientific exams and show convincing results
Alternative medicine	A way to communicate values in union with spirituality	Primitive or vulgar version of medicine
Diagnosis and recommendations	Diagnosis to be shared with important members of the family. Attempt to reach understanding. Recommendations are examined and may be modified through additions of elements of traditional medicine	Exact diagnosis only to be shared with patient, who will submissively follow the recommendations
Medication	May combine traditional and modern medicine	The patient takes what's been prescribed
Healing	Process into which an individual embarks on a lifetime journey	Disappearance of symptoms or visible traces of the disease
Condoms	A contraceptive mechanism that goes counter to the conception of life	Effective means of protection against HIV/AIDS and other diseases
Enlightened consent	Notion that is likely to arouse mistrust, as a result of past experience with medical treatments that were imposed on many people	Self-explanatory notion in accordance with suggested treatments
Silence	Means often used to take a break or to regain contact with one's emotions	Often perceived as a sign of passivity, an awkward moment that has to be filled
Questions	Means of communication that may be perceived as intrusion	Means of communication demonstrating interest or curiosity associated with intelligence
Eye contact	In some Aboriginal cultures looking an authority figure in the eye is a sign of disrespect	Maintaining eye contact is seen as a sign of sincerity
Notion of time	Little importance, a notion which is not linked to a specific time, but to times in the day, during the day, e.g., the sunrise, the sunset, midday	Dominated by a belief that the more punctual we are the better everyone will get along

Source: Dumont (1993).

majority. Some may blend traditional healing practices and Western medicine—for instance, by practising acupuncture or by taking herbal medicine while also undergoing conventional drug therapy. On the other hand, however, they may have completely adopted Canadian health care norms. Cunningham (2003) suggests that there are three modern ways of knowing about the world: the Western, the Eastern and the Aboriginal. Patients, regardless of background or origin, may

Traditional First Nations Prayer Ceremony
Source: VK Douglas.

exhibit ways of knowing about the world, and approaches to both their health and the people they interact with, that does not fit into the Canadian definition of "normal."

It is important for health care professionals in every field to be alert to this difference and to respond to it appropriately. The health care professional's behaviour and the patient's diagnosis may set the tone for Aboriginal and other patients' experience with the health care system. It is a truism, however, that nurses are often the front-line health care professionals and their response is particularly important in this context.

RECOGNIZING INDIVIDUALITY

The corollary to this is that nurses must be flexible enough to realize that all individuals are unique. People of the same ethnic or cultural background may have radically different approaches to health and healing. Even the same person, over time, may change beliefs, habits and expectations. Some people blend traditional and modern medicine in idiosyncratic ways (e.g., participating in smudging, taking medications and undergoing acupuncture throughout the healing journey). All of these are valid approaches to health that may be important to individual patients. Recognizing that patients are individual human beings and deserve to be treated as such is the first step toward cultural accommodation.

EPISTEMOLOGY AND ONTOLOGY

Epistemology and ontology are terms drawn from philosophy to describe how people think. Although they can be very complicated (and usually are when philosophers use them), they can also be very simple approaches to understanding different world views, which is how we will use them. Both terms are important for understanding how people think about the world, and as important, about their health.

Ontology

Ontology refers to ways of "being" or "existing." For example, most things exist independently of humans—rocks are rocks and stars are stars irrespective of what humans choose to think about them. However, some things, such as the economy or population health, require humans for their existence. These things also change their very nature when people think about them and act on them.

This sounds confusing, but is actually quite simple. Population health exists only as long as we think about people in the aggregate, or in populations, rather than just about the health of individuals. When we start thinking about populations and their collective health, we see health differently and we treat it differently.

A good example of this is vaccination campaigns. Many people will never catch a dangerous infectious disease, such as smallpox, whether or not they are vaccinated. Yet public health campaigns try to immunize everyone in a population, because we know that if the population is vaccinated, individuals are also less likely to contract infectious diseases. So the health of the population changes because we thought about it and made a change that would be for everyone's good, not just individual people. As a consequence, smallpox is now extinct, which has permanently changed population health. We will not use ontology much in this book, but it is a useful term to remember and contrasts with one we will use: epistemology.

Epistemology

Epistemology refers to "ways of knowing," or systems of thinking about the world and everything in it. Seeing a rock as a piece of inanimate mineral and a star as a giant ball of flaming matter far off in space are ways of knowing or thinking about rocks and stars. Epistemology is a means of describing how we relate to the world around us. It is also highly dependent on our cultural preconceptions. Although modern, Western Canadians tend to see rocks and stars as inanimate matter, through most of human history people have not followed this way of knowing and have seen rocks and stars quite differently. So, for example, astrology, the art of reading the future from the stars, explicitly assumes that there is a mystical connection between people and the stars and that the stars are not inanimate matter. Although astrology is a marginalized activity today and was relegated to that status during the Enlightenment some 300 years ago, it was once very popular and influential throughout Europe and versions of astrology remain influential in some non-Western societies.

BEING AND KNOWING IN TIME

Human beings do change considerably, both in how they think about the world, and how they interact with it. While a rock will always be a rock, people may not always think about rocks the same way and may change the ways they use them. In this light, health care practitioners have to be aware that patients are not inanimate objects that passively receive care and treatment. Their ways of knowing and being change from person to person and also across cultures and over time. These changes and differences are at the root of the problems that some health care practitioners face working in Aboriginal health, as Aboriginal patients and health care workers may not share the same ways of knowing and of being as other Canadians.

HISTORICAL EPISTEMOLOGY

"Modern" and "modernism" are terms generally associated with the world view that emerged from a shift in the European world view in the 16th century. This has been referred to as the "disenchantment of the world" by Pickstone (2000) and refers to the separation of nature from society; that is, the belief that nature can be comprehended directly and objectively through science, rather than through cultural representation. Premodern epistemologies, on the other hand, did not perform this act of separation—their cosmos remained laden with significance for human affairs, and vice versa. Thus, in the Inuit case, human actions, such as breaking pittilinaat (taboos), would have a direct effect on nature, causing storms and other natural events.

Similarly, natural events, such as stellar motions or positions, also had the potential to signify events on Earth. The world was, as it were, animated by occult correspondences and influences, which human beings had to navigate their way through. According to Foucault (1971), this perception of the cosmos was replaced with the modernist one in the 18th century, in which nature is an objective, rationally defined entity quite separate from human society. Pickstone, on the other hand, points out that premodern epistemologies continued to coexist with modern epistemology of science, and in fact continue to do so, although he also implies that they remain incommensurable.

This interpretation is altered somewhat by Latour (1993) who suggests instead that modernism, including scientific epistemology, is a cultural artifact of European society. Although a useful tool for the generation and utilization of knowledge, it does not reflect the fundamental relationship between human society and the natural world. In Latour's model, the fundamental difference between modern and nonmodern societies is one of power and knowledge, and has not always been to the modern advantage.

This suggests that modernism is largely an illusion, but instead Latour considers it to be a culturally shaped approach to the world that is differentiated from premodernism only by the enormous amount of knowledge it has generated, and hence the power it is able to accrue. He argues that premodern epistemologies are not necessarily incompatible with modern knowledge, even with scientific epistemology, as they simply deny it its totalitarian status, its claim to an exclusive understanding of nature. This approach receives some practical support from Latour's (1988) analysis of the relationship between the French hygiene movement and Louis Pasteur's version of the germ theory of disease. The germ theory ultimately became the basis for modernist biomedicine, particularly in Anglo-Saxon nations (Rosenberg, 1992). On the other hand, the hygiene movement, in France and elsewhere, was predicated on a premodern view of disease as rooted in cultural, economic and moral causes as much as physical ones. Its leaders seized on the germ theory as an additional causative agent, one that strengthened their own program of social reform by solidifying their control over disease. Thus, in the short term, at least in France, the biomedical model of disease appears to have both coexisted and been incorporated into quite a different model, one which was essentially premodern in its identification of disease as a social, moral and physical phenomenon.

Obviously then, "biomedicine," is a term that carries considerable cultural baggage. Traditionally it is defined as the application of scientific epistemology to medicine, a practice that became dominant in the second half of the 19th century. More specifically, it refers to a curative, technological model that focuses on the physical basis of illness—the microbe. Foucault (1976) traces the cultural practices that shaped biomedicine to another epistemological shift in the late 18th century, one that produced a revolution in the nature and application of state power. It is a classic example of what he terms a "totalitarian theory"—one that, by its exclusive claim to understand the world, refuses to accept the equality of any other.

TRADITIONAL ABORIGINAL EPISTEMOLOGY

Traditional Aboriginal cultures did not follow the biomedical approach to health, as their conception of the body was essentially premodern and sharply different from the modern perspective on a number of principles. First, there was no sharp distinction between physical and spiritual health. They viewed health as a matter of balance between different forces acting in the world, either physical or spiritual. Health was maintained through the authority of the community and the force of tradition through consensus. Second, the health of individuals was seen in the context of the health of the family and community. Thus, healing focused not only on individual illness, but also on maintaining the health of the community as a whole. This approach could be described as communal health, not community health, because health was a resource shared by the entire community.

However, Aboriginal communities exist today in the modern world, not in isolation. Over time there has been considerable penetration by modern Western ideas, and modern biomedicine has made undoubted advances in treating ill health and disease. Aboriginal people are as interested as any other Canadians in benefiting from the techniques and technology that biomedicine has to offer. They know that they can no longer be premodern, and indeed seldom wish to be so. Yet, they want the tools and techniques of biomedicine, but not necessarily the epistemology that accompanies it. The challenge for nurses is to provide the care, but not the prejudices that so often accompany biomedicine.

The Medicine Wheel

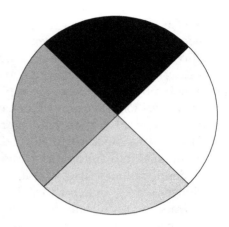

One of the most common *leit motifs* of Aboriginal health and Aboriginal epistemology is the medicine wheel. A design, also called a sacred hoop that originated as a physical artifact among the Prairies First Nations, it has been adopted as symbol of health by a number of Aboriginal groups across Canada. The wheel has a number of levels of symbolism. The colours may be taken as meaning the four directions (North, South, East, West), the four stages of life (birth, youth, adulthood, death), the four seasons (spring, summer, fall, winter), the four elements (Sun, Air, Water, Earth), the four aspects of human life (spiritual, emotional, intellectual, physical) or even of four animal species (varying depending on the group interpreting the wheel and their preferred animal species). Some may consider it to represent four human races (Black, White, Yellow, Red). The medicine wheel has also been adapted by different groups into many forms. Its basic symbolism is that of the holistic relationship between health, the community and the natural world. It is also a nonhierarchical way of considering human and natural relationships. This makes it fundamentally different from the standard "top down" hierarchical way in which Europeans have traditionally viewed the world.

Health care professionals working with the Aboriginal population will almost certainly encounter the medicine wheel, and may choose to use it, when appropriate. It is, however, important to remember that many Aboriginal groups do not use the medicine wheel at all, and it has come under attack from some Aboriginal historians, in particular Andrea Bear Nicholas (2008), who has identified it as a modern construct and an example of cultural reductionism. Aboriginal groups may be either indifferent to it or even actively hostile to its use in their cultural context. Among others, the Inuit and many British Columbian First Nations make little or no use of the medicine wheel. They have their own culturally appropriate approaches to health that do not draw on that iconography, even if they share many values with other groups who do.

PROFESSIONAL FLEXIBILITY

Negotiating an approach toward improving Aboriginal health requires flexibility on the part of both the Aboriginal participants and the front-line health care workers. Each party must recognize that they are faced with practices and authority that are rooted in an approach to health and a way of knowing different from their own. However, each must also recognize that the world view of the other should be respected, even as they maintain their own epistemological integrity.

BIOMEDICINE VERSUS TRADITION

Many nurses and physicians, although well meaning, do attempt to impose their values and world view on their patients, thus creating a problem. The problem arises out of something as simple as holding the expectation that the medical treatment prescribed will take priority over family and community

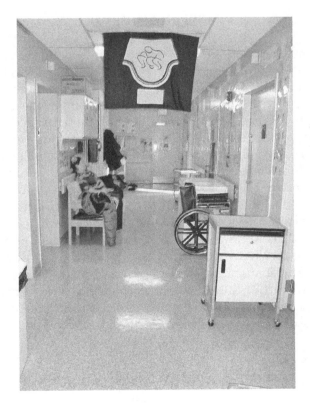

Two Choices

Culturally Relevant Health Care Should Not Mean Choosing Between Modern Care and Premodern Care:
The Waiting Area at the Inuulitsivik Maternities.
Source: V. K. Douglas.

concerns or input. For the health care professional this may seem a basic assumption. After all, individual patient health is what nurses foster and community and public health is often felt to flow from individual health. Yet, for people raised in a belief system that focuses on the communal over the individual, this is exactly backward. For someone from a traditional Aboriginal world view, individual health flows from the community itself. In other words, a healthy community leads to healthy individuals within it. While individuals may become ill and suffer injuries, these are overcome within the framework of the community.

This fundamental disjuncture in approaches to health is why many Aboriginal communities and individuals have difficulty dealing with the health care system. Their values and mores may conflict with biomedical authority in ways that health care professionals do not recognize. However, Aboriginals do not wish to reject the advantages of modern medicine, but only its authority over their lives and culture.

NONMODERN EPISTEMOLOGY

The problem seems insoluble—how to reconcile an epistemology of health focused on the individual body/machine ethos with one that considers the health of the community as the source of individual health. However, anthropologist Bruno Latour (1993) suggested that there is a third way to see the world, one which draws on the power of modern knowledge and modern medical systems, but combines it with premodern sensibilities. He describes this as neither a premodern nor a modern epistemology, but a nonmodern epistemology. Although this sounds like a difficult concept, in practice it is quite easy: Latour suggests that as the human and natural worlds do influence each other all the time, we should simply recognize this and use the tools which biomedicine and science provide us with to improve our lives, all within our existing world views. In Latour's formulation, rather than Aboriginal peoples abandoning their approach to health, they will use the tools and techniques that modern medical systems provide, without necessarily abandoning their own communally centered epistemology. This, however, requires health care professionals, especially nurses, to modify their own approach to health and healing in order to provide care that does not attempt to impose biomedical values on their patients and their communities.

EPISTEMOLOGICAL ACCOMMODATION

The process in which both Aboriginal patients and health care professionals must accommodate and respect each others' world views is epistemological accommodation. Some Aboriginal communities in Canada have already developed a form of epistemological accommodation with the health care system, notably the Inuit of Northern Québec, through the Inuulitsivik Maternities, and the Mohawk of Kahnawake, Québec, through the Kahnawake Diabetes Prevention Project. Both groups use the techniques and knowledge of biomedicine, but their approach to health care is still rooted in their own culture.

RECOGNIZING AND RESPECTING DIFFERENCE

Nurses are key front-line professionals in providing health care to both patients and populations. As the interface between the biomedical system and Aboriginal patients and communities, they play an important role in making the health care system work for the Aboriginal population. By learning to recognize and accommodate different ways of knowing when they are encountered in practice, nurses can provide the epistemological accommodation that will allow Aboriginal patients to receive culturally appropriate care. This requires the professional flexibility and education to recognize what a patient regards as acceptable care and to respect that, all the while maintaining the standards and ethics of the profession.

CRITICAL THINKING EXERCISE—HOW MODERN ARE YOU?

First divide a sheet of paper into two columns. Entitle one Premodern, entitle the other one Modern.

Now, think about your cultural and social background and ask yourself the following questions, placing the answers under the appropriate column heading:

1. Do you follow a particular religion? If so, do you believe that it influences what happens to you in your life?
2. Do you ever read the astrology columns in newspapers?
3. Have you ever participated in a traditional healing ceremony from any culture?
4. Have you ever used a sauna or a steam room? (Saunas were originally a traditional healing practice in Scandinavia.)
5. Do you see your doctor regularly?
6. Do you always follow your physician's advice?
7. Have you ever used a traditional practice to avoid bad luck? (Hanging a dream catcher, knocking on wood, hanging a horseshoe, etc.)

Look at your list and think about your answers and where they have gone. Compare your answers with those of others and what they have chosen. How modern are you?

Discussion Questions

1. Different people have different ways of knowing and world views. How can they interact with each other in the clinical setting?

2. What is the difference between ontology and epistemology? How is this important for understanding how Aboriginal patients view the world and how their world views change over time?

3. What would be more important, Sophie Thomas's medicines or her administration of them?

4. One of the key ingredients of Sophie Thomas's traditional medicine was red willow. How does this make superficial sense in biomedical terms? Is it missing the point?

5. Is the medicine wheel still a useful concept in Aboriginal healing, irrespective of its origins?

REFERENCES AND FURTHER READING

Cunningham, C. (2003). Indigenous by definition, experience or world view. *BMJ British Medical Journal, 327,* 403–404.

Dumont, J. (1993). *"Justice and Aboriginal people" in Aboriginal peoples and the justice system.* Ottawa, ON: Minister of Supply and Services Canada.

Foucault, M. (1971). *The order of things.* New York, NY: Random House.

Foucault, M. (1976). *The birth of the clinic.* London, UK: Routledge.

Jacks, T. (2000). *The warmth of love, The 4 seasons of Sophie Thomas (DVD).* Vanderhoof, BC: Sophie Thomas Foundation.

Latour, B. (1988). *Pasteurization of France.* Chicago, IL: University of Chicago Press.

Latour, B. (1993). *We have never been modern.* Cambridge, MA: Harvard University Press.

Nicholas, A. B. (2008). The assault on Aboriginal oral traditions: past and present. In R. Eigenbrod, & R. Hulan, *Aboriginal oral traditions: theory, practice, ethics,* 13–43 Halifax, NS, and Winnipeg, MB: Fernwood Publications.

Pickstone, J. (2000). *Ways of knowing: a new history of science, technology and medicine.* Chicago, IL: University of Chicago Press.

Rosenberg, C. (1992). *Explaining epidemics and other studies in the history of medicine.* Cambridge, UK: Cambridge University Press.

Useful Websites

McMaster University, Aboriginal Health Sciences Programme, educational videos: http://fhs.mcmaster.ca/ashs/video.html

Sophie Thomas's website on traditional healing: www.sophiethomas.org

University of Ottawa, School of Medicine, Traditional Aboriginal Medicine: www.med.uottawa.ca/sim/data/Aboriginal_Medicine_e.htm

Cultural Competency, Cultural Sensitivity and Cultural Safety

Chapter Objectives

- To explain the important differences among the three models of intercultural care.

- To explain the concept of cultural safety, its origins and development.

- To explain how it can be adapted to the Canadian multicultural context.

- To demonstrate how epistemological accommodation can be used to implement cultural safety in Canada.

Key Concepts

Cultural Competency

Cultural Safety

Cultural Sensitivity

Epistemological
   Accommodation

Ethnic Origin

Intercultural Nursing

Multicultural

Patient-Centered Care

Professional Standards

Sharps Safety

Key Terms

Awareness

Beliefs

Competency

Cooperation

Cultural Relevance

Demean

Diminish

Disempower

Dominance

Hierarchy

Legislation

Method

Practice

Recognize

Regulation

Respect

Safety

Sensitivity

Standards

Values

MODERN HEALTH CARE IN THE 21ST CENTURY

Over the last 25 years modern health care systems and governments in Canada and other Western countries have been facing changes to their users and citizenry. This period has seen increased non-Western immigration to all industrialized countries. Immigrants to Canada no longer come from other industrialized parts of the West, such as those who entered from the large urbanized centres of Europe following the Second World War. This change in immigration patterns has led to increased population diversity and has broadened the extent of Canada's multiculturalism (Figure 3.1).

Even as the ethnic make-up of Canada's population has changed, so too has its attitude toward authority. In company with other populations in the world, Canadians are more assertive, more willing to claim rights and privileges. This change in attitude is also apparent among Canada's ethnic minorities, both foreign in origin and Aboriginal. Groups as diverse as Japanese-Canadians, Ukrainian-Canadians and the First Nations have begun calling for redress for past wrongs or their fair share of the Canadian polity today.

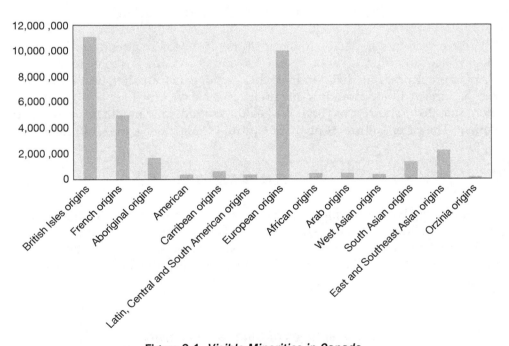

Figure 3.1 *Visible Minorities in Canada*

Canadian population by ethnic origins.
Source: Statistics Canada Census of Population 2011.

A KINDER, GENTLER HEALTH CARE?

The problem is that the old, authoritarian models of health care delivery assumed that the population was homogeneous, that everyone could be treated in the same way, and that everyone would do as they were told. This no longer holds true of even the European-descended segments of the population, much less for those who do not recognize the cultural authority of biomedicine.

However, Canada has had universal health care for over 40 years now. This means that every person in Canada has the right to their share of public health. More importantly, allowing the health care of certain groups to fall behind risks creating perpetual reservoirs of disease and ill health that ultimately threaten everyone's well-being. Although public health regulations allow non-cooperative patients with contagious conditions to be forcibly treated, this is both expensive and risks creating long-term social problems. It also risks the potential for charges being made that health care authorities are violating patients' civil rights.

Instead, modern health care systems have been learning to accommodate this new reality through models of intercultural care. In effect, nurses, doctors and administrators have been trying to find ways of meeting the cultural needs of patients while also treating their physical health.

THREE MODELS OF INTERCULTURAL CARE

There are various approaches to intercultural care used in nursing and medicine, all of which have their advantages and drawbacks. In Canada, there are three models of intercultural care that dominate the discourse in Canadian health care. They can be ranked in an ascending hierarchy of their effectiveness and the commitment that they require from both the health care provider and, to some extent, the patient. They are: Cultural Sensitivity, Cultural Competency and Cultural Safety.

CULTURAL SENSITIVITY

Cultural sensitivity is the most superficial and least demanding form of intercultural care. As the name suggests, the nurse is asked to be aware of the existence of different cultural practices and beliefs. No specific actions are either required or suggested of either the nurse or the patient. Instead the focus is on awareness of difference.

Advantages of Cultural Sensitivity

Although this may appear to be superficial, in reality the act of awareness may be enough to put patients at ease in the health care setting. It is also likely to put the practitioner more at ease by preparing her/him for culturally diverse patients. In an administrative sense, cultural sensitivity is relatively simple to teach, and very easy to practise, as no action is required from the nurse beyond a simple awareness of cultural difference. It is also, in a sense, the foundation for all other types of intercultural care, as awareness of cultural difference is necessary before any concrete action can be undertaken.

Disadvantages of Cultural Sensitivity

On the other hand, cultural sensitivity is not generally viewed as helpful in the clinical setting. It is more of a useful first step but leads to no real change in the institutional environment. Most authorities suggest a more activist approach to a culturally diverse patient population.

CULTURAL COMPETENCY

The most common practical approach to intercultural care is cultural competency. It was developed in the United States, partly by the U.S. military. As this suggests, cultural competency is more common in the United States than elsewhere, although some health care institutions in Canada have also adopted it as their model for intercultural care.

Although there are a few dissenting approaches to cultural competency, the overwhelming majority stress a checklist approach to intercultural care. In practice, this means that nurses, and other practitioners, become culturally competent by learning to react to patients identified as being part of a distinct and recognized ethnic group in a way that has been predefined as appropriate to their culture. Indeed, practitioners, nurses and otherwise, can be certified as culturally competent by satisfying a list of requirements. This proves that they can react in a culturally competent way when faced with a patient from a culture in which they have been certified to be culturally competent. Although there are a number of institutions offering courses and certifications in cultural competency, the National Center for Cultural Competence, Georgetown University, Washington, DC, is the most prominent one. It issues certificates and administers this program for the United States government and military.

Advantages of Cultural Competency

Cultural competency does have advantages. The creation of a list of skills and requirements for certification creates a defined goal to which practitioners, whether nurses or other health care professionals, can aspire. Achieving this goal then becomes the definition of what cultural competency is.

In addition, the centralized organization that is a feature of cultural competency and the uniform standards that are inherent to it create a reliable definition of what it is that everyone can understand, and is readily both achievable and easily recognized in the health care community. Effectively, cultural competency provides a simplified approach to intercultural care that is both activist (unlike cultural sensitivity) and testable: Cultural competence is proven through the certification test. It has proved remarkably popular with institutional authorities for that very reason.

Drawbacks of Cultural Competency

However, there are some serious flaws with cultural competency as well. The certification approach only certifies the practitioner within the limits of the exam—it says nothing about their cultural awareness or ability to interact with patients beyond that limited metric. As well, the checklist approach that cultural competency certification fosters tends to pigeon-hole people, including patients, according to cultural norms they may not all hold. Even people from the same ethnic background may not all hold the same values and views, but cultural competency assumes that they do and will necessarily react according to fixed cultural values. Variations then become departures from the norms defined by cultural competency exams, and a failure on the patient's part to be a "real" First Nation, or "real" Inuit. This has obvious implications both for the patient and the nurse in the relationship.

CULTURAL SAFETY

The highest level of intercultural care is cultural safety, which was developed by Irihapeti Ramsden, a Maori nurse and academic, in New Zealand in the 1980s. It was designed to overcome the barriers to accessible health care experienced by the Maori population. Cultural safety has become part of the official health policy in New Zealand and has been integrated into the nursing, midwifery, medicine and social work curricula there. The concept has since spread, with variations to account for cultural, political and constitutional differences, to Australia, Canada and other jurisdictions with significant Aboriginal or immigrant populations.

Sharps Safety and Cultural Safety

Cultural safety transfers the concept of safety in nursing from physical behaviour to cultural behaviour. Ramsden explicitly modelled the term and concept on "Sharps Safety". Nurses are taught to engage in certain behaviour around sharp

---

Irihapeti Ramsden

Irihapeti Ramsden, RN, PhD (1946–2003), was a New Zealand Maori nurse, anthropologist and educator. She was noted for her passion for Maori health and culture and was regarded as one of the most influential Maori leaders of her generation. In her practice as a general duty and obstetric nurse, she noticed the cultural obstacles to health care that Maori faced, and was able to analyze them both as a nurse and as a Maori. From this experience she developed the concept of cultural safety, which has evolved into the dominant paradigm for intercultural nursing in New Zealand and Australia. Her efforts to promote knowledge of Maori issues and well-being included public lectures on the New Zealand constitution, the Treaty of Waitangi and cultural safety. She also took part in publishing ventures (including publishing a Booker Prize-winning novel), was a fellow of the New Zealand College of Nurses and was appointed to the New Zealand Order of Merit shortly before her death (Ellison-Loschmann, 2003).

---

objects, such as syringes, in order to render them safe. However, far from being simple awareness of sharps, or a checklist of actions to take when encountering a sharp object, sharps safety requires nurses to exercise active care when practising. Nurses must undertake constant self-evaluation to determine that their environment is safe from sharp objects. As such, sharps safety is an ongoing process of education and self-reflection. Although safety checklists and procedures have their place, as do safety engineered sharps, self-awareness and constant reflection on one's practice is the core of successful sharps safety.

Patient-Centred Cultural Care

Like sharps safety, cultural safety requires the professional to exercise safe behaviour. However, whereas sharps safety is largely internalized by the practitioner, cultural safety is externalized. It places the responsibility for determining whether cultural safety is being observed on the patient. That is, the patient determines if the nurse is culturally safe, not the nurse. This ensures that culturally appropriate care is consistently delivered irrespective of the ethnic origin or outlook of the patient, as the focus of care remains the individual patient, not the patient's presumed cultural background. It also requires the practitioner to constantly engage in self-evaluation to ensure that the patient's need for culturally safe care is fulfilled. This is difficult, as it requires nurses and other practitioners to be constantly aware of their patient's response to care and be actively engaged in modifying their own behaviour in response to its feedback. Cultural safety focuses on the individual patient, but considers the patient within the context of power relationships that originate in the colonial encounter between Europeans and non-Western people and that are institutionalized in both Western society and the health care system. Cultural safety is a means for health care professionals to alter this colonial relationship by making a safe space for Aboriginal patients within the health care system, and in doing so to reshape the system itself.

Nurses practising cultural safety must avoid the three *D*s. They must not: *Diminish, Demean or Disempower* the cultural identity and the well-being of the individual. Instead they must follow the three *R*s: *Recognize* and *Respect* the *Rights* and nurture the unique cultural identity of the Aboriginal people (Polaschek, 1998). This is not an easy prescription, however. Yet, successful, culturally safe practice is extremely rewarding, as it maintains a strong nurse–patient bond, and ultimately improves the standard of care for all patients, regardless of their cultural background.

A key component of culturally safe care is creation of space in which patients can feel safe while expressing concern about their care. This requires institutional rules that explicitly protect patients' right to appeal their treatment and make patients aware they can do so without facing retaliation.

Rules for Cultural Safety

Payne (2005) compiled a list of practices that nurses can do to ensure that they are culturally safe. The culturally safe nurse:

1. Values diversity and recognizes the importance of enhancing cultural values and social practices in the lives of individuals, families and communities.
2. Is culturally aware and engages in self-examination and in-depth exploration of his/her own cultural background to identify biases, prejudices and assumptions about people who are different.
3. Has the motivation and desire to become more culturally safe and actively seeks experiences to reshape his/her epistemology and appreciate the epistemology of others.
4. Has cultural humility and is aware that becoming culturally safe is a life-long commitment.
5. Is willing to invest the time and commitment to foster relationships of mutual benefit, mutual respect and mutual trust.
6. Tries not to impose his/her cultural values on others and is non-judgmental.
7. Is alert to new forms of racism and oppression; views situations through a cultural safety lens and has the ability to recognize cultural issues.
8. Is willing to ask daily how his/her practice might be recreating the traumas inflicted on First Nations people.
9. Brings a service delivery philosophy that emphasizes the importance that access to health services, education, decent housing, social support systems and satisfying employment provides for life-changing behaviour.

10. Recognizes that individuals, families and community members must participate in and ultimately gain control over decision making regarding their health and health services; is willing to work with the community to build these partnerships.

11. Recognizes that health is more than physical; it is also closely related to a whole set of personal values and social resources.

12. Understands that the historical and socio-economic context creates dependency on Western medical technology, and acknowledges that healing in First Nations communities is about reclaiming their own historical practices.

13. Is a good listener; listens to others' values, beliefs, concerns, resources, abilities and motivations.

14. Is willing to work together with others, celebrate their differences and use complementary talents and skills to build a more effective health care team.

PROFESSIONAL STANDARDS AND ABORIGINAL UNDERSTANDING

Cultural safety is now an official policy of the Canadian Nurses Association, which has adopted it in an effort to improve standards of practice with both the Canadian Aboriginal population and the increasing immigrant population of non-Western origin. Provincial nursing associations, the Canadian Association of Schools of Nursing and the Canadian Medical Association have all endorsed the concept of cultural safety and are working on integrating it into practice in Canada.

However, there are some obstacles to implementation of cultural safety in Canada. Canada is a multicultural society, which is working hard both to recognize its cultural diversity and to maintain core standards that will bind together a society within that diversity. New Zealand, on the other hand, is an essentially bicultural society split between the Maori minority and a majority of largely British descent. Non-Maori, non-British immigrants have largely been absorbed into the majority population and the values of both Maori and European New Zealanders have had a century and a half of convergence. This makes cultural safety straightforward to adopt in New Zealand as Maori and European New Zealanders share enough fundamental values to make compromise workable. New Zealand nurses are unlikely to have their professional standards compromised through culturally safe practice (Spence, 2001).

Canada's cultural diversity poses more of a challenge. Canadian health care professionals are unlikely to implement cultural safety if it means compromising their own values or those of mainstream Canadian society. In essence, the professionals need to feel culturally safe as much as the patients do. Thus a compromise is needed.

EPISTEMOLOGICAL ACCOMMODATION AND CULTURAL SAFETY

The Canadian version of cultural safety requires epistemological accommodation. While the practitioner must respect and understand the culture of the patient and practise culturally safe care, at the same time the patient must practise a form of

The Limits of Safety: Female Circumcision

Some urban regions of Canada have a significant population that has emigrated from places in the world where female infant circumcision and infibulations are accepted cultural practices. Although most abandon these practices in Canada, some wish to continue them. In Canada, female circumcision is regarded as mutilation and assault on a minor and is a crime under the Canadian Criminal Code. Any nurse, or other health care provider, would face serious assault charges, in addition to being guilty of professional misconduct, if they either assisted in such a procedure or were aware of it and failed to report it. In this case, societal norms in Canada limit the extent of cultural safety, requiring culturally safe practice to conform to the limits of Canadian professional regulations, as well as to consider the cultural milieu of the patient.

reciprocal cultural safety, by respecting the professional limits of the practitioner. Both health care practitioners and patients keep their own values and practices, but actively accommodate each other's culture and values within the clinical setting.

Although we have presented cultural safety as a form of care that is applicable to all patients in Canada, in practice most nurses encounter patients drawn from the Aboriginal population, especially First Nations, but increasingly Métis and Inuit as well, who actively require a commitment to culturally safe care. With the growth of the urban Aboriginal population, virtually every nurse, anywhere in Canada, will encounter Aboriginal patients who will expect respect for their culture and values.

Three Canadian Models

There are three Canadian models for culturally safe care with Aboriginal populations. These are: the Inuulitsivik Maternities in Nunavik, Québec; the Kahnawake Schools Diabetes Prevention Project in Kahnawake, Québec and the Aboriginal Healing Foundation's Healing Centres, which are found in every part of Canada. Although each of these will be explained in more detail in later chapters, their significance for cultural safety and epistemological accommodation is particularly noteworthy.

Inuulitsivik Maternities

The Inuulitsivik Maternities are a network of Inuit birthing centres, served by Inuit midwives, in Northern Québec. Their creation in 1986 ended the practice of routinely evacuating women to Montreal for childbirth, allowing women to give birth in the community and allowing prenatal and postnatal care to be seam-lessly integrated. Only high-risk patients are still evacuated and the definition of high-risk is not made by physicians, or even by using a score sheet for risk assessment. Instead a community board, with representatives from the medical staff, the community and the midwives who actually attend births, make the decisions based on community priorities and desires. The outcome is that more children are now born in the community than previously, perinatal outcomes are equal to the best hospitals in Southern Canada, and levels of interventions (caesarian sections) are falling to much lower than national averages. This com-bination has made the Maternities successful clinically, culturally and economi-cally (Douglas, 2010).

Kahnawake School Diabetes Prevention Project

The Kahnawake Schools Diabetes Prevention Project (KSDPP) was created in the early 1990s as a long-term solution to high rates of diabetes on the Kahnawake Reserve in Southern Québec. The project has both professional staff and academic advisors, but its core is the Community Advisory Board, which directs the Project and has been instrumental in recruiting support for it from within the community. By promoting traditional Mohawk values and diet, and also advancing techniques in blood glucose monitoring and evaluation of the clinical outcomes of the Project, the KSDPP has made a success of integrating clinical skills, research facilities and traditional knowledge in addressing diabetes in the population.

Aboriginal Healing Centres

The Aboriginal Healing Foundation was created in 1998 to manage community-directed healing programs that would treat the trauma caused by generations of Aboriginal children attending residential schools. The foundation created a network of traditional healing centres spread across Canada. Their methods vary accord-ing to the cultural norms and wishes of the local native communities, but they are generally directed by First Nations personnel and utilize a blend of traditional and medical techniques to treat collective trauma caused by the residential schools. Although the total number of residential school survivors and their descendants far outnumber those fortunate enough to attend the healing centres, they have had some success in connecting those who have received treatment with their cultures and helped them to resume normal lives (Aboriginal Healing Foundation, 2003).

CRITICAL THINKING EXERCISE—SENSITIVITY, SAFETY AND COMPETENCE

List the ways in which the triage nurse in the case study was or was not cultur-ally sensitive, culturally competent and culturally safe. What could have been done differently?

Case Study

A young Aboriginal woman enters the emergency room at a major urban hospital with two young children. She seems quiet and composed, registers the children and herself with the triage nurse and states that they have all been feeling ill and coughing for some time, but are now feeling worse. The nurse asks where they are from and discovers that they live in the city. The nurse then asks what Aboriginal group she belongs to and finds out that the young woman is a member of a local First Nation. Their temperatures are taken and are slightly elevated, and the nurse notes that one of the children, a boy, has a black eye. She asks the mother whether they would like the services of an Aboriginal counsellor, but the mother refuses and states that her son fell off the equipment at a playground. The nurse notes on their file a possible case of child abuse and assesses the family as otherwise low priority and sends them to the waiting room to wait to be seen.

The family remains in the waiting room for 6 more hours, during which their coughing becomes worse. After 6 hours, the family is seen by a physician, who diagnoses tuberculosis (TB). Over 100 patients who passed through the waiting room have to be screened, as well as the staff in the emergency room.

The little boy's eye injury was caused by falling off a schoolyard playground, while visiting his father's family at a remote northern community, where TB is endemic.

Discussion Questions

1. What sort of reaction to pain might a culturally sensitive nurse expect from a First Nations patient? How should the nurse react in turn?

2. How would you describe the process of two or more cultures adapting to one another so that people from both respective cultures can interact with each other?

3. How does sharps safety inform the Cultural Safety theory?

4. What is the relationship between Cultural Sensitivity, Cultural Competency and Cultural Safety?

5. Which organizations tend to routinely use cultural competency for nursing practice and why do they do so, rather than using cultural safety?

6. Does a nurse have to be culturally sensitive in order to be culturally safe? Why?

7. How should health care professionals respond to requests that exceed their professional practice boundaries?

REFERENCES AND FURTHER READING

Aboriginal Healing Foundation. (2003). *Third interim evaluation report of Aboriginal Healing Foundation program activity.* Ottawa, ON: Aboriginal Healing Foundation.

Anderson, J., Perry, J., Blue, C., Browne, A., Henderson, A., Basu Kahn, K.,…Smye, V. (2003). Rewriting cultural safety within the postcolonial and postnational feminist project: Toward new epistemologies of healing. *Advances in Nursing Science, 26*(3), 196–214.

Atleo, M. (1997). First Nations healing: Dominance or health. *The Canadian Journal for the Study of Adult Education, 11*(2), 63–67.

Douglas, V. K. (2010). The Inuulitsivik Maternities: Culturally appropriate midwifery and epistemological accommodation. *Nursing Inquiry, 17*(2), 111–117.

Ellison-Loschmann, L. (2003). Obituary: Irihapeti Ramsden. *British Medical Journal, 327*(7412), 453.

Payne, H. (2005). *Closing the gap: A journey to cultural safety.* Nanaimo, BC: Inter Tribal Health Authority, Transfer Department. www.intertribalhealth.ca/publications.html

Polaschek, N. R. (1998). Cultural Safety: A new concept in nursing people of different ethnicities. *Journal of Advanced Nursing, 27*(3) 452–457.

Smye, V., & Browne, A. (1999). "Cultural Safety" and the analysis of health policy affecting Aboriginal people. *Nurse Researcher, 9*(3), 42–56.

Spence, D. (2001). Prejudice, paradox and possibility: Nursing people from cultures other than one's own. *Journal of Transcultural Nursing, 12*(2), 100–106.

Useful Websites

Anishnawbe Health Toronto: Aboriginal Cultural Safety Initiative. www.aht.ca/Aboriginal-culture-safety

Cultural Competency: Registered Nurses Association of Ontario, Embracing Cultural Diversity in Health Care: Developing Cultural Competence: http://rnao.ca/bpg/guidelines/embracing-cultural-diversity-health-care-developing-cultural-competence

National Center for Cultural Competence, Georgetown University. http://nccc.georgetown.edu/

University of Victoria online course on cultural safety:

Module 1: http://web2.uvcs.uvic.ca/courses/csafety/mod1/

Module 2: http://web2.uvcs.uvic.ca/courses/csafety/mod2/

Module 3: http://web2.uvcs.uvic.ca/courses/csafety/mod3/

4

Historical Overview

Chapter Objectives

1. To outline the history of Aboriginal peoples in Canada from pre-contact to the present
2. To explain how their historical experiences have informed their health status today
3. To illustrate the uniqueness of the Canadian experience for both Aboriginal and non-Aboriginal peoples of Canada
4. To survey Aboriginal history and Aboriginal–White relations in Canada, while also indicating how this differs from Aboriginal–European relations in other national contexts. The goal is to provide a sense of the historical context that informs the Aboriginal relationship with the health care system today.

Key Concepts

Assimilation

Traditional Medicine

Biomedicine

Pre-Contact

Depopulation

Decolonizing

Sovereignty

Virgin Soil Epidemic

Devolution

Decentralization

Resistance

Fur Trade Economy

Key Terms

Contact

Smallpox

Measles

Mumps

Rubella

Syphilis

Tuberculosis (TB)

Tokenism

Royal Proclamation

Residential Schools

Land Claims

Constitution Act
(1982)

Charter of Rights and
Freedoms

Terra Nullius

Racism

Chauvinism

Matrilineal

Enfranchisement

PRE-CONTACT HISTORY

Although there are no direct historical records of the pre-contact period in Canadian history, we can reconstruct it from explorers' accounts, archaeology and oral history. It is certain that the Aboriginal peoples of North and Central America existed in a diversity of cultures at least as wide as Europe and Asia. While Aboriginal peoples in Central and South America developed very complex societies with large urban areas (such as pre-contact Mexico City), the Canadian environment limited the lifestyle and material culture options for most pre-contact cultures here. There were, however, exceptions.

ABORIGINAL FARMERS

A significant number of pre-contact Aboriginal cultures were agricultural and based their economies and societies on farming. The heartland of pre-contact Aboriginal agriculture lay in southern North America, Central America and the Andean Highlands, but in Eastern Canada the Iroquois of the St. Lawrence Valley and the Huron of the Niagara Peninsula developed sophisticated societies based on agriculture. Further east, the Micmac and other peoples on the Eastern seaboard developed sophisticated societies based on a seasonal round of fishing, hunting and gathering.

Overall, the Aboriginal farmers of the Americas domesticated a wide range of crops from their wild ancestors, including corn, beans, potatoes, melons, squash, avocados, tomatoes, cacao (chocolate), tobacco and vanilla. Despite the difficult environment, even a few groups on the Canadian Prairies managed to grow some hardy varieties of corn shortly before contact. The Iroquois and Huron also faced climatic restrictions due to the harsh winters, but still managed to grow beans, maize, melons, squash and tobacco, as their summers were long and warm, and the soils of the Niagara Peninsula and St. Lawrence Valley were very fertile.

VILLAGES AND LAWS

The Iroquois, who composed the Six Nations Confederacy, the Huron Confederacy and other smaller groups, in particular developed a complex agrarian society, characterized by substantial villages and intensive cropping of corn, beans and squash. Although fishing and hunting were also important sources of food, farming provided most of the diet. The Iroquois (Six Nations Confederacy) developed a strong legal tradition and highly complex society characterized by villages of several hundred people. Their laws and traditions included a complex federal system of government with approximately equal rights for women, including veto rights over treaties and policy. Within Iroquois society, inheritance was matrilineal and women retained their property and their children through marriage and divorce. These features of Iroquoian society were very

Joseph Brant

Thayendanega, better known in Canada as Joseph Brant, was a leader of the Mohawk Nation in the 18th century. His intellectual and social abilities were recognized by members of the British and colonial aristocracy before the American Revolution. His mansion in New York was the site of the leading social circle of the day. When war broke out he allied his people with the British, and led them to Canada, where they were given a large land grant on the Grand River in Southern Ontario. The city of Brantford is named after him.
Source: Library and Archives Canada, ACC. 1970–188-2367 Purchased with a grant from the Secretary of State / MIKAN 2833416.

advanced over European norms of the time. Their system of government was admired by the British colonists and may have served as one of the models for the United States Constitution.

NOMADIC HUNTERS

Throughout most of Northern Canada and the Prairie West, Aboriginal cultures depended on hunting and gathering. The basis of their diet was large game animals—bison on the Prairie and caribou in the North. Since their major food sources were migratory, these peoples were also highly mobile, moving with their food supplies.

Those peoples who relied on the bison developed a sophisticated hunting culture and strong social organization centred around hunting and raiding bands. The bison herds were large enough to support substantial nomadic

Bison Hunters

George Catlin: The Bison Hunt on the Canadian Prairies. The arrival of the horse revolutionized
Prairie First Nations' hunting and military strength.
Source: Library and Archives Canada, Catlins American Indian collection ACC. No. 1960–50-2.6 / MIKAN 2837384.

communities, especially during the summer months. After horses captured from the Spanish were introduced in the 17th century, the Prairie First Nations became powerful and well-organized military forces that organized into large alliances based on shared language and culture, such as the Blackfoot Confederacy, the Crow, the Plains Cree, the Sioux and other groups.

Farther north smaller hunter-gatherer groups among the Cree and Dene followed the caribou herds through the boreal forest, although large gatherings for trade and social interaction were also regular features of the yearly cycle. On the East Coast, the harsh climate restricted farming for the Micmac, Maliseet, Beothuk and Innu, but they developed an economy focused around fishing and hunting.

FISHERS OF THE COAST

Although the climate on the Northwest Coast is not suitable for agriculture, it does abound in marine life that is sufficient to support substantial communities. Pre-contact Aboriginal cultures of the Pacific Coast developed a village culture focused on fishing for oceanic species, marine mammals and salmon. Although they moved between summer and winter villages, their food resources allowed them to develop a complex hierarchical society and elaborate material culture, reflected in their artwork and the potlatch.

The potlatch was one of the most important cultural practices among Northwest Coast peoples. It was a gift-giving ceremony, in which the prestige and social standing of the gift-giver depended on how much could be given away. Rivals would in turn hold their own potlatch ceremonies and attempt to increase their own prestige by outdoing the others. European colonists found the concept of, and economy founded on, gift giving rather than on the accumulation of wealth to be both alien and repulsive, and did their best to suppress the practice by passing laws to forbid potlatching. In Canada the potlatch was banned in 1884, through an amendment to the Indian Act. Despite this, First

Haida Village at Skidegate

A photograph of the village of Skidegate on Haida Gwai'i in 1878.
Source: George M. Dawson / Library and Archives Canada / PA-037756 / MIKAN 3368507.

The Governess-General's Sketch of Skidegate

The village of Skidegate as drawn by Lady Dufferin, wife of the Governor General, in 1876:
The large villages of the Pacific Coast fascinated European travellers.
Source: Library and Archives Canada / MIKAN 2837685.

Nations on the coast continued practising the potlatch in secret, as most Indian Agents and the police were either unable or unwilling to enforce the ban. The ban was rescinded in 1951, and since then the practice has been increasing in popularity and frequency.

Salmon resources were abundant enough to support village life in the Pacific interior (west of the Rocky Mountains), wherever the salmon runs extended to. Although their villages were smaller, and most members dispersed onto the land to hunt and gather in the summer, the Interior peoples also practised the potlatch and forged strong trade links with the coastal First Nations.

THE INUIT

Despite differences in languages, specific cultural practices and location, there are strong cultural similarities among different First Nations peoples in North America. Their world views were similar, if not identical, and radically different from the dominant European epistemology.

Notably, a different Aboriginal culture, the Inuit, inhabited the High Arctic. The Inuit are closely related to other circumpolar populations in Russia and Alaska, with whom they traded. The Inuit see themselves, and in turn are seen, as very different from the First Nations to the south. In a few regions, such as the Mackenzie Delta, whaling supported seasonal Inuit villages of up to 1,000 people. Elsewhere, the Inuit lived in small family groups in a marginal lifestyle focused on survival in a very inhospitable environment.

The environment shaped Inuit society and culture, enforcing a world-view that was based on consensus and group survival. The Inuit, then and now, avoid conflict and competition, as their environment is so harsh that sharing is the only way for communities to survive—and individuals without a community ultimately die out.

This perspective has both helped and hindered the Inuit in the modern world. On the one hand, their avoidance of conflict and their culture of cooperation and sharing have opened them to exploitation, first by whalers and fur traders, and later by government officials, businessmen and missionaries. On the other hand, they have also exhibited a quiet determination to maintain their traditional culture, while adopting Southern technology when it suits their principles.

HEALTH AND WELFARE

Archaeological evidence has suggested that in general pre-contact Aboriginal peoples were well nourished—helped by a generally low population density and diet high in protein and low in fat. It may seem surprising, but hunter-gatherers were particularly well nourished, as they were quite mobile and were able to travel widely in pursuit of their food supply. Although prone to famine in the winter and spring, most still maintained an adequate diet helped by their low population density.

Burial practices of the Assiniboine

Tombs of Assiniboine Indians in trees (1840–43): While different Aboriginal groups had had very
different burial practices, many placed their dead on platforms. This was both practical and respectful.
As the picture suggests, it kept the bodies out of reach of wild animals, and also allowed them to
decompose with a low risk of contamination.
Source: Wikimedia Commons, Karl Bodmer. Plate 30 in Maximilian zu Wied-Neuwied. Maximilian Prince of Wied's
Travels in the Interior of North America, during the years 1832–1834. Ackermann & Company, London 1843–1844.

The farmers of the East did engage in frequent conflict over land and
resources. Their lifestyle, however, limited most intercommunity conflict to raiding, rather than large-scale warfare, as did their lack of modern technology. As
such, most pre-contact Aboriginal peoples lived a life that, although it required
unceasing hard work to sustain life, was nonetheless harmonious with their
environment and largely peaceful.

Death could come through accident, injury, or through wounds sustained
in warfare, but most died of old age. Even the more warlike of the Plains First
Nations seldom engaged in large scale conflict or suffered mass casualties. Only
the complex and wealthy civilizations of Central America seem to have engaged
in systematic and large-scale warfare with high casualty rates.

DISEASE BEFORE CONTACT

There is little evidence that disease was present in the Americas before contact with Europe. There are some signs of tuberculosis (TB) in human remains present in archaeological excavations, but these are disputed, and do not seem to reflect any widespread diffusion of the disease, since Aboriginal peoples were notably vulnerable to European strains of TB when exposed to the disease after contact, suggesting that there was little or no inherent resistance to TB.

Other infectious diseases were completely absent. Even the common cold does not appear to have infected Aboriginal peoples of the Americas before Europeans brought it with them after contact.

EUROPEAN CONTACT

Europeans, on the other hand, had millennia of exposure to all the diseases that had been developed in Europe, Asia and Africa, as there had been widespread contact between these regions since the prehistoric period. Repeated epidemics over hundreds, even thousands of years, slowly built up resistance in European populations to most infectious diseases. Even smallpox and the Black Plague, historically major sources of mortality in Europe, killed a relatively small proportion of the European population by the 16th century. As well, mortality was concentrated in infants and children, as they possessed weaker and immature immune systems. Most adults, especially adult men, were resistant to disease, although still capable of carrying them and infecting others. Most significantly, when Europeans began exploring and settling the Americas in substantial numbers they brought their diseases with them.

DISEASE AND CONQUEST

Previous generations of historians emphasized the technological gap between Aboriginal cultures and Europeans, particularly the gap in military technology to explain the rapid collapse of Aboriginal societies in the face of European settlement and colonization. While it is true that Aboriginal technology was Stone Age, most Aboriginal peoples were quick to adopt metal implements, weapons and European techniques like reading and writing—as quick as the Europeans were to trade these tools and ideas to them. Nor were Aboriginal techniques and technologies as backward, when compared to early European technologies, as most have assumed. Before mass production of breech-loading rifles and rapid firing artillery, Aboriginal weaponry faced primitive European muzzle-loading muskets, which was not that large of a technological gap. The well-organized, urbanized cultures of the Eastern seaboard and Mexico were both ready and willing to respond to European aggression. Centuries of conflict among themselves had made them quite capable in both war and diplomacy.

On the Pacific Coast, when European ships arrived at the end of the 18th century, First Nations traders were quick to see and seize advantages, dominating the fur trade there for at least two decades.

However, within a little over a century, Europeans had established themselves as the dominant group everywhere they went. What defeated Aboriginal peoples was neither technology nor intellectual superiority (although literacy was a significant advantage, it was quickly lost as Aboriginal peoples adapted European writing systems to their own requirements), but rather infectious disease.

DISEASE IMPACTS

Centuries of European exposure to infectious diseases gave them partial immunity as a population, even though individuals could and did succumb to diseases. However, Aboriginal populations had no such immunity. The results were what are called virgin soil epidemics.

Virgin soil epidemics were characterized by diseases that were more virulent, spread faster and caused a much higher mortality rate in the populations they infected, which were without any inherited resistance or immunity to any infectious diseases. These diseases had once caused similar mortality rates in European populations, but that had occurred centuries, even millennia earlier, and without the accompanying waves of invasions by immune populations.

Among the Aboriginal populations of the Americas, up to 90% mortality rates for diseases such as smallpox were the result of these early disease encounters (among Europeans the equivalent mortality rate was 30%). Survivors were often weakened and succumbed to exposure and hunger. Other diseases, such as TB, which was a slow wasting disease in Europe, could kill Aboriginal victims in weeks. There were many diseases that travelled the Atlantic with explorers and settlers and all of them proved to be far more virulent among the Aboriginal population than they had been in Europe for some time.

SOME IMPORTED DISEASES

Smallpox: This was the most serious disease, even in Europe. It remained an acute global public health hazard until the 20th century, until international mass vaccination programs eliminated the disease. However, its effects on the Aboriginal population when smallpox first arrived in the Americas were much more severe, and indeed often preceded physical contact with Europeans. It was usually spread through the Aboriginal population by existing trade routes, allowing the epidemic that started in Mexico in 1775, for instance, to spread as far as the Pacific Northwest.

Measles, mumps and rubella: These had become largely pediatric diseases in Europe by the 16th century, as illness in childhood usually conferred lifetime immunity. They were major contributors to high pediatric mortality rates in the European population, but were less significant among the adult population. Among the Aboriginal population, adults did not have immunity initially, leading to community-wide epidemics that devastated whole populations.

Tuberculosis: This was, and remains, a major public health issue among the Aboriginal population. Although TB was endemic among the European population until antibiotic therapy reduced its prevalence in the 20th century, its progression was usually slow. Most people carried TB, but were not ill until their immune systems weakened enough for it to become active. Without the presence of antibodies to the TB bacillus, and with exposure to a host of other diseases to weaken their immune systems, Aboriginal peoples often died of TB in weeks rather than years, and developed "galloping consumption," where tubercular infection spread throughout the body, often eating holes through the chest cavity from the lungs.

Syphilis: Scientific evidence suggests that the spirochete bacterium that causes syphilis originated as a pediatric skin disease in the Caribbean and South America. The disease was contracted and transformed into its venereal form by the sailors of Christopher Columbus's ships on his first voyage to the Americas. Once established in Europe it spread rapidly, with the first outbreak occurring in Naples in 1494. As a virgin soil epidemic, syphilis was extremely virulent in Europe, progressing rapidly from primary through secondary to tertiary stages in as little as a year. Often patients literally rotted to death from the tertiary form of the disease, or became demented. It was not until the 19th century that the virulence of the disease abated, while it remained a severe public health risk until the development of antibiotics in the 20th century. Tragically, it was transmitted back to the Americas by infected explorers and colonists, where its virulence matched that of Europe and its effects were only mitigated by the lower population densities caused by other epidemic diseases.

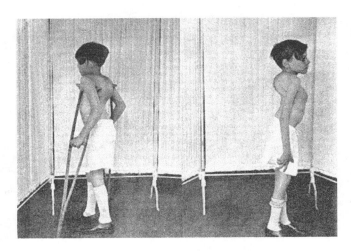

Spinal Tuberculosis (TB) Victim

Visible deformities in a boy recovered from TB infection of the spine.
Source: Canadian Lung Association, from the *Valley Echo*, February 1928. 9(2);18.

MAP OF THE 1775–1782 SMALLPOX EPIDEMIC

This smallpox epidemic began in Mexico in 1775 and progressed across North America, transmitted along existing Aboriginal trade routes, before finally reaching the limits of transmission in the Arctic. Both the Inuit and the North Coast First Nations of British Columbia escaped this epidemic as they were too remote for disease carriers to reach them before dying of the disease themselves. This was the largest and best documented of early epidemics, but there were many more. The massive mortality caused by epidemics like this damaged Aboriginal cultures and severely reduced their populations, allowing European settlement to supplant the survivors.

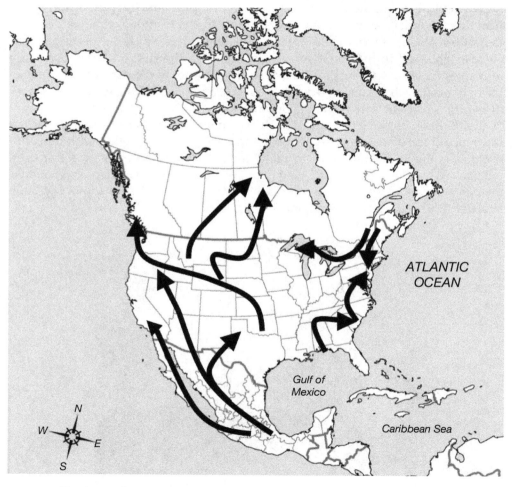

The Approximate Route of Smallpox Across North America. 1775–1782

Source: V. K. Douglas.

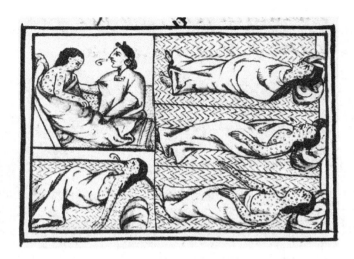

Mexican Aboriginals With Smallpox, 16th Century

Source: From the Florentine Codex (~1590), World Digital Library: http://www.wdl.org/en/item/10096.

THE FUR TRADE

In Canada early contact with the Aboriginal population was dominated by the fur trade, rather than the actual settlement and domination by Europeans that marked the experience of Aboriginal peoples farther south. Fur traders exploited and replaced existing Aboriginal trade networks with ones focused solely on the trade in furs. Effectively they brought the Aboriginal population into a global economy, even if most Aboriginal fur traders were not aware of it.

The fur trading companies, dominated by the Hudson's Bay Company, created a network of European trading posts that covered Canada. As the map indicates, the trade was both complex and widespread across western and northern Canada. The traders brought European goods, European diseases and European religion to the Aboriginal population. They did not seek to dominate the Aboriginal population politically, but the fur traders prepared the way for further European economic and political penetration by promoting dependence on European trade goods.

TRADE PARTNERSHIPS

Yet, the Aboriginal population was not helpless in the face of the fur trade. Aboriginal peoples exploited the fur trade for their own benefit, too. Most furs were traded between Aboriginal traders, who only passed them on to European fur traders at trading forts. Native middlemen often tried, and often succeeded, in monopolizing trade with the Europeans, forcing both their native competitors and the traders to deal only with them. Maquinna, the chief of the Nuu-Chah-Nulth First Nation (previously known as the Nootka), established a trading empire on the west coast of Vancouver Island in the late 18th century that lasted for at least two decades. He established his control early and forced European traders to trade at only one location, Nootka Sound, which he controlled.

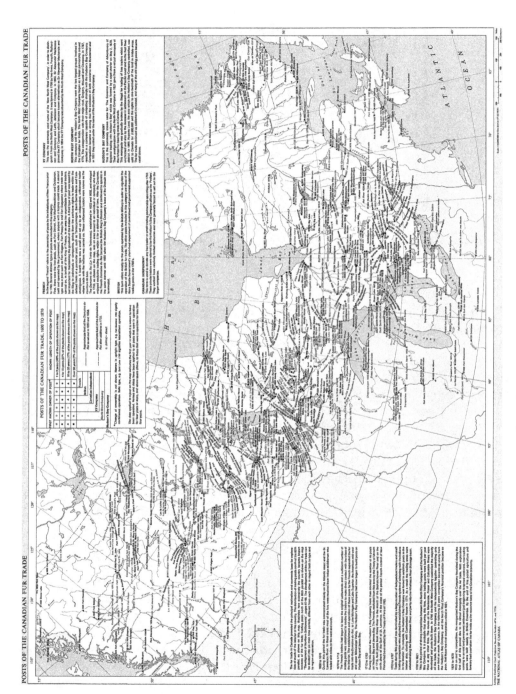

Map of the Fur Trade

The extent of fur trade routes and posts across Canada and parts of the northern United States.
Source: Natural Resources Canada. (1974) The National Atlas of Canada, 4th Edition.

Beyond examples such as this, other Aboriginal people worked as guides, hunters and labourers for European fur traders. Since they were able to leave their employment and return to their communities, they enjoyed much more freedom than the European employees, who were forced to fulfil employment contracts that severely limited their freedom.

Even after settlement began, Aboriginal traders and entrepreneurs were able to maintain some autonomy, especially at the margins of settlement. For example, Tlingit packers and traders had traditionally controlled the passes between the Yukon and tidewater on the Alaska Panhandle, providing both transportation services, by carrying goods over the Chilkoot Pass, and by trading independently as well. When the Klondike Gold Rush began in 1898, the Tlingit continued this role, by transporting goods over the pass for hopeful gold miners, as well as participating in gold prospecting themselves. Only after the railway from Skagway to Whitehorse was built were the Tlingit marginalized economically.

POLITICAL ISSUES AROUND THE FUR TRADE TODAY

Overall, the fur trade brought both benefits and problems. Today the problems are seen as outweighing the benefits, but most Aboriginal peoples were content to trade with the European fur traders at the time—not seeing them as any

Packing Up the Chilkoot Pass

Packing Supplies up the Chilkoot Pass into the Klondike Gold Fields. Most of the packers
were First Nations men.
Source: E.A. Hegg / Library and Archives Canada C-005142 / MIKAN 3192704.

different than their previous Aboriginal trading partners. However, the fur trade ultimately paved the way for settlement of much of Canada—with the forts and infrastructure of the Hudson's Bay Company providing both a template for settlement, and facilitating the incorporation of Aboriginal peoples into European economic networks, which were, in due course, followed by European political networks and European settlers. This sequel to the fur trade has made it a very controversial and politically charged topic today.

SETTLEMENT AND TRADITIONAL ECONOMIES

While the fur trade led to some economic changes, Aboriginal economies and societies remained relatively intact where the trade dominated the economy. The Hudson's Bay Company's policy of conducting its trade through Aboriginal middlemen, and its resistance to anything that might damage its relations with its trading partners, contributed to this continuity.

Settlement was another matter. Once the fur trade was displaced by settlers, so too were Aboriginal peoples and their traditional economies. Everywhere, whenever European settlers appeared, the Aboriginal population was moved onto reserves and restricted in their traditional lifestyles. Some, such as the Iroquois and the Coastal First Nations of British Columbia, were able to adapt to the new economy by becoming commercial farmers and fishermen, but most were never given these opportunities.

SETTLEMENT AND COLONIZATION

Settlement proceeded somewhat differently in most of Canada than it did in the United States or Latin America. For the most part, neither settlers nor their colonial governments could simply take lands whenever they wanted them. The Royal Proclamation of 1763 recognized Aboriginal title and sovereignty to land in Canada everywhere but the Maritimes and Southern Ontario/Québec, which were already settled by this time. It was a product of British fear of an outbreak of warfare between First Nations in British North America and its colonists in the 13 colonies. It required the government to legally extinguish native sovereignty to land (by purchasing it through treaties) before it could be settled. Effectively, it recognized First Nations as sovereign entities, although subject to the Crown. The Royal Proclamation ceased to be valid in the United States after the American Revolution (and was one of the factors that caused the revolt by the American colonists), but it has remained in legal force in Canada to this day.

When the Canadian colonies joined in Confederation in 1867, the right to manage Aboriginal affairs was explicitly granted to the new Dominion government in the British North America Act. This ensured that the process of negotiating Aboriginal title would remain largely uniform and directed by the highest civil power in Canada. The Dominion government (now known as the Federal

Royal Proclamation of 1763

And whereas it is just and reasonable, and essential to our Interest, and the Security of our Colonies, that the several Nations or Tribes of Indians with whom We are connected, and who live under our Protection, should not be molested or disturbed in the Possession of such Parts of Our Dominions and Territories as, not having been ceded to or purchased by Us, are reserved to them, or any of them, as their Hunting Grounds.—We do therefore, with the Advice of our Privy Council, declare it to be our Royal Will and Pleasure that no Governor or Commander in Chief in any of our Colonies of Québec, East Florida or West Florida, do presume, upon any Pretence whatever, to grant Warrants of Survey, or pass any Patents for Lands beyond the Bounds of their respective Governments as described in their Commissions: as also that no Governor or Commander in Chief in any of our other Colonies or Plantations in America do presume for the present, and until our further Pleasure be known, to grant Warrants of Survey, or pass Patents for any Lands beyond the Heads or Sources of any of the Rivers which fall into the Atlantic Ocean from the West and North West, or upon any Lands whatever, which, not having been ceded to or purchased by Us as aforesaid, are reserved to the said Indians, or any of them.

And We do further declare it to be Our Royal Will and Pleasure, for the present as aforesaid, to reserve under our Sovereignty, Protection, and Dominion, for the use of the said Indians, all the Lands and Territories not included within the Limits of Our said Three new Governments, or within the Limits of the Territory granted to the Hudson's Bay Company, as also all the Lands and Territories lying to the Westward of the Sources of the Rivers which fall into the Sea from the West and North West as aforesaid.

And We do hereby strictly forbid, on Pain of our Displeasure, all our loving Subjects from making any Purchases or Settlements whatever, or taking Possession of any of the Lands above reserved without our especial leave and Licence for that Purpose first obtained.

And We do further strictly enjoin and require all Persons whatever who have either wilfully or inadvertently seated themselves upon any Lands within the Countries above described. or upon any other Lands which, not having been ceded to or purchased by Us, are still reserved to the said Indians as aforesaid, forthwith to remove themselves from such Settlements.

And whereas great Frauds and Abuses have been committed in purchasing Lands of the Indians, to the great Prejudice of our Interests and to the great Dissatisfaction of the said Indians: In order, therefore, to prevent such Irregularities for the future, and to the end

(*continued*)

Royal Proclamation of 1763   (continued)

that the Indians may be convinced of our Justice and determined Resolution to remove all reasonable Cause of Discontent, We do with the Advice of our Privy Council strictly enjoin and require that no private Person do presume to make any purchase from the said Indians of any Lands reserved to the said Indians, within those parts of our Colonies where, We have thought proper to allow Settlement: but that if at any Time any of the Said Indians should be inclined to dispose of the said Lands, the same shall be Purchased only for Us, in our Name, at some public Meeting or Assembly of the said Indians, to be held for that Purpose by the Governor or Commander in Chief of our Colony respectively within which they shall lie: and in case they shall lie within the limits of any Proprietary Government they shall be purchased only for the Use and in the name of such Proprietaries, conformable to such Directions and Instructions as We or they shall think proper to give for that Purpose: And we do by the Advice of our Privy Council, declare and enjoin, that the Trade with the said Indians shall be free and open to all our Subjects whatever provided that every Person who may incline to Trade with the said Indians do take out a Licence for carrying on such Trade from the Governor or Commander in Chief of any of our Colonies respectively where such Person shall reside and also give Security to observe such Regulations as We shall at any Time think fit by ourselves or by our Commissaries to be appointed for this Purpose, to direct and appoint for the Benefit of the said Trade:

And we do hereby authorize, enjoin, and require the Governors and Commanders in Chief of all our Colonies respectively, as well those under Our immediate Government as those under the Government and Direction of Proprietaries, to grant such Licences without Fee or Reward, taking especial Care to insert therein a Condition, that such Licence shall be void, and the Security forfeited in case the Person to whom the same is granted shall refuse or neglect to observe such Regulations as We shall think proper to prescribe as aforesaid.

And we do further expressly conjoin and require all Officers whatever, as well Military as those Employed in the Management and Direction of Indian Affairs, within the Territories reserved as aforesaid for the use of the said Indians, to seize and apprehend all Persons whatever, who standing charged with Treason. Misprisions of Treason. Murders, or other Felonies or Misdemeanors. shall fly from Justice and take Refuge in the said Territory, and to send them under a proper guard to the Colony where the Crime was committed of which they, stand accused, in order to take their Trial for the same.

Given at our Court at St. James's the 7th Day of October 1763, in the Third Year of our Reign.

King George III

King George III of Great Britain and Ireland. Although later derided as "Mad King George," he was an active and politically astute monarch when he first ascended the throne in 1760.
Source: Library and Archives Canada, No. R9266-3147 / MIKAN 4321177. Peter Winkworth Collection of Canadiana.

British North America Act, 1867

VI. DISTRIBUTION OF LEGISLATIVE POWERS

91. It shall be lawful for the Queen, by and with the Advice and Consent of the Senate and House of Commons, to make laws for the Peace, Order, and good Government of Canada, in relation to all Matters not coming within the Classes of Subjects by this Act assigned exclusively to the Legislatures of the Provinces; and for greater Certainty, but not so as to restrict the Generality of the foregoing Terms of this Section, it is hereby declared that (notwithstanding anything in this Act) the exclusive Legislative Authority of the Parliament of Canada extends to all Matters coming within the Classes of Subjects next hereinafter enumerated; that is to say,—

... 24. Indians, and Lands reserved for the Indians.

FATHERS OF CONFEDERATION IN LONDON
The scene is laid in the Westminster Palace Hotel in the year 1866, when, on the eve of Christmas, the Fathers of Confederation completed the drafting of the Constitution of Canada—The British North America Act.
From the original painting by J. D. Kelly, in possession of Confederation Life Association

The Fathers of Confederation

The Fathers of Confederation in conference in London, England, during the negotiations
to unify the British North American colonies.
Source: Library and Archives Canada, Acc. No. R1300-360 / MIKAN 3000888: Kelly, J.D. (1935)
The Fathers of Confederation in London.

Government, or simply the Canadian government) was also the one entrusted with the responsibility for enforcing the results of treaties on both colonists and Aboriginals.

ABORIGINAL TITLE IN CANADA

Recognition of Aboriginal title was a political move intended to control relations between settlers and the Aboriginal population. It reduced tensions and allowed governments to control settlement. It explicitly granted the right to purchase Aboriginal territory to the Crown, but not to individuals, so that conflict between settlers and Aboriginals could be avoided.

Canadian governments have not always wanted to recognize Aboriginal title and have not always negotiated in good faith to transfer it. However, the Royal Proclamation has generally helped reduce tension between the Aboriginal and non-Aboriginal populations to this day, since conflicts over territory are usually between governments, not individuals.

In the United States, which rejected this principle, relations between the Aboriginal population, government and settlers were much more violent. Since individuals had the right to purchase land from Aboriginals, conflicts involving the settler population often drew in the U.S. government, leading to repeated use of the U.S. Army to suppress native resistance on the Great Plains. In contrast, Canada, directed by Britain, organized the orderly transfer of title from much of the native population on the Prairies before settlement had even begun. Other parts of Canada had different experiences.

RESERVE SYSTEM IN CANADA

When Aboriginal groups surrendered title to their land they were granted land to live on which are known as reserves and are held directly under the Crown. Their status and origins depend on where the reserves are located and what the rules regarding Aboriginal title were when they were established. Reserves in Eastern Canada often have different historical origins than reserves in Western Canada, while British Columbia is a different case again, as is Northern Canada.

In general, however, reserves are under federal jurisdiction, not provincial jurisdiction. They are also held in common by the First Nation itself, rather than by its individual members as their private property. Historically, reserves were under a great deal of control by the Indian Affairs Department, although most now have much more autonomy. The political status of reserves is still controversial because to many First Nations they are sovereign entities—that is, independent nations—although Canadian governments also wish to exercise sovereignty over them. It is important to remember that not all First Nations live on reserves, and neither do Métis nor Inuit.

RESERVES IN EASTERN CANADA

Much of Eastern Canada was settled before the Royal Proclamation regulated relations between Aboriginal and colonist populations. There were either no rules, or only ad hoc rules governing Aboriginal–settler relations. Reserves exist, especially in the Northern regions of Ontario and Québec, which were settled later and fell under post-Confederation treaty-making processes.

However, reserves in the South were often granted under different circumstances. The Iroquois reserves in Southern Ontario and Québec were granted to Iroquois allies of the British after the American Revolutionary War, who fled to Canada after their territory was seized by the United States. As sovereign allies of the British, the Iroquois regarded themselves as an autonomous people who never surrendered their independence. The Canadian government, on the other hand, regards them as settling on reserves held under the Crown like any other in Canada. This has made defining the status of Iroquois reserves quite controversial and was one of the factors that influenced the Oka Crisis.

In the Maritimes the precedent for treaties was set in the 17th century. Treaties there, although allowing First Nations communities to remain in their villages, extinguished Aboriginal title and recognized Crown sovereignty without any explicit grants of land. The Crown did, however, grant First Nations in the Maritimes hunting and fishing rights.

RESERVES ON THE PRAIRIES

The Canadian Prairies were transferred to Canada from the Hudson's Bay Company by the British government, on the condition that Canada negotiate surrender of Aboriginal title through a treaty process. Consequently, the Canadian government signed a series of numbered treaties with First Nations on the Prairies to pave the way for settlement. Each First Nation was given a reserve and a guarantee of a stipend to pay for the land surrendered. Although negotiations were not always conducted in good faith, substantial land grants were provided under the treaties and are the basis for the extensive Prairie reserve system today.

RESERVES IN BRITISH COLUMBIA

British Columbia was, for a long time, a special case in Canada. The first governor of the Crown Colony of British Columbia, James Douglas, signed a number of treaties with First Nations on Vancouver Island in the early 1850s. However, subsequent colonial and provincial governments refused to follow his precedent, claiming that the doctrine of terra nullius applied. This was the only part of Canada in which there was an attempt to apply this perspective, and it led to generations of litigation by First Nations in British Columbia, including appeals directly to the monarch in Britain. Reserves were assigned in British Columbia, but they were arbitrarily chosen by the provincial government from land that was not wanted by European settlers and were generally considered too limited to sustain their populations. These parcels of land were then transferred to the Canadian government, allowing the provincial government to claim no further role in Aboriginal affairs.

Only recently has a series of court judgments and the threat of unrest reversed this stance. Faced with the aftermath of the Oka Crisis and coupled with the Gustafsen Lake Incident in the Southern Interior of British Columbia and increasing international attention, the provincial government recognized Aboriginal title and created the British Columbia Treaty Commission in 1993 to

---

Terra Nullius

Terra nullius is a principle used by some colonial and settler governments to justify displacing Aboriginal peoples. It literally states that the land was unoccupied prior to the arrival of European colonists. Usually a combination of low population density and a hunter-gatherer lifestyle were used as evidence that there was no one there. It made a European definition for occupation—fixed dwellings, cultivation, property ownership—an excuse to claim that existing populations were not actually there.

negotiate land claims. It also negotiated a separate agreement with the Nisga'a First Nation of Northwest British Columbia. Under the terms of the Nisga'a Final Agreement the Nisga'a have received self-government, but remain subject to provincial and federal sovereignty.

RESERVES IN THE NORTH

The Northern Territories of Canada have only a few reserves, since all are underpopulated and underdeveloped enough that there has been little historical pressure to create them. The Yukon Territory does have a number of small reserves, but it also has larger traditional territories where First Nations have harvesting rights. The Northwest Territories has only three small reserves located in communities where the non-Aboriginal presence is substantial. Most Northwest Territories communities have majority Aboriginal populations anyway, and see no advantage in creating reserves.

Although other First Nations and Inuit settlements do not have reserve status, their Aboriginal regional corporations and governments, such as the Inuvialuit Regional Corporation, exercise powers considerably greater than most reserve councils do.

Canada's newest territory, Nunavut, created in 2000, has a majority Inuit population and no reserve system, although the Inuit population did surrender its title through a land claims process. The legal representative of the Inuit of Nunavut to both the Territorial government and the Canadian government is a treaty corporation, Nunavut Tunngavik Incorporated.

INDIAN ACT, 1876

The legal framework that governs relations between the Canadian government and the Aboriginal population of Canada is the Indian Act. Originally signed in 1876, it was the first attempt to create a unified Aboriginal policy by the new Dominion of Canada. It replaced the separate Aboriginal legislation created by the independent colonies that joined the Confederation, but recognized the treaties and reserves that they had previously signed.

The Act established a bureaucracy to handle native affairs that eventually evolved into the modern Department of Aboriginal Affairs and Northern Development. It also created a framework to govern the process of signing treaties with the First Nations on land under federal jurisdiction. This essentially meant the Canadian Prairies, which had then recently been incorporated into Canada from the Hudson's Bay Company control.

However, it also created a framework to create regulations to control many aspects of native life, including what they could do, where they could go, and what all their interactions with non-natives would be. It had the explicit goal of assimilating the Aboriginal population of Canada into the Canadian population. Until

Excerpt From the Indian Act

RESERVES

4. All reserves for Indians or for any band of Indians, or held in trust for their benefit, shall be deemed to be reserved and held for the same purposes as before the passing of this Act, but subject to its provisions.
5. The Superintendent-General may authorize surveys, plans and reports to be made of any reserves for Indians, shewing and distinguishing the improved lands, the forests and land fit for settlement, and such other information as may be required; and may authorize that the whole or any portion of a reserve be subdivided into lots.
6. In a reserve, or portion of a reserve, subdivided by survey into lots, no Indian shall be deemed to be lawfully in possession of one or more of such lots, or part of a lot, unless he or she has been or shall be located for the same by the band, with the approval of the Superintendent-General:

    Provided that no Indian shall be dispossessed of any lot or part of a lot, on which he or she has improvements, without receiving compensation therefor, (at a valuation to be approved by the Superintendent-General) from the Indian who obtains the lot or part of a lot, or from the funds of the band, as may be determined by the Superintendent-General.
7. On the Superintendent-General approving of any location as aforesaid, he shall issue in triplicate a ticket granting a location title to such Indian, one triplicate of which he shall retain in a book to be kept for the purpose; the other two he shall forward to the local agent, one to be delivered to the Indian in whose favor it was issued, the other to be filed by the agent, who shall permit it to be copied into the register of the band, if such register has been established:
8. The conferring of any such location title as aforesaid shall not have the effect of rendering the land covered thereby subject to seizure under legal process, or transferable except to an Indian of the same band, and in such case, only with the consent of the council thereof and the approval of the Superintendent-General, when the transfer shall be confirmed by the issue of a ticket in the manner prescribed in the next preceding section.
9. Upon the death of any Indian holding under location or other duly recognized title any lot or parcel of land, the right and interest therein of such deceased Indian shall, together with his goods and chattels, devolve one-third upon his widow, and the remainder upon his children equally; and such children shall have a like estate in such land as their father; but should such Indian die without

(*continued*)

Excerpt From the Indian Act   (continued)

issue but leaving a widow, such lot or parcel of land and his goods and chattels shall be vested in her, and if he leaves no widow, then in the Indian nearest akin to the deceased, but if he have no heir nearer than a cousin, then the same shall be vested in the Crown for the benefit of the band: But whatever may be the final disposition of the land, the claimant or claimants shall both be held to be legally in possession until they obtain a location ticket from the Superintendent-General in the manner prescribed in the case of new locations.

10. Any Indian or non-treaty Indian in the Province of British Columbia, the Province of Manitoba, in the North-West Territories, or in the Territory of Keewatin, who has, or shall have, previously to the selection of a reserve, possession of and made permanent improvements on a plot of land which has been or shall be included in or surrounded by a reserve, shall have the same privileges, neither more nor less, in respect of such plot, as an Indian enjoys who holds under a location title.

PROTECTION OF RESERVES

11. No person, or Indian other than an Indian of the band, shall settle, reside or hunt upon, occupy or use any land or marsh, or shall settle, reside upon or occupy any road, or allowance for roads running through any reserve belonging to or occupied by such band; and all mortgages or hypothecs given or consented to by any Indian, and all leases, contracts and agreements made or purported to be made by any Indian, whereby persons or Indians other than Indians of the band are permitted to reside or hunt upon such reserve, shall be absolutely void.

12. If any person or Indian other than an Indian of the band, without the license of the Superintendent-General (which license, however, he may at any time revoke), settles, resides or hunts upon or occupies or uses any such land or marsh; or settles, resides upon or occupies any such roads or allowances for roads, on such reserve, or if any Indian is illegally in possession of any lot or part of lot in a subdivided reserve, the Superintendent-General or such officer or person as he may thereunto depute and authorize, shall, on complaint made to him, and on proof of the fact to his satisfaction, issue his warrant signed and sealed, directed to the sheriff of the proper county or district, or if the said reserve be not situated within any

(continued)

Excerpt From the Indian Act   (continued)

county or district, then directed to any literate person willing to act in the premises, commanding him forthwith to remove from the said land or marsh, or roads or allowances for roads, or lots or parts of lots, every such person or Indian and his family so settled, residing or hunting upon or occupying, or being illegally in possession of the same, or to notify such person or Indian to cease using as aforesaid the said lands, marshes, roads or allowances for roads; and such sheriff or other person shall accordingly remove or notify such person or Indian, and for that purpose shall have the same powers as in the execution of criminal process; and the expenses incurred in any such removal or notification shall be borne by the party removed or notified, and may be recovered from him as the costs in any ordinary suit:

Provided that nothing contained in this Act shall prevent an Indian or non-treaty Indian, if five years a resident in Canada, not a member of the band, with the consent of the band and the approval of the Superintendent-General, from residing upon the reserve, or receiving a location thereon.

13. If any person or Indian, after having been removed or notified as aforesaid, returns to, settles upon, resides or hunts upon or occupies, or uses as aforesaid, any of the said land, marsh or lots, or parts of lots; or settles, resides upon or occupies any of the said roads, allowances for roads, or lots or parts of lots, the Superintendent-General, or any officer or person deputed and authorized as aforesaid, upon view, or upon proof on oath made before him, or to his satisfaction, that the said person or Indian has returned to, settled, resided or hunted upon or occupied or used as aforesaid any of the said lands, marshes, lots or parts of lots, or has returned to, settled or resided upon or occupied any of the said roads or allowances for roads, or lots or parts of lots, shall direct and send his warrant signed and sealed to the sheriff of the proper county or district, or to any literate person therein, and if the said reserve be not situated within any county or district, then to any literate person therein, and if the said reserve be not situated within any county or district, then to any literate person, commanding him forthwith to arrest such person or Indian, and commit him to the common gaol of the said county or district, or if there be no gaol in the said county or district, or if there be no gaol nearest to the said reserve in the Province or Territory there to remain for the time ordered by such warrant, but which shall not exceed thirty days.

(continued)

Excerpt From the Indian Act *(continued)*

14. Such sheriff or other person shall accordingly arrest the said party, and deliver him to the gaoler or sheriff of the proper county, district, Province or Territory, who shall receive such person or Indian and imprison him in the said gaol for the term aforesaid.

15. The Superintendent-General, or such officer or person as aforesaid, shall cause the judgment or order against the offender to be drawn up and filed in his office, and such judgment shall not be removed by certiorari or otherwise, or be appealed from, but shall be final.

16. If any person or Indian other than an Indian of the band to which the reserve belongs, without the license in writing of the Superintendent-General or of some officer or person deputed by him for that purpose, trespasses upon any of the said land, roads or allowances for roads in the said reserve, by cutting, carrying away or removing therefrom any of the trees, saplings, shrubs, underwood, timber or hay thereon, or by removing any of the stone, soil, minerals, metals or other valuables off the said land, roads or allowances for roads, the person or Indian so trespassing shall, for every tree he cuts, carries away or removes, forfeit and pay the sum of twenty dollars; and for cutting, carrying away or removing any of the saplings, shrubs, underwood, timber or hay, if under the value of one dollar, the sum of four dollars, but if over the value of one dollar, then the sum of twenty dollars; and for removing any of the stone, soil, minerals, metals or other valuables aforesaid, the sum of twenty dollars, such fine to be recovered by the Superintendent-General, or any officer or person by him deputed, by distress and sale of the goods and chattels of the party or parties fined: or the Superintendent-General, or such officer or person, without proceeding by distress and sale as aforesaid, may, upon the non-payment of the said fine, order the party or parties to be imprisoned in the common gaol as aforesaid, for a period not exceeding thirty days, when the fine does not exceed twenty dollars, or for a period not exceeding three months when the fine does exceed twenty dollars: and upon the return of any warrant for distress or sale, if the amount thereof has not been made, or if any part of it remains unpaid, the said Superintendent-General, officer or person, may commit the party in default upon such warrant, to the common gaol as aforesaid for a period not exceeding thirty days if the sum claimed by the Superintendent-General, upon the said warrant does not exceed twenty dollars, or for a time not exceeding three months if the sum claimed does exceed twenty dollars: all such fines shall be paid to the Receiver-General, to be disposed of for the use and benefit of

(continued)

Excerpt From the Indian Act   (continued)

the band of Indians for whose benefit the reserve is held, in such manner as the Governor in Council may direct.

17. If any Indian, without the license in writing of the Superintendent-General, or of some officer or person deputed by him for that purpose, trespasses upon the land of an Indian who holds a location title, or who is otherwise recognized by the department as the occupant of such land, by cutting, carrying away, or removing therefrom, any of the trees, saplings, shrubs, underwood, timber or hay thereon, or by removing any of the stone, soil, minerals, metals or other valuables off the said land; of if any Indian, without license as aforesaid, cuts, carries away or removes from any portion of the reserve of his band for sale (and not for the immediate use of himself and his family) any trees, timber or hay thereon, or removes any of the stone, soil, minerals, metals, or other valuables therefrom for sale as aforesaid, he shall be liable to all the fines and penalties provided in the next preceding section in respect to Indians of others bands and other persons.

18. In all orders, writs, warrants, summons and proceedings whatsoever made, issued or taken by the Superintendent-General, or any officer or person by him deputed as aforesaid, it shall not be necessary for him or such officer or person to insert or express the name of the person or Indian, summoned, arrested, distrained upon, imprisoned, or otherwise proceeded against therein, except when the name of such person or Indians is truly given to or known by the Superintendent-General, or such officer or person, and if the name be not truly given to or known by him, he may name or describe the person or Indian by any part of the name of such person or Indian given to or known by him, and if no part of the name be given to or known by him he may describe the person or Indian proceeded against in any manner by which he may be identified; and all such proceedings containing or purporting to give the name or description of any such person or Indian as aforesaid shall primâ facie be sufficient.

19. All sheriffs, gaolers or peace officers to whom any such process is directed by the Superintendent-General, or by any officer or person by him deputed as aforesaid, shall obey the same, and all other officers upon reasonable requisition shall assist in the execution thereof.

20. If any railway, road, or public work passes through or causes injury to any reserve belonging to or in possession of any band of Indians, or if any act occasioning damage to any reserve be done under the authority of any Act of Parliament, or of the legislature of any province, compensation shall be made to them therefor in

(continued)

> ### *Excerpt From the Indian Act   (continued)*
>
> the same manner as is provided with respect to the lands or rights or other persons; the Superintendent-General shall in any case in which an arbitration may be had, name the arbitrator on behalf of the Indians, and shall act for them in any matter relating to the settlement of such compensation; and the amount awarded in any case shall be paid to the Receiver General for the use of the band of Indians for whose benefit the reserve is held, and for the benefit of any Indian having improvements thereon.
>
> 21. In all cases of encroachment upon, or of violation of trust respecting any special reserve, it shall be lawful to proceed by information in the name of Her Majesty, in the superior courts of law or equity, notwithstanding the legal title may not be vested in the Crown.
> 22. If by the violation of the conditions of any such trust as aforesaid, or by the breaking up of any society, corporation, or community, or if by the death of any person or persons without a legal succession of trusteeship, in whom the title to a special reserve is held in trust, the said title lapses or becomes void in law, then the legal title shall become vested in the Crown in trust, and the property shall be managed for the band or irregular band previously interested therein, as an ordinary reserve.

that goal could be reached, however, the Act essentially treated the Aboriginal population as children to be educated to grow into their positions as full citizens of Canada.

OFFICIAL IDEOLOGY OF ASSIMILATION

The stated goals of the Indian Act reflected Canadian government policy for over a century. This was a common position taken at the time and was widely seen as a liberal (small "l" liberal, not Liberal Party) position. It was NOT a racist policy, since it envisaged the Aboriginal population being Canadians like any other. However, it was a strong example of cultural chauvinism, as it implicitly assumed that Aboriginal society and culture was inferior to Canadian/European society and culture and that it would give way to the latter.

There were two fatal problems with the Act and the policy and regulations that it produced. First, most First Nations did not want to assimilate and resisted fiercely, although mostly peacefully. Unlike the immigrants to whom they were implicitly compared, Aboriginals had never made a conscious decision to leave their homeland and move to a new and alien place—they were IN their homeland and saw no reason to give up their traditions. Second, although the policy may not have been racist, many of the people who actually implemented the Act

Duncan Campbell Scott, Indian Affairs Branch

Duncan Campbell Scott was the Deputy Superintendent of the Department of Indian Affairs
Branch from 1913 to 1932. As the bureaucrat in charge of Aboriginal affairs, he had tremendous influence on the
development of Aboriginal policy in Canada. His reign at Indian Affairs saw the creation of a policy of compulsory
residential school attendance for all Registered Indian children. A noted poet and writer, he romanticized the
"noble savage" in his writing, but as a government official he was noted for his budgetary controls and his
rigourous adherence to an ideology of assimilation: "I want to get rid of the Indian problem. I do not think as a
matter of fact, that the country ought to continuously protect a class of people who are able to stand alone.... Our
objective is to continue until there is not a single Indian in Canada that has not been absorbed into the body politic
and there is no Indian question, and no Indian Department..." (Leslie 1978 p. 114).
Source: Yousuf Karsh / Library and Archives Canada / PA-165842 / e010752290 / MIKAN 3220952.

were, as were elements in the general population. This left Aboriginal peoples
with two unpalatable choices: retain their culture and suffer legal discrimination
from the government, or attempt to assimilate and suffer racial discrimination
from their European neighbours. Those who attempted a third way and tried to
succeed on their own terms in Canada, by retaining their culture, but participating in the market economy, were prevented from doing so. The Canadian government was not willing to allow Aboriginals to become successful in Canada
unless they ceased to be Aboriginal. A few managed it, but at the cost of their
culture and heritage. Most refused.

GOVERNMENT POLICY AND THE INDIAN ACT

If the Indian Act and government policy were to consider Aboriginals wards of
the state in need of education and protection until they could be integrated, then
reserves were seen as steps on the road to integration, not as permanent endowments. As well, after the Northwest Rebellion of 1885, the government feared that
First Nations on the Prairies would resort to armed resistance.

This led to the creation of a system of regulations restricting even daily life.
Travel, whether off-reserve, or even to other reserves within the same First Nation,
was restricted, with individuals requiring a signed pass from a government official

Multiracial Picnic in Ontario

A picnic on W. S. Piper's farm in Fort William Ontario in 1920. Canada was never as segregated
as some other settler states, and social interaction between the Aboriginal population and the
non-Aboriginal population still existed, especially in rural areas.
Source: Canada Patent and Copyright Office / Library and Archives Canada / MIKAN 3260170.

to leave their reserve. Aboriginals were forbidden from engaging in business without
authorization from the Indian Agent present on the reserve. They also had to receive
permission to engage in celebrations and public gatherings, while traditional dancing was prohibited outright. Particular ceremonies, such as the potlatch in British
Columbia and the Sun Dance on the Prairies were also forbidden. Drinking alcohol was also forbidden, with penalties enforced for both drinking and for supplying
alcohol to any First Nations person. It was typical of the regulations, however, that
while the penalty for drinking was prison, the non-Aboriginal who supplied the
drink only received a fine. Basically First Nations suffered the same restrictions on
their lives that citizens of a totalitarian state would (nor could they vote, of course).

ASSIMILATION AND RESISTANCE

However, any First Nations individual could, in theory, escape these restrictions
by giving up status and leaving the reserve. This process was known as enfranchisement, as those who qualified and accepted it became Canadian citizens.
Most of these restrictions were difficult to enforce anyway, for several reasons.
First, Aboriginal affairs was and is chronically underfunded, leaving the Indian
Department short-handed and unable to even identify, let alone prevent, minor
infractions. Overly enthusiastic prosecution of government policy could and did
spark some public sympathy for First Nations, reflected in newspaper editorials protesting restrictions on public dance performances. The police also often

Residential School, Manitoba

Children at Poplar River Residential School, Manitoba 1890.
Source: J.B. Tyrrell / Library and Archives Canada / PA-053620/MIKAN 3194038.

Before and After

Removing the Indian within: Thomas Moore before and after residential school in Regina.
Source: Department of Indian Affairs Annual Report, 1897. Library and Archives Canada, NL-02247.

refused to enforce unreasonable policies, particularly the prohibition on dancing and the travel restrictions. Unfortunately, the most notorious of the government assimilation policies, and by far the most destructive, was the residential school system, which was also the most rigidly enforced.

RESIDENTIAL SCHOOLS

Residential schools were one of the more prominent means to enforce assimilation. They were boarding schools for Aboriginal children designed to inculcate mainstream Canadian culture in Aboriginal children. Although some were initially created on reserves as day schools, most were explicitly designed to remove children from their families and societies as a more efficient means of assimilating them. Some were initially run directly by the government and were called Industrial Schools, but this proved expensive and qualified teachers were difficult to find. This led the government to allow various churches to operate them as agents. The government paid the basic operating budget, while the churches provided the staff. Since members of religious orders seldom required high salaries, this proved a significant economy over civil service run schools.

Some select non-Aboriginal groups who refused to either assimilate or accept Canadian legal authority were also given the same treatment, most notably the extremist members of the Russian religious sect, the Doukhobors, who were known as the Sons of Freedom and followed a form of primitive communism. Living in the Kootenay region of British Columbia, their children were also removed from them and placed in a residential school in New Denver from 1953 to 1960, where they were forbidden to speak their language (Russian), practice the Doukhobor religion or wear traditional clothing. Allegations of both physical and sexual abuse have also emerged from this residential school experience.

RESIDENTIAL SCHOOLS AND ABUSE

The residential school system has become a byword for all that was wrong with Canadian Aboriginal policy. The system was chronically underfunded and mismanaged, with very high levels of epidemic disease, including tuberculosis, smallpox, measles and cholera, leading to a conservative estimate by the Medical Inspector in 1909 that at least 24% of the children sent to residential schools died. In addition, many who became ill were sent home to their families, where they perished, and spread disease to their communities as well.

Even when the hygiene and physical conditions of the residential schools were improved after the Second World War, other problems remained. Severe punishment exacted on children for speaking their own languages, or for any infraction of the rules, was prevalent in many of the schools. However, beyond this, some schools were sites of horrific sexual and physical abuse of children that occurred for decades, leaving generations of children emotionally scarred. At best, graduates lost their ties to their own families and culture, without being fully accepted by general society.

This abuse remained hidden, both by the government, the churches and the survivors, who were afraid to speak out. Only after a public scandal in 1989 over long-term abuse of orphans (who were largely non-Aboriginal) at a church-operated orphanage and school in Newfoundland, Mount Cashel Orphanage, was the silence of generations broken and the abuse in the residential schools also became public.

TESTIMONIES OF ABUSE

Subsequent to these revelations of physical and sexual abuse in the Aboriginal residential school system, the churches that operated them have made varying attempts to make amends. Some churches, notably the Anglican Church of Canada and the United Church of Canada, have made public apologies and financial settlements with former students. For its part, the Government of Canada established the Aboriginal Healing Foundation to find ways to heal the emotional wounds inflicted on generations of Aboriginal Canadians by the residential schools experience.

HEALTH AND WELFARE

The Canadian government accepted responsibility for the health and welfare of the Status Indian population in the Indian Act, and had furthermore explicitly guaranteed to provide medicine when government agents signed Treaty 6 with different groups from 1876–1898. The Cree and Stoney First Nations across what is now central Alberta, Saskatchewan and Manitoba negotiated a "medicine chest" clause, in which the government agreed to provide medical services as part of the land claims agreement.

In reality, however, support was minimal and largely directed through the Indian Agents on each reserve. In general, health services did not begin to improve until after Second World War, when responsibility for the health of Status Indians and Inuit was transferred to the Department of Health and Welfare (now Health Canada), which began directly providing health services to the Aboriginal population on reserves and in the North. Non-Status Indians and Métis remained outside all of these provisions, and still remain the responsibility of their respective provincial governments.

CONSTITUTION ACT OF 1982

The Aboriginal situation began to change with Canada's constitutional arrangement. The Canadian constitution had resided in London as an Act of the United Kingdom's Parliament from Confederation to 1982. Although successive Canadian governments wanted to patriate it—to replace it with a constitution entirely located in Canada—this required the agreement of both the United Kingdom's Parliament and of each of the Canadian Provinces, which proved hard to get.

By the late 1970s Canadian Aboriginal leaders were more assertive, and were well aware that Canada had signed a number of international conventions stating

---

Excerpt from the Constitution Act, 1982

RIGHTS OF THE ABORIGINAL PEOPLES OF CANADA

35. 1. The existing Aboriginal and treaty rights of the Aboriginal peoples of Canada are hereby recognized and affirmed.

    2. In this Act, "Aboriginal peoples of Canada" includes the Indian, Inuit, and Métis peoples of Canada.

    3. For greater certainty, in subsection (1) "treaty rights" includes rights that now exist by way of land claims agreements or may be so acquired.

    4. Notwithstanding any other provision of this Act, the Aboriginal and treaty rights referred to in subsection (1) are guaranteed equally to male and female persons. (17)

35. 1. The government of Canada and the provincial governments are committed to the principal that, before any amendment is made to Class 24 of section 91 of the "Constitution Act, 1867", to section 25 of this Act or to this Part,

    (a) a constitutional conference that includes in its agenda an item relating to the proposed amendment, composed of the Prime Minister of Canada and the first ministers of the provinces, will be convened by the Prime Minister of Canada; and

    (b) the Prime Minister of Canada will invite representatives of the Aboriginal peoples of Canada to participate in the discussions on that item. (18)

---

that it would protect human rights and minority rights. The Canadian government was also a leader in opposing the apartheid government in South Africa and the white minority government in Rhodesia. Aboriginal leaders argued that as the original inhabitants of Canada, their interests should be taken into account too with regard to the patriation of the constitution.

This was done in two ways. First, when the constitution was patriated, the rights of Aboriginal peoples were explicitly included in it, effectively acknowledging that Canada was a partnership among three founding peoples, the English, the French and the Aboriginals. More significantly the constitution explicitly recognized all Aboriginal peoples, First Nations, Métis and Inuit, and Aboriginal women were also explicitly given equal status with Aboriginal men. This last principle led directly to Bill C31, a revision to the Indian Act, which restored Status to First Nations women who had married non-Status men. The second way in which Aboriginal rights were acknowledged was through the Charter of Rights and Freedoms.

The Charter on Aboriginals

25. The guarantee in this Charter of certain rights and freedoms shall not be construed so as to abrogate or derogate from any Aboriginal, treaty or other rights or freedoms that pertain to the Aboriginal peoples of Canada including

(*a*) any rights or freedoms that have been recognized by the Royal Proclamation of October 7, 1763; and

(*b*) any rights or freedoms that now exist by way of land claims agreements or may be so acquired. (94)

CHARTER OF RIGHTS AND FREEDOMS

The Charter of Rights and Freedoms enshrined human rights in the Canadian Constitution, but it also included protection for group rights—English, French, minority and Aboriginal. Aboriginal rights were specifically located in the 1763 Royal Proclamation and the treaties that had been signed since then, and that might be signed in the future. Furthermore, the Charter explicitly exempted the rights of the Aboriginal peoples of Canada granted by the Royal Proclamation and treaties from the actions of the Charter in protecting and promoting individual rights. In other words, the Charter could not be used to take away Aboriginal title or to take treaty rights away from any Aboriginal group or individual.

DEVOLUTION OF THE HEALTH CARE SYSTEM

Constitutional changes did lead to increased autonomy and self-government in the 1980s, reflecting primarily the structural changes in Canadian society. These societal changes, however, also coincided with structural changes in the Canadian government, which combined decentralization with downsizing of federal government services. Health Canada began transferring administration of health services to local authorities, including band councils and village administrations. Health care services in the Territories were also devolved to the territorial governments. The federal government, through Health Canada, continued to provide some funding and retained a role in health promotion and provision to non-insured health benefits (such as eyeglasses, hearing aids and other prosthetics).

This movement accelerated in the 1990s as federal budgetary cutbacks increased in severity and calls for greater Aboriginal self-government became more insistent. Devolution has mainly affected Status First Nations and Northern Aboriginals, as these two groups have traditionally been the responsibility of the federal government. The effect on these peoples is that responsibility is now largely limited to arms-length funding and health promotion. The health of other Aboriginals, including Métis, non-status First Nations and those with status living away from their reserves, remains a provincial responsibility.

THE MOVEMENT TOWARD AUTONOMY

The movement toward autonomy began in the 1980s, encouraged by a new sense of self-reliance by many Aboriginal groups and the willingness of the federal government to withdraw from direct supervision of the services it once provided. Equally, the political fallout from incidents in the 1990s such as the Oka Crisis, the Gustafsen Lake Standoff, the Ipperwash Crisis and the Burnt Church Crisis encouraged the Canadian government to accelerate the movement to self-government in order to reduce the chances for further violence.

As always, there are other motives present, however. The Canadian government also began to wrestle with its long-standing budgetary deficits in the 1990s. Self-government and devolution of powers was also viewed as a cost-cutting measure, which allowed Health Canada and Indian and Northern Affairs to reduce their staffing, thus achieving significant cost savings. Just as importantly, self-government removed the federal government from direct responsibility for Aboriginal health and well-being. This allowed the government to essentially off-load responsibility onto territorial governments, regional councils and local First Nations, thus short-circuiting Aboriginal anger at the shortcomings of the government itself.

PROBLEMS IN HEALTH COVERAGE

Cost cutting and self-government also have had some less desirable effects. The existence of an increasingly fragmented set of overlapping federal, provincial and local health jurisdictions sometimes leaves Aboriginal patients to "fall through the cracks." This has led to a tendency for different authorities to argue over who should pay for care, while withholding care until one of the jurisdictions actually paid. This has materially affected the health of the Aboriginal population and has led to increasing calls for reform, driven by prominent scandals, notably the Jordan Case.

JORDAN'S PRINCIPLE

Jordan River Anderson, a 5-year old from Norway House Reserve in northern Manitoba, fell ill with Carey Fineman Ziter syndrome, a rare, but treatable muscular disorder when he was 2 years old and was evacuated to Winnipeg for treatment. He was treated in a hospital in Winnipeg and responded well to care, so his physicians recommended he return to his community with appropriate home care. Instead, Jordan died in hospital in Winnipeg 2 years later, while the federal and provincial governments argued over who should pay for his care.

This caused an international scandal, and led to angry editorials in the *Canadian Medical Association Journal* accusing the federal and provincial governments of racism. This was followed by a highly critical report in 2009 by the United Nations Children's Fund (UNICEF) on the state of Aboriginal children's health in Canada.

The result was the creation of Jordan's Principle. This states that the first agency to come into contact with an Aboriginal child in need of care is obligated to pay for that care within the child's home community, if medically possible. The Principle has been implemented by the Federal Government and the provincial governments of Manitoba and British Columbia. Work is proceeding on having it enshrined in legislation in every province in Canada. This movement has been supported by both the Canadian Nurses Association and the Canadian Medical Association, as both organizations advocate for a pan-governmental approach to Aboriginal health.

Canadian Medical Association Statement of Aboriginal Health Entitlement

That the federal government adopt a comprehensive strategy for improving the health of Aboriginal peoples that involves a partnership among governments, non-governmental organizations, universities and the Aboriginal communities.

(Canadian Medical Association: The Health of Aboriginal Peoples, 2002.)

Canadian Nurses Association Open Letter on Aboriginal Health

The marked gap between the health of Aboriginal Peoples and the health of the general population in Canada is well-documented. ... Yet more illness care services for Aboriginal Peoples alone will not turn the tide. It is recognized that there are unique social determinants of health for Aboriginal Peoples, which are associated with such factors as culture, colonization, racism, residential schools and their current situations. Through culturally appropriate research, developed jointly with Aboriginal health professionals and peoples, and through greater understanding of the impact of social determinants of health, we can develop new models of health care and achieve better health outcomes for Aboriginal Peoples.

(Canadian Nurses Association: Open letter on Aboriginal health, 21 June 2012.)

ABORIGINAL HEALTH AND WELFARE TODAY

Self-government and devolution have created varying conditions for the Aboriginal population. Some Aboriginal people have outstanding primary care systems. For example, the system in Nunavut has been described as superior to any in Southern Canada. On the other hand, some urban populations and many rural populations have very poor primary care. All Aboriginal populations, irrespective of their primary care systems, have ongoing problems with the determinants of health and without improvements in these underlying causes of ill health, increasing the availability of primary care cannot have much impact.

ECONOMIC AND CULTURAL SECURITY

The problems faced by Aboriginal communities are compounded by the socio-economic and geographical barriers they face. Most native reserves and Northern communities are remote and far from sources of advanced education and employment. This leads to poor economic security and widespread dependence on government assistance. Subsistence hunting and fishing is still practised, though it is becoming increasingly harder to afford. Ammunition, tools and transportation all cost money, which is hard to find in small, impoverished communities.

This problem of poor economic security is linked to the anti-fur campaigns of the 1980s and 1990s, which led directly to the collapse of the fur industry in Canada after the European Union banned fur imports. Most Canadians and North Americans also ceased wearing fur outerwear as a response to the attitudes expressed in Europe. Whatever the moral and ethical issues of fur farming, the fur industry in Northern Canada was intimately tied into the traditional economy. Animals were hunted and trapped, eaten and their furs sold, and the income generated was used to support this lifestyle. When the fur industry collapsed, so did the fur trade and the economic support for traditional harvesting. As a consequence, the levels of social assistance have increased markedly, and diets have shifted from consumption of traditional foods to unhealthy and expensive market foods from the stores.

Aboriginal communities face distinctly modern technological challenges to their culture as well. Modern technology means that even the most remote Arctic community has access to modern media, including satellite TV and the internet. This tends to undermine their cultural security as well, by encouraging youth to neglect their traditions and assimilate to modern popular culture.

FINDING OPPORTUNITIES

There have been some successes in Aboriginal health. Some communities have taken control of their devolved health care and have both run it well and integrated it into their lives. The Nisga'a Valley Health Authority has assumed the burden of providing both primary and secondary care. It also administers Non-Insured Health Benefits to its beneficiaries on behalf of Health Canada, and has created an integrated system that blends local control with professional service delivery. In practice, this has reduced bureaucratic red tape and has given more autonomy to the Nisga'a people, as the Nisga'a Lisims Government is smaller and closer to the people than the federal government. Similarly, the Inter Tribal Health Authority has united a variety of smaller reserves and functions to provide both integrated health and social services to a diverse population on Vancouver Island and the Inner Coast region of British Columbia.

THE MEANING OF HEALTH IN DIFFERENT CULTURES

Yet, the successes in Aboriginal health care are little known and less appreciated. Part of the problem is how we define health in Canada. Traditionally Canada has defined health as the absence of disease in individuals. The health care system reflects this by being orientated toward treating individual patients rather than populations. Many Aboriginal cultures value family and community health as highly as individual health. To traditional Aboriginal culture, healthy family and community relationships may take priority over the health of individuals. This has led to misunderstanding when these values clash. In most devolved Aboriginal health care systems, success in administering devolved programs is dependent on a certain economy of scale (Sommerfeld & Payne, 2001). Often small reserve populations find it difficult to develop the infrastructure to ensure control of devolved programs, which leaves their health care subject to a patchwork of overly bureaucratic Health Canada oversight and small local administrations that may have problems in recruiting and coordinating health care for their population. The result can be seen as a failure by both the Aboriginal population and the non-Aboriginal population.

DECOLONIZING HEALTH?

The result is misunderstanding on both sides, and a sense that Aboriginal health is still "colonized" by the Canadian health care system. That is, the lack of respect and understanding for Aboriginal values and priorities reflects "colonial" attitudes inherent to the health care system.

Generally decolonizing involves empowering Aboriginal populations within the health care system. This can take different forms. It may involve devolving more services to Aboriginal health authorities, thus permitting more Aboriginal agency within the health care system. The creation of a First Nations Health Authority in British Columbia in 2011 is one example of this approach. There are also attempts to incorporate Aboriginal rituals and beliefs into the health care system. This may include creating smudging rooms in hospitals or incorporating traditional ceremonies into childbirth. These approaches emphasize blending biomedical and traditional approaches to health and may range from tokenism—adding a ritual to an essentially biomedical procedure to give it a traditional "flavour"—to engaging Aboriginal traditions as the core of practice, while using biomedical techniques to improve outcomes. Finally, there is the option of abolishing the biomedical system altogether and returning to traditional healing as it was practised before Contact. Very few Aboriginal or non-Aboriginal people would seriously advocate this.

ABORIGINAL HEALTH INDICATORS

Overall, there have been some improvements in Aboriginal health, taken from the historical context, but there are still many areas of concern. Although primary care services have improved, secondary and tertiary care, as well as population health, remain problematic.

CANCER AND HEART DISEASE

Among the few areas in which the Aboriginal population has shown definite signs of good health are cancer and heart disease. Both are signal successes in their population health. Cancer and heart disease rates among the Canadian Aboriginal population are low compared with the general population. Although genetic factors may play a role, the traditional diet that many members of the Aboriginal population living on reserve or in remote areas still consume appears at least partly responsible. This is possibly an advantage that will be eliminated with time and changing diets and lifestyles, but for now remains both an historical and current health indicator in which the Aboriginal population outstrips the general population.

ABORIGINAL AND NON-ABORIGINAL HEALTH CONCERNS

Unfortunately, there are many other areas of concern in Aboriginal health and well-being. Diabetes, other chronic and infectious diseases, mental health and women and children's health all remain areas where substantial improvement would improve both the health of Canada's Aboriginal population and also the health of the general population, by mediating a source of poor health and human misery. Nineteenth-century public health theorists believed that an invisible miasma of ill health flowed from areas of public poverty and misery to infect everyone else. While we do not believe that today, leaving a large segment of the population in poor health still endangers everyone else through the creation of the conditions in which disease and social misery can affect, indeed infect, everyone.

CONCLUSION—A TURBULENT PASSAGE

Canadian Aboriginals have travelled from a traditional past through profound social and economic disruption to face an uncertain future. Canadian government attempts to enforce assimilation of the Aboriginal population were well meant, but were very badly executed, leading to generations scarred by their experiences of residential schools and the restrictive paternalism of the Canadian government. Self-government and belated attempts by Canadian governments to live up to treaty obligations have led to changes, as have reforms to the health care system, but they have also introduced their own problems. A cultural and social gulf still separates many in the Aboriginal population from the health care system, and that gulf has been complicated by the mistrust and fear engendered by past attitudes of Western cultural superiority. A century of failed policy still has its repercussions on Aboriginal life and health today, leading to the ineluctable conclusion that the state of Aboriginal health was manufactured and that it is not inherent to their population. It is incumbent on health care professionals to find ways to bridge this gap and overcome the historical legacy that poisons Aboriginal participation in the health care system today.

CRITICAL THINKING EXERCISE—SITUATING THE ABORIGINAL PEOPLES OF CANADA IN OUR HISTORY

There is often a sense expressed in Canada that Aboriginal peoples receive special treatment, which can cause resentment among non-Aboriginals. Divide a piece of paper into two columns, give one the title "Benefits" and the other the title "Drawbacks." Using the examples and description given in this chapter, list the benefits of Indian Status from the beginning of documented history until the present in the first column. List the drawbacks to Indian status in the second column. The lengthy abstract from the Indian Act of 1876 is a good place to start. Remember that free schools and education were probably benefits, but residential schools were not.

Look at your results. Do Aboriginal peoples receive "special treatment"? Does it look desirable?

Discussion Questions

1. Why are virgin soil epidemics characterized by high mortality in all age groups?

2. Which pre-Contact diseases can be diagnosed in skeletal remains?

3. How do traditional Aboriginal health views differ from traditional Western medicine?

4. What was the predominant pattern of disease among Aboriginal people following Contact? What is it today? Why?

5. The trade routes of the northern plains and boreal forest were the hub for disease contact and concomitant spread of many epidemics. Which diseases fulfil the criteria for depopulating epidemics?

6. What was the title given to children born of one Aboriginal parent and one of European descent? Were there other identities they could assume?

7. What did Bill C31, an amendment to the Indian Act enacted by Parliament, change?

8. What ceremony did Pacific Northwest First Nations use to redistribute wealth, to announce names, weddings, and so on?

9. The Indian Act provided for the enfranchisement of Aboriginal people. What did this mean?

10. How did (and do) Canadian governments attempt to assimilate the Aboriginal population?

REFERENCES AND FURTHER READING

Bryce, P. (1922). *The story of a national crime*. Ottawa, ON: James Hope.

Bumsted, J. M. (2007). *A history of the Canadian peoples*. Oxford , UK: Oxford University Press.

Fenn, E. A. (2001). *Pox Americana: The great smallpox epidemic of 1775–82*. New York, NY: Hill and Wang.

Leslie, J. (1978). *The historical development of the Indian Act*, (2nd ed). Ottawa, ON: Department of Indian Affairs and Northern Development, Treaties and Historical Research Branch.

Newhouse, D., & Voyageur, C. (2005). *Hidden in plain sight: Contributions of Aboriginal peoples to Canadian identity and culture*. Toronto, ON: University of Toronto Press.

Nichols, R. L. (1998). *Indians in the United States and Canada: A comparative history*. Lincoln, NE: University of Nebraska Press.

Sproule-Jones, M. (1996). Crusading for the forgotten: Dr. Peter Bryce, public health, and prairie native residential schools. *Canadian Bulletin of Medical History, 13*, 199–224.

Titley, E. B. (1986). *A narrow vision: Duncan Campbell Scott and the administration of Indian Affairs in Canada.* Vancouver, BC: UBC Press.

United Nations Children's Fund (UNICEF). (2009). *Not there yet: Canada's implementation of the general measures of the Convention on the Rights of the Child.* Florence, Italy: UNICEF Canada and UNICEF Innoscenti Research Centre.

Useful Websites

Aboriginal Canada Portal: Recent Legislation and Legal Issues: www.aboriginalcanada.gc.ca/acp/site.nsf/eng/ao20021.html

Aboriginal Healing Foundation: www.ahf.ca

Intertribal Health Authority: www.intertribalhealth.ca/

Natural Resources Canada. (1774) The National Atlas of Canada, 4th Edition. http://atlas.nrcan.gc.ca/site/english/maps/archives/4thedition/historical/079_80/#download

Sommerfeld, M., & Payne, H. (2001). Small Independent First Nations: Evolving Issues and Opportunities In the Administrative Reform of Community Health Programs. Nanaimo: Intertribal Health Authority. www.intertribalhealth.ca/publications.html

Aboriginal Health and the Canadian Health Care System

Understanding the Determinants of Health and Canada's Native Population

Chapter Objectives

- This chapter will place the major health care issues facing native peoples in Canada today in the context of the determinants of health.

- It will introduce the determinants as fundamental guides to both a deeper analysis of the health status of the Aboriginal population and to its improvement.

Key Concepts

Determinants of Health

Income and Social Status

Social Support Networks

Education and Literacy

Employment and Working
Conditions

Social Environment

Personal Health Practices

Healthy Child Development

Biology and Genetic
Endowment

Health Services

Gender

Culture

Physical Environment

Ecosystem Health

Gaia Theory

Cultural Identity

Key Terms

Population Health

Primary Health Care

Vaccination

Community

Genetics

Primary Care

Secondary Care

Tertiary Care

Education

Health

By far the greatest share of health problems is attributable to broad social conditions. Yet health policies have been dominated by disease-focused solutions that largely ignore the social environments. As a result, health problems persist, inequalities have widened and health interventions have obtained less than optimal results.

— World Health Organization Commission on Social Determinants of Health. Report of First Meeting. Geneva. March, 2005.

WHAT IS POPULATION HEALTH?

We tend to think of health as an individual concern, but individual health is hard to achieve in an unhealthy environment. Population health tries to improve the health of individuals by measuring and improving the health of the population they live in. This does not mean everyone will be healthy, but it makes it more likely that most people will be, thus decreasing the burden on primary care services. Essentially, a healthy population does not ensure individual health, but it creates the conditions in which it can occur. Conversely, if one particular part of the population suffers from poor health, it reduces the health of everyone else by providing a reservoir of misery and disease that affects everyone in society, statistically and individually.

To achieve good population health it is important to measure the health of populations. This provides a means of determining how public health measures, like changes in socioeconomic status or even public works measures such as building sidewalks, can improve population health and thus individual health.

WHAT ARE THE DETERMINANTS OF HEALTH?

This brings us to the determinants of health. These are the different factors in people's physical, social, economic and biological environments that affect their health. By breaking the environmental causes of health into individual determinants, they can be measured and analyzed. This provides a way of measuring the health of a population, and more importantly how it can be improved, and in doing so also improve the health of the individuals within that population.

Although different authorities debate the exact number of determinants of health, for the purposes of analyzing Aboriginal health in Canada there are 13 of them. They are:

1. Income and Social Status
2. Social Support Networks
3. Education and Literacy

4. Employment and Working Conditions

5. Social Environment

6. Personal Health Practices

7. Healthy Child Development

8. Biology and Genetic Endowment

9. Health Services

10. Gender

11. Culture

12. Physical Environment

13. Ecosystem Health

INCOME AND SOCIAL STATUS

Income and social status are related health indicators. Statistically, health status improves at each step up the income and social hierarchy. Fundamentally, income determines living conditions such as safe housing and the ability to buy sufficient good food. The degree of control people have over life circumstances and their discretion to act in health-promoting ways are key influences. Higher income generally results in more control and discretion.

Social status is partly, but not entirely, correlated with income in Canadian society. In general, self-esteem improves with social status as does the ability to use social status to engage in health promoting behaviour, even if income is low. Higher status individuals are usually able to access better health and social services due to improved community standing. Although social status can be difficult to measure effectively, income is not (Figure 5.1). The Canadian Aboriginal population ranked as one of the lowest income groups in Canada, suggesting that social status, at least for individuals away from their own communities and their traditional social networks, is also low.

Income is, however, only one means of measuring poverty. Poverty is also a function of lifestyle and cost of living. Remote Aboriginal communities have always been cash poor and in this sense have for some time fallen below Canadian income-based poverty lines. However, as long as the traditional economies in many communities provided a basic income, sufficient nutrition and traditional lifestyles, Aboriginal peoples were less "poor" than income cut-off levels reflected. This is the case because much of their well-being was not wholly measurable in terms of income, public education or even urban standards of housing. As early as 1975, Brody observed that Canadian Arctic communities with high levels of social assistance, but which had active traditional economies, were more socially functional than communities where most Aboriginals worked in wage labour, made high incomes, but had no time to hunt, trap or fish. Unfortunately, the decline of the fur trade and other traditional economic activities has also altered this balance. With a cash economy increasingly prevailing, Aboriginal communities increasingly match non-Aboriginal measures of poverty.

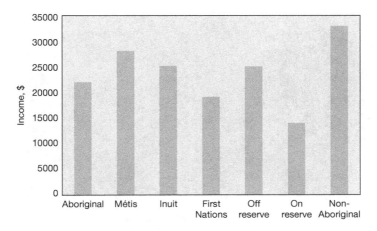

Figure 5.1 *Income In the Aboriginal Population*
Source: Statistics Canada, 2006 Census of Population.

SOCIAL SUPPORT NETWORKS

Social support networks are the connections within a community that individuals use to enlist others in solving problems and dealing with adversity, as well as maintaining a sense of mastery and control over life circumstances. The caring and respect that occur in social relationships, and the resulting sense of satisfaction and well-being, seem to act as buffers against health problems. They also create a reservoir of physical assistance that can act to support both individuals and families when they do experience ill health. Although hard to measure in statistical studies, qualitative research has suggested that traditional Aboriginal societies have very strong social support networks, but that these have been eroded by generations of assimilation, and particularly through the disruption caused to individual emotional growth by the residential schools experience. The strength of social support networks can be partly measured through participation in family and community events and festivals, and in how common these are within communities.

EDUCATION AND LITERACY

Education is closely connected to income and social status. Education equips people with knowledge and skills for problem solving, and helps provide a sense of control and mastery over life circumstances. It increases opportunities for job and income security and job satisfaction. It improves people's ability to access and understand information to help keep them healthy. However, those with higher income and social status also tend to confer the ability to access education to their families, simply because they have the resources to afford more education. On the other hand, those with poor income and social status may face barriers to education tied closely to their socioeconomic status. In other words, without programs to encourage universal participation in education, it can become the restricted preserve of only those who can afford it and also their children.

Traditional Social Networks

Festival in Kinngait, Nunavut, Canada: Traditional Aboriginal lifestyle revolves around the community.
Source: V. K. Douglas.

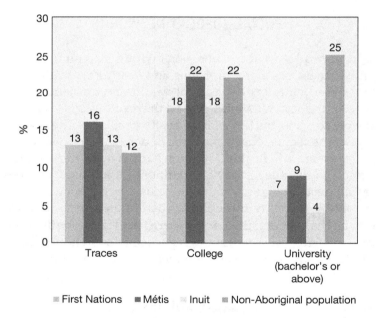

■ First Nations   ■ Métis   ■ Inuit   ■ Non-Aboriginal population

Figure 5.2 *Education in the Aboriginal and Non-Aboriginal Population*
Source: Statistics Canada, 2006 Census of Population.

Among Canada's Aboriginal population there are deep inequities in educa-tional achievements (Figure 5.2). For example, among the First Nations population living on reserves, as many as 50% have never received a high school diploma, while among the urban First Nations population only 30% have never graduated from high school. According to the 2006 Census, in other fields of education the picture is brighter: More Aboriginal Canadians have trades certification than the general population, while graduation from college diploma programs is only slightly behind the non-Aboriginal population. However, university education is lacking for Canada's Aboriginal population: As many as 25% of the non-Aboriginal population have university degrees, but among Canada's Métis, First Nations and Inuit populations, the rates of university graduation range from only 4% to 9%.

EMPLOYMENT AND WORKING CONDITIONS

Employment and working conditions have a direct impact on the health of the individual, as well as the health of the family, and by extension the health of the community. Unemployment, underemployment, stressful or unsafe work are associated with poorer health. People who have more control over their work circumstances and have fewer stress-related demands of the job are healthier and often live longer than those in more stressful or riskier work. Paid work provides money, a sense of identity, social contacts and opportunities for personal growth. Unemployed people have a reduced life expectancy and suffer significantly more health problems than people who have a job.

Beyond the individual, unsatisfactory working conditions or unemployment have knock-on effects on the family, through lower income or the effects of higher stress on the household and the effects of workplace injuries on family income. For the community, collective problems with employment and working conditions can eventually affect the community itself, its cohesion and sense of collective self worth.

Due to the systemically high rates of unemployment and underemployment, the Aboriginal population in Canada has poor employment and working conditions. As Figure 5.3 indicates, employment rates in the Aboriginal population are significantly lower than those for the non-Aboriginal population. First Nations on-reserve populations and Inuit tend to suffer even higher rates of unemployment, due to lack of opportunities in rural and remote areas, although these may be alleviated by the opportunity to engage in traditional activities, such as hunting and trapping, that do not register as employment.

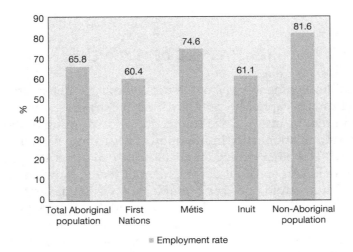

Figure 5.3 *Employment in the Aboriginal and Non-Aboriginal Population, Ages 25 to 54*

Source: Statistics Canada, 2006 Census of Population.

SOCIAL ENVIRONMENT

The social environment refers to membership in a distinctive group of people. This can include ethnic groups, social groups or family. Group membership can contribute to problem solving by allowing individuals to recruit assistance from other members or their group, or even use the collective social status of their group to resolve issues. Social groups include fraternal organizations, such as the Freemasons, while both individual First Nations, and even larger pan-ethnic organizations such the Assembly of First Nations or the Inuit Tapirisat Kanatami, can act to focus membership in a distinctive group. High levels of trust within group membership indicate a strong social environment. These tend to be associated with reduced mortality rates. Social or community support can add resources to an individual's strategies to cope with changes and foster health.

PERSONAL HEALTH PRACTICES

Personal health practices refer to the specific practices grouped under the heading of hygiene (tooth brushing, hand washing, etc.) and broader actions, such as diet or anger management. These practices constitute lifestyle choices that allow individuals to prevent diseases, promote self-care, cope with challenges and develop self-reliance.

However, other determinants of health also influence personal health practices. These influences impact lifestyle choice through at least five areas: personal life skills, stress, culture, social relationships and belonging, and a sense of control. Personal "life choices" are greatly influenced by socioeconomic environments.

HEALTHY CHILD DEVELOPMENT

Healthy child development is one of the most important determinants of health. Experiences from conception to age six years have the most important influence of any time in the life cycle on the connection and sculpting of the brain's neurons. Positive stimulation early in life improves learning, behaviour and health into adulthood. The other determinants of health all affect the physical, social, mental, emotional and spiritual development of the child, which then go on to influence health in adulthood. For example, low weight at birth is linked with high rates of perinatal mortality and morbidity and developmental problems that manifest later in childhood. In adulthood, health issues persist in individuals born with low birth weight, including the development of chronic diseases, such as diabetes and cardiovascular problems.

Feeding a Young Child Traditional Food
Feeding an infant country food at a community feast.
Source: V. K. Douglas.

BIOLOGY AND GENETIC ENDOWMENT

Biology and genetic endowment refers to inherited predisposition or resistance to various health conditions. It is the only determinant of health which is (barring dramatic improvements in genomics) invariant. We are all born with a certain genetic inheritance, which we cannot change.

However, while some diseases are genetically determined (e.g., sickle cell anemia), often biology and genetics may influence health, but do not determine it. There has been much debate over a genetic predisposition to diabetes among the Aboriginal population, given the very high Aboriginal diabetes rates today, but historically Aboriginal rates of diabetes were extremely low—obviously other factors are playing a role. Biology and genetic endowment are important factors to consider when taking action to improve individual health, but should be treated with caution when considering population health, since most populations experience a wide range of genetic diversity.

HEALTH SERVICES

Health services, particularly those designed to maintain and promote health, to prevent disease and to restore health and function, all contribute to population health. The health services continuum of care includes primary treatment, secondary prevention and tertiary care. Health services provide a variety of vital health-supporting functions, from vaccination and other preventative health measures, such as mammograms or Pap smears, to emergency medical treatment and palliative care.

The health care services provided to the Aboriginal population of Canada vary in quality and effectiveness depending on location and service provider, but overall access to health services lags behind that of the general population (Figure 5.4) and levels of satisfaction with those services are significantly lower (Figure 5.5). Urban Aboriginal populations tend to have primary care services equivalent to the general population they live among—for better or worse. Interestingly, primary care services for remote populations are often of a higher standard. Vaccination levels among the Aboriginal population are actually higher than among the general population (Figure 5.6).

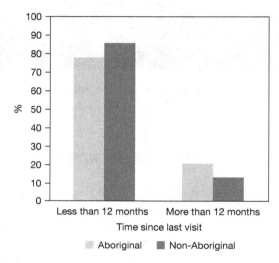

Figure 5.4 *Physician Visits*

Source: Statistics Canada, 2003 Canadian Community Health Survey.

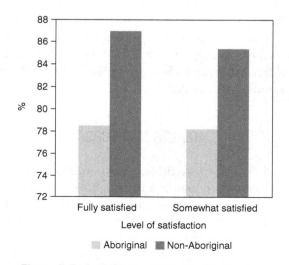

Figure 5.5 *Satisfaction With Health Services*

Source: Statistics Canada, 2003 Canadian Community Health Survey.

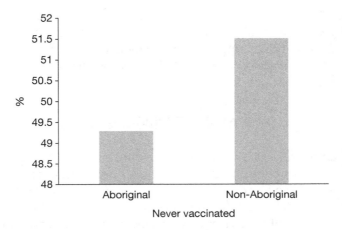

Figure 5.6 *Influenza Vaccination Rates*

Source: Statistics Canada, 2003 Canadian Community Health Survey.

GENDER

Gender refers to the array of society-determined roles, personality traits, attitudes, behaviours, values, and the relative power and influence that society ascribes to the two sexes on a differential basis. Many health issues are a function of gender-based social or status roles. In Canada, men are more likely to die younger than women largely as a result of heart disease, injuries, cancer and suicide. Women are more likely to suffer depression, stress overload, and chronic conditions such as arthritis. However, since gender roles vary from culture to culture depending on cultural norms, the effect of gender on health also varies considerably. Gender can have very real physical consequences on individual and community health, since socially assigned gender roles guide individual actions.

Contravention of socially assigned gender roles also has health consequences. It can lead to discrimination, violence, loss of social support networks and group membership. Gender roles in traditional Aboriginal cultures may have been quite different from modern Western norms. Some historians and anthropologists have identified the existence of third gender societies in pre-Contact Aboriginal societies, something some groups, such as the Navaho, still practice. However, most of the Aboriginal population in Canada has adopted Western gender norms.

CULTURE

Culture is informed by the historical and material conditions that people live in. It is very difficult, although not impossible, to abandon one's culture, because it is, for most people, a strong component of their identity. Some persons or groups may face additional health risks due to their socioeconomic environment, which is largely determined by the dominant cultural values that contribute to the perpetuation of conditions such as marginalization, stigmatization, loss or devaluation of language and culture and lack of access to culturally appropriate health care and services.

PHYSICAL ENVIRONMENT

The physical environment is the state of the natural world that people live in. A clean, healthy physical environment is an essential component of good health. Polluted air, water, food and soil can cause a variety of adverse health effects, including cancer, birth defects, respiratory illness and gastrointestinal ailments. Just as a dirty and polluted environment makes a strong contribution to ill health, a clean, healthy environment promotes good health.

ECOSYSTEM HEALTH

While the physical environment may directly cause ill health, it can also have indirect effects that can have serious implications for individual and community health. For instance, heavy metal contamination in the environment cascades up the food chain and concentrates at the top. This has direct implications for individual health, since humans are near the top of the food chain, but it also affects the health of large animal species, such as whales or caribou, which also have contaminants

Sanitation in Remote Northern Communities

The weekly sewage truck removing household waste in a northern community.
Few communities have central sewage systems, and environmental conditions may not permit either underground sewage disposal or sewage lagoons.
Source: V. K. Douglas.

concentrated in their tissues. This has important implications for the entire eco-system. It also has important implications for traditional Aboriginal culture, since large animals are an important part of the traditional diet and hunting and har-vesting them are culturally significant. Even if alternative food supplies are found, the loss of a major cultural resource will affect the health of the population.

As a determinant of health, ecosystem health is connected to the physical environment, but is more complex. It considers the health of the ecosystem that individuals and groups live in and depend on for their well-being. Thus, even if shortcomings in ecosystem health do not affect populations directly, they will affect them indirectly.

Gaia Theory

Ecosystem health is closely connected to the Gaia Hypothesis. The Gaia Hypothesis, also known as the Gaia Theory, was developed by environmental scientist James Lovelock in the 1970s. He named it after the Ancient Greek Earth goddess, Gaia. The theory claims that living organisms interact with the inorganic environment to produce complex, interactive cybernetic systems that create the conditions that make it possible for life to exist on Earth. This theory ultimately considers the Earth as a cybernetic system, in which living organ-isms, by modifying the planet's atmosphere, hydrosphere and lithosphere, make life itself possible. Feedback loops from the changes to the inorganic environment then lead the biosphere to modify itself in response to changes in the Earth (Figure 5.7). The implication is that people are an integral part of

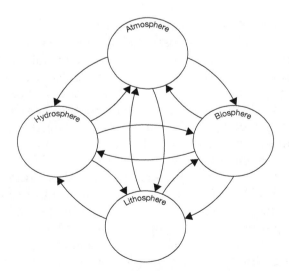

Figure 5.7 *The Gaia Theory*

The Gaia Theory sees the Earth as a single complex organism, in which
the organic and nonorganic processes interact with each other.
Source: Lovelock (2000).

this system and dependent on it for our existence as a species. Although the Gaia Theory was initially controversial, it is finding more and more adherents among physical scientists, as more evidence of the effects of the biosphere on the Earth emerges.

Gaia and Aboriginal Epistemology

The Gaia Theory, although a strictly physical theory, bears a striking resemblance to traditional Aboriginal epistemology of knowledge. Both see human beings as an integral part of Nature, not standing outside it, and both view ecosystem health as fundamental to the health of human populations.

Gaia, Ecosystems and the Determinants of Health

The Gaia Hypothesis provides a theoretical context and justification for considering ecosystem health as a fundamentally important determinant of health. Although the Gaia Theory has no spiritual component, its world view is remarkably close to that of traditional Aboriginal culture because it too considers the world holistically, as an interconnected web of living and nonliving things.

ABORIGINAL CULTURAL IDENTITY

The determinants of health are general measures of the physical health of populations. However, physical health is closely tied to a secure sense of identity. For the Canadian Aboriginal population this means their cultural identity. While some Aboriginal Canadians may identify themselves as bicultural (Cree-Canadian, Inuit-Canadian), others may reject a Canadian identity altogether. Those who lose their Aboriginal identity altogether either assimilate and disappear into the non-Aboriginal population, or become a marginalized and disenfranchised group on the periphery of Canadian society.

Berry (1999) independently identified 12 events and experiences that have either a positive or negative impact on a distinct Aboriginal cultural identity (Table 5.1). These could be considered the "determinants of Aboriginal cultural health" as they include elements, such as the connection to the land, the residential schools experience and the importance of Elders, which are either rare or nonexistent in the non-Aboriginal population. It is worth considering these briefly, as they are closely parallel to the determinants of health, although more specific to the Canadian Aboriginal population. When a healthy influence, they contribute to a healthy population—both culturally and physically. Otherwise, they can, by impacting the Aboriginal sense of identity, lead to

Table 5.1 *Events and Experiences That Contribute to Aboriginal Cultural Identity*

1. Traditional Culture	Language, Elders, Spirituality, Arts, Community
2. Family	Parents, Siblings, Children, Grandparents, Aunts, Uncles, Abuse (Sexual, Physical, Emotional)
3. Land and Environment	Bush, Hunting, Trapping, Fishing, Nature, Land Rights
4. Social Relations	Friends, Clubs, Recreation, Sports, Fights
5. Residential School	Abuse, Discrimination, Lack of Education, Forced Religion, Forced Work
6. Education	Schooling (Nonresidential), Teachers, Curriculum
7. Prejudice	Discrimination, Racism, Stereotyping
8. Addictions	Alcohol, Drugs, Cigarettes, Gambling, Bingo
9. Economy	Employment, Unemployment, Poverty
10. Government Institutions	Police, Courts, Prisons, AAND*, Social/Welfare Services, Foster Homes, Health
11. Church	Conversion, Priests/Ministers
12. Media	Television, Radio, Magazines, Films

Source: Berry (1999).

(Department of) Aboriginal Affairs and Northern Development.

both cultural insecurity and poor physical health. Improving the determinants of health almost always leads to improvement in the "determinants of Aboriginal cultural health," especially when attention is paid to the cultural and social context that is the foundation that healthy determinants of health are built on.

CRITICAL THINKING EXERCISE

We all experience the determinants of health. Some find them a support for their individual health, others find them detrimental.

1. On a piece of paper, make three columns. List the determinants of health in the first column. Give the last two the titles "Positive" and "Negative." List the positive and negative aspects of your personal health and the health of your community in the appropriate columns. How healthy do you feel? How healthy is your community?

2. Create another table for an Aboriginal community that has been in the news for severe health problems. (e.g., the NFLD Innu community in Davis Inlet or the Ontario Cree community of Attawapiskat, or choose your own). Using news reports, government press releases and the community website, use the same method as in the previous exercise to determine where the community stands with respect to the determinants of health. What do they say about the health of the population?

Discussion Questions

1. What effect does education have on Canadians' health? Why?

2. How does our social environment influence our health?

3. What effect does the physical environment have on the social environment?

4. How does the Gaia Theory lend support to Aboriginal epistemology?

5. Can an individual's biological and genetic endowment be modified by other determinants of health?

6. How does a healthy population contribute to healthy individuals?

7. How are some of women's health concerns determined by their gender roles, rather than by biology?

8. Why would Aboriginal communities experience poor health, when many have better primary care than that available to the general population?

9. What is the difference between primary, secondary and tertiary care?

10. How can the strength of social support networks be assessed?

REFERENCES AND FURTHER READING

Berry, J. W. (1999). Aboriginal cultural identity. *The Canadian Journal of Native Studies, XIX*(1), 1–36.

Brody, H. (1975). *The People's Land.* Toronto, ON: Penguin Books.

Health Canada. (2009). *A Statistical profile on the health of First Nations in Canada: Self-rated health and selected conditions, 2002 to 2005.* Ottawa, ON: Health Canada. Available at: www.hc-sc.gc.ca/fniah-spnia/pubs/aborig-autoch/2009-stats-profil-vol3/index-eng.php#a537.

King, M., Smith, A., & Gracey, M. (2009). Indigenous health part 2: The underlying causes of the health gap. *The Lancet, 374*(9683), 76–85.

Lovelock, J. (2000). *Gaia: A new look at life on Earth.* Oxford, UK: Oxford University Press.

Reading, C. L., & Wien, F. (2010). *Health inequalities and the social determinants of Aboriginal peoples' health.* Prince George, BC: National Collaborating Centre for Aboriginal Health.

Useful Websites

Public Health Agency of Canada (PHAC) – What Determines Health?: www.phac-aspc. gc.ca/ph-sp/determinants/index-eng.php

World Conference on the Social Determinants of Health: www.who.int/sdhconference/ en/

World Health Organization (WHO) – Determinants of Health: www.who.int/hia/ evidence/doh/en/

Diabetes, Diet and Nutrition

Chapter Objectives

▦ This chapter will introduce the issues surrounding diabetes as a major health issue among the Aboriginal population.

▦ It will introduce students to the particular features of diabetes as it is increasingly affecting the Aboriginal populace and will review examples of successful treatment approaches.

Key Concepts

Diet

Gestational Diabetes

Type 1 Diabetes

Type 2 Diabetes

Thrifty Gene Theory

Poverty

Key Terms

End-Stage Renal Disease

Chronic Kidney Disease

Amputation

Erectile Dysfunction

Polydipsia

Polyuria

Polyphegia

Cardiovascular Disease

Insulin

Among Aboriginals, the overall prevalence of diabetes and its complications are expected to increase in the next years and would represent a huge burden for health authorities. A study done in Manitoba shows the magnitude of this problem. It estimated that between 1996 and 2016, there will be a 10-fold increase in the rate of cardiovascular disease; a five-fold increase in strokes, 10 times as many dialysis starts; 10 times the rate of lower extremity amputations; and 5 times the rate of blindness.

— Health Canada, *Diabetes in Canada*, 2nd edition

GROWTH OF ABORIGINAL DIABETES SINCE 1980

Diabetes is rising throughout the Canadian and world populations. The World Health Organization predicts a 39% rise in the worldwide prevalence of diabetes. It is particularly high, however, among the Aboriginal population and is rising even more rapidly, driven by changes to diet, lifestyle and longevity.

Diabetes rates are complicated by the proportion of the Aboriginal population that lives in remote, impoverished communities. This also complicates the process of gathering accurate statistics, as many Aboriginal diabetes sufferers may not be immediately diagnosed. As well, the Canadian Aboriginal population is much younger than the general population, so high rates of diabetes are more significant and tend to be adjusted higher when the raw data are age standardized, as is suggested in Figure 6.1. Diabetes rates in the Aboriginal population are thus conservative estimates, and may be considerably higher.

According to Health Canada's collated statistics from 2008 to 2010, 17.2% of First Nations individuals living on-reserve, 10.3% of First Nations individuals living off-reserve, and 7.3% of Métis individuals suffer from diabetes, compared to 5.0% in the non-Aboriginal population. The age-standardized prevalence rate of diabetes in Inuit populations (5%) was comparable to the one seen in the general Canadian population.

However, diabetes rates are a moment frozen in time. The rate of increase is more significant for long-term population health. This gives a somewhat different outlook. Diabetes is a health problem that faces the entire Canadian population. Between 2001/2002 and 2006/2007, the age-standardized prevalence of diagnosed diabetes in Canadians (aged 1 year and older) increased by 26.8% and shows no signs of ceasing its growth since then (see Figure 6.2). Aboriginal populations present different figures for different time periods. There are no reliable national statistics for the Aboriginal population as a whole, only regional estimates and data for specific subpopulations, such as the off-reserve First Nations population surveyed by the Statistics Canada Aboriginal Peoples Survey in 2001. These figures present wide variations in numbers. Some populations recorded increases lower than the general population (e.g., the British Columbian First Nations population saw a 15.5% increase in diabetes rates between 2002/2003 and 2006/2007). Others, such as the Inuit population, saw their diabetes rates

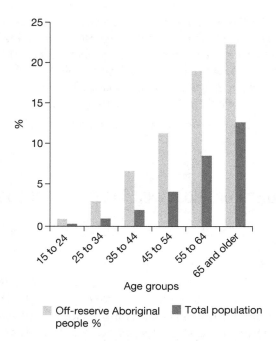

Figure 6.1 *Diabetes Mellitus in the Aboriginal Population*

Source: Statistics Canada, Aboriginal Peoples Survey, 2001 and Canadian Community Health Survey, 2000/2001.

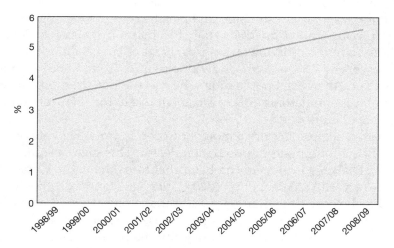

Figure 6.2 *Prevalence of Diabetes in Canada*

Source: Public Health Agency of Canada (PHAC), 2011.

double (100% increase) over the same time period, while the Cree population in Northern Québec experienced a growth in diabetes rates of over 36%.

Much also depends on the baseline data. Inuit diabetes rates are currently no higher than that of the general population, but they are increasing rapidly from a level close to zero in the 1980s. This suggests that diabetes rates among the Inuit population will rapidly approach the rates seen among other Aboriginal populations. Similarly, the First Nations population across Canada had no record of diabetes prior to 1950, but sustained increases in the prevalence of diabetes since then have led to the highest rate in the country. Overall, diabetes is an increasing health issue for the entire population, but rates are much higher among most Aboriginal populations and are increasing at higher rates among most as well.

GROWTH OF ABORIGINAL DIABETES AND NON-ABORIGINAL DIABETES

The health consequences of diabetes can be severe. They include organ dysfunction and failure of the: Kidneys; Eyes; Nerves; Blood vessels; Heart.

These secondary conditions often result from chronic hyperglycemia and concomitant decreased blood flow to the organs and extremities. Over time this leads to both reduced quality of life and reduced life span (by 15 years on average). As rates of diabetes increase so do rates of co-morbidities and complications. Diabetes is already the leading cause of blindness, end-stage renal failure and non-traumatic amputation in all Canadian adults. Cardiovascular disease, the leading cause of death in individuals with diabetes, occurs two to four times more often in diabetics compared to people without diabetes. Diabetics also have high rates of diagnosed depression, which often leads to non-compliance with treatment regimes—most especially with diet—which in turns leads to more secondary physical ailments. This is one of the reasons why diabetics are four times more likely than members of the general population to be admitted to hospital. In 2006, 10% of hospital admissions were due to diabetes/complications (PHAC, 2011).

STATISTICS

Diabetes was virtually unknown in the Canadian Aboriginal population before 1940. Rates have been rising in the general population, but are rising much faster in the Aboriginal population, as Figure 6.3 demonstrates.

DISEASE ETIOLOGY

Diabetes is a chronic condition that is caused by the body's inability to sufficiently produce and/or properly use insulin. Insulin is produced by the pancreas and is required by the body for the metabolism of sugar (glucose). Insulin assists glucose molecules to cross from the blood stream and into the cells, providing them with nourishment and allowing them to function normally. Lack of insulin in the bloodstream, usually caused by malfunction of the pancreas, leads to

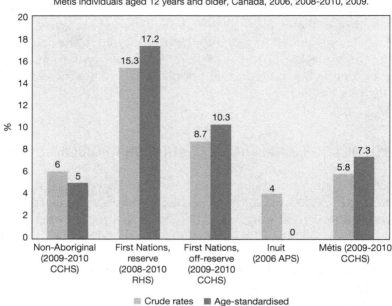

Figure 6.3 *Prevalence of Self-reported Diabetes*

Age-standardised to the 1991 Canadian population.
Gestational diabetes cases excluded from Canadian Community Health Survey (CCHS)
and Regional Health Survey (RHS) data.
Source: Public Health Agency of Canada (2011), using data from 2009 to 2010 Canadian Community Health
Survey (Statistics Canada); First Nations Information Governance Centre (2011), using data from the 2008 to 2010
First Nations Regional Longitudinal Health Survey (Phase 2) (First Nations Information Governance Centre);
Social and Aboriginal Statistics Division, Aboriginal Peoples Survey, 2006: Inuit Health and Social Conditions:
Ottawa, Ontario: Statistics Canada; 2008.

concentration of sugars in the blood, also known as hyperglycemia, and starvation of the cells in the body as they are unable to use the sugar in the bloodstream. This ultimately can lead to death.

TYPES OF DIABETES

There are three types of diabetes. Type 1 diabetes is hereditary, quite rare, and is usually (but not always) diagnosed in childhood. It is characterized by cessation in insulin production caused by pancreatic beta cell destruction, which leads to the condition where the sugars that should feed the body's cells build up in the blood, while the body literally starves to death. Type 1 diabetes patients are characterized by ketoacidosis (of which one symptom is sweet breath). Type 1 can strike adults, when an autoimmune process that is poorly understood causes beta cell destruction and thus halts insulin production. Type 1 diabetes cannot be prevented, but it can be treated through diet, rigorous monitoring of patients' blood sugar levels and insulin replacement. With proper care most patients with type 1 diabetes are able to live normal lives.

Type 2 diabetes, also known as "adult onset" diabetes, was formerly quite rare, but is increasing in frequency. It is characterized by inadequate insulin production or utilization (insulin resistance). Type 2 diabetes is now considered to be one part of a group of disorders called metabolic syndrome, which includes insulin resistance, cholesterol and lipid disorders, obesity, high blood pressure, a high risk of blood clotting and disturbed blood flow to many organs. Type 2 can be either prevented through lifestyle changes, or its complications can be minimized.

Gestational diabetes occurs during pregnancy and refers to glucose intolerance with onset or first recognition during pregnancy. The condition typically resolves after birth. Rates of gestational diabetes are rare in the general population with only 0.5% of women suffering from the condition during pregnancy. The Aboriginal population has a much higher incidence, with rates reaching 4.8% in the First Nations population, 4% in the Inuit population and 2% in the Métis population. The causes of gestational diabetes are poorly understood, but women who experience it have a significantly higher chance of developing type 2 diabetes later in life, as do their children.

SYMPTOMS

As cells are starved of the glucose needed to perform metabolic activities, the following symptoms may become apparent, although signs and symptoms differ depending on type—everyone is different and not everyone will experience the same symptoms:

Excessive thirst or polydipsia: As the concentration of glucose increases in the blood, the brain receives signals for diluting it, which leads to a sense of thirst.

Frequent urination or polyuria: An increase in urine production is due to excess glucose present in the body. The body gets rid of the extra sugar in the blood by excreting it through urine. This leads to dehydration because, along with the sugar, a large amount of water is excreted out of the body.

Excessive hunger or polyphegia: The hormone insulin is also responsible for stimulating hunger. In order to cope with high sugar levels in blood, the body produces insulin which leads to increased hunger. This is a symptom of type 2 and gestational diabetes, since it is dependent on the body's ability to continue to produce insulin, which is not a factor in type 1 diabetes.

Weight fluctuation: This is caused by factors like water loss (polyuria), glucose secretion in the urine (glucosuria) and metabolism of body fat and protein due to low insulin levels (ketoacidosis). A few cases may show weight gain due to polyphegia, although this will be reversed as the body becomes unable to metabolize nutrients.

Fatigue: Due to the inefficiency/inability of the cell to metabolize glucose, reserve body fat is metabolized to gain energy. When the fat is broken down in the body, it uses more energy to do so than glucose, hence triggering the body to negative calorie effect, which results in fatigue.

Blurry vision or hyperosmolar hyperglycemic nonketotic syndrome: This is caused when body fluid is pulled out of tissues including the lenses of the eye, which affects its ability to focus, resulting in blurry vision.

Irritability: This condition is caused by inefficient glucose supply to the brain and other body organs, which leads the individual to feel tired and uneasy.

Infections: They become more frequent due to suppression of the immune system, which is caused by high blood sugar levels that suppress white blood cell production. The result is more frequent fungal or bacterial skin infections or urinary tract infections.

Poor wound healing: Another effect of immune system suppression, this is also caused by gradual thickening of the blood vessel walls as the disease progresses. This impairs circulation to the extremities and can lead, in the worse cases, to the development of gangrene (anaerobic bacterial infection of the flesh).

ASSOCIATED HEALTH CONDITIONS

In general, diabetes leads to increased strain on the entire body and its organs. Thus, organ dysfunction and failure are common health conditions associated with diabetes. This includes failure of the kidneys, eyes, nerves, blood vessels and heart. These conditions result in part from the chronic hyperglycemia and decreased blood flow characteristic of people suffering from diabetes. On an average, diabetes reduces the life span by 15 years, and has varying effects on the quality of life remaining. Due to the effects of diabetes on the organs, it is the leading cause of blindness, end-stage renal failure and nontraumatic amputation in Canadian adults. Cardiovascular disease is the leading cause of death in individuals with diabetes and, as noted, is much more common than in the nondiabetic population.

In addition, the physical effects of diabetes, including high blood sugar levels and poor nutrient absorption, lead to higher rates of clinical depression, which in turn often leads to non-compliance with treatment regimes, causing further progression of the disease and its complications. Overall, diabetics are approximately four times more likely to be admitted to hospital than the non-diabetic population. As rates of diabetes increase, both in the Aboriginal and non-Aboriginal populations, so will rates of comorbidities and complications, and inevitably hospital admissions, and thus will increase economic strain on the health care system.

POST-DIABETIC END-STAGE RENAL DISEASE

The combination of high blood pressure, thickening and weakening of the capillary walls and high blood sugar levels leads many diabetics to develop chronic kidney disease (CKD). Without treatment CKD progresses to post-diabetic end-stage renal disease, in which renal failure requires replacement therapy, either through dialysis or a kidney transplant.

GANGRENE

As noted, impaired wound healing and an impaired circulatory system can lead to gangrene in unhealed wounds. Although treatable by antibiotics, gangrene progresses extremely rapidly (particularly virulent infections can lead to death within 24 hours if untreated) and often requires amputation of the infected body part in order to remove the necrotic tissue. Amputation rates in the Aboriginal population are much higher than in the non-Aboriginal population, due to geographical remoteness, poverty and poor secondary health care services. In these circumstances, factors as simple as poor footwear can lead to infection and gangrene, if unchecked (Martens et al., 2006).

CORONARY ARTERY DISEASE

Damage to the walls of the blood vessels and high blood pressure symptomatic of diabetes also leads to cardiovascular disease and, without treatment, eventually to myocardial infarction (heart attack).

ERECTILE DYSFUNCTION

In men, a common and often emotionally distressing side effect of diabetes is erectile dysfunction. This is primarily caused by impaired circulation, but the other comorbidities associated with diabetes also effect sexual function, which in turn may lead to depression and non-compliance with treatment.

FINANCIAL BURDEN OF DIABETES

Diabetes carries with it a heavy financial burden that lies on the shoulders of the individual, the community and ultimately the health care system and the nation as a whole. Individuals suffering from diabetes experience reduced quality of life, reduced life span and, even when costs of treatment are covered through social benefits, including Medicare and Non-Insured Health benefits, may not be able to work, leading to a significant loss of income. Even with assistance, medical costs for diabetic individuals are two to three times higher than for the non-diabetic population.

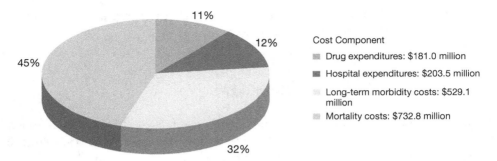

Figure 6.4 *Economic Burden of Diabetes*

Source: Public Health Agency of Canada (2011).

These costs, and the burden of disability that affects many people with diabetes, also impair the functioning of their communities. Where a significant proportion of the population is diabetic, the financial burden weighs down the entire community, as does the loss of productivity. In some Aboriginal communities diabetes may affect traditional harvesting, since sufferers may not be able to hunt or gather traditional food, leading to dependence on imported market foods that, being high in sugars and processed fats, contribute to the development of diabetes in the community.

For the health care system, the costs of diabetes are thought to add as much as 1.6 billion dollars a year to the cost of health care in Canada. It is also a factor in over 40,000 deaths a year. As rates of diabetes rise, in both the Aboriginal and non-Aboriginal population, this burden can also be expected to rise (Figure 6.4).

CAUSES OF ABORIGINAL DIABETES

Dietary Factors

The growth in Aboriginal diabetes is closely tied to changes in diet. More than any other factor, diet is extremely important to the increase in Aboriginal diabetes rates. In particular, the nutrition transition, meaning the transition from a traditional to a modern diet, that virtually all Aboriginal communities have either passed through or are passing through, is a prime cause of Aboriginal diabetes.

Traditional Diet

Traditional Aboriginal diets, rich in animal fats, lean meat, fish and produce gathered from the land, provided a strong barrier against diabetes and other chronic diseases. Although fat intake in the traditional diet is high, the fats in question are both unprocessed and high in essential nutrients, including vitamin B, omega-3 and omega-6 fatty acids. The presence of trans fatty acids (hydrogenated fats) is very rare. This diet is, however, becoming increasingly uncommon.

Drying Muktuk

Muktuk, or whale blubber, drying. Traditional foods, although often high in fat and protein,
also exert a protective effect against many chronic diseases, including diabetes.
Source: V. K. Douglas.

Labrador Tea

A relaxing tea made from the leaves of Labrador Tea (such as this variety, *Rhododendron
tomentosum*, for example) is traditionally made by Aboriginal peoples throughout Canada.
Source: V. K. Douglas.

Market Diet

Market, or store-bought, foods are rapidly replacing traditional foods in the
diet of Aboriginal Canadians. However, these are often processed foods high
in simple carbohydrates, high in processed fats and high in sodium. One of the
most commonly consumed market foods is soda pop, often sweetened with high

fructose corn syrup and lacking in other nutrients. Frozen, pre-packaged foods, such as breaded chicken, are also prevalent in the market diet. Conspicuously absent from the market diet are fresh vegetables and fruit. This diet leads to high blood sugar levels, increasing the body's insulin production and eventually leading to insulin resistance and type 2 diabetes.

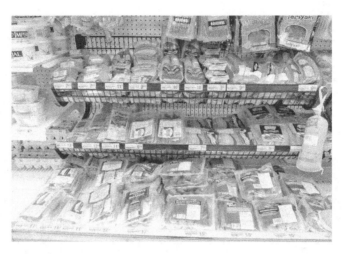

The Northern Store Shelves

Processed foods on the shelves in a Northern grocery store: Poor selection, low nutritional content, but high in calories.
Source: V. K. Douglas.

Vegetables in the Northern Store

More Northern grocery store shelves: When fruits and vegetables are available, they are very expensive in remote Aboriginal communities.
Source: V. K. Douglas.

Market and Traditional Foods

Traditional foods often co-exist with less healthy market foods: Traditional food
(dried fish) and market foods in an Inuit kitchen.
Source: V. K. Douglas.

From Traditional to Market Foods

The transition from a traditional diet to a market diet is called the "nutrition transition" and appears to be common to peoples throughout the world. It is attributable to increasing urbanization and the economic decline of traditional lifestyles. Most people in the developed world, including most Canadians, have already passed through this process, but the Aboriginal population is still undergoing it. It is complicated by the nature of market foods available, which increasingly tend to be heavily processed, high in simple carbohydrates, salt and fat.

The effects of this transition on the Aboriginal population are directly linked to the dietary causes of diabetes; they have led to either extremely high rates of diabetes, extremely high rates of increase in diabetes rates, or both.

BARRIERS TO A HEALTHY MARKET DIET AMONG ABORIGINAL POPULATIONS

There are significant barriers to developing a healthy market diet among the Aboriginal population. First, a significant number of Aboriginal people live in rural and remote areas of Canada. Of the Inuit population, only two communities, Tuktoyaktuk and Inuvik, in the Inuvialuit Settlement Region have all-weather road access to southern Canada. All other Inuit communities across Arctic Canada are dependent on seasonal water transport (usually in the form of the annual summer sea lift), winter ice roads or air freight to bring in market food supplies. This contributes to high market food costs and a tendency to rely on food with a very long shelf life that can be brought in during the summer. Many remote First Nations and Métis communities also face similar transport costs.

The costs of transportation also lead many merchants to opt for foods with a long shelf life, permitting them to be imported as bulk cargos. This preference favours frozen foods and processed foods and discriminates against fresh fruits and vegetables, both of which must be air freighted in at higher cost. This is compounded by the lack of competition in the retail sector in many Aboriginal communities. There is usually only one grocery store in all but the largest communities and the managements of these monopolies are thus free to charge whatever rates they wish for their goods, knowing that the populace has no choice but to buy. Even when two different retailers exist, there is rarely intensive competition between them to offer lower prices. Among the urban Aboriginal population, eating a traditional diet is even less feasible, while socio-economic factors also mitigate against a healthy market diet.

Low education and low income are often linked with diabetes rates. In the 1998/1999 National Population Health Survey of the Canadian population, 21.4% of individuals with diabetes reported low income and 42.7% had not completed secondary school. In the general population, the proportions were 12.8% and 22.5%, respectively. Low education is directly linked both to a lack of awareness of the health risks that lead to diabetes and its complications, and to low income. Low income earners may not possess the resources to diversify their diet beyond a poor quality market diet. Even in remote rural communities, low nutrition market foods are often cheaper than incurring the expense of hunting and gathering traditional foods. Hunting and fishing require time and expensive equipment to travel and stay on the land and since the collapse of the fur industry due to the European Union ban on fur imports, there is little economic incentive to do so.

OBESITY

Diets rich in simple carbohydrates and processed fats have also led to increased obesity. While also a chronic disease in its own right, obesity is a primary cause of type 2 diabetes. As we shall see, Aboriginal obesity rates are high and continue to climb, driven by the change in diet and other lifestyle changes.

LIFESTYLE FACTORS

One of the most marked lifestyle changes in the Aboriginal community is a decline in physical exercise. While the Canadian population as a whole has become more sedentary, the decline among the Aboriginal population is more recent and is closely tied to changes in diet. The traditional diet required constant physical exertion to gather the animals, fish or plants that comprised it. This exercise, as much as the diet itself, provided a buffer against diabetes and was a factor in the extremely low levels of diabetes historically prevalent in the Aboriginal population.

The market diet foods require little exercise to acquire; this and other factors combine to reduce the exercise levels of the Aboriginal populace. These include lack of facilities for physical recreation in most Aboriginal communities, socio-economic factors and cultural resistance to exercise as a recreational activity.

Many Aboriginal communities find that distance and cost are barriers to physical recreation. Small villages can seldom afford all-season recreational facilities, while families and individuals in a low income bracket find there are economic barriers to physical recreation on the individual level as well. While exercises as simple as walking or running might seem possible for everyone, physical environmental conditions, including the harsh winters prevalent in many parts of Northern Canada or the unexpected appearance of predatory animals, can render even these activities problematic. Few families are willing to risk an encounter with a polar or grizzly bear in order to take their children for a casual walk.

Beyond the socio-economic and geographic barriers to physical exercise, there is also a cultural barrier. Aboriginal cultures share with many others an emphasis on physical activity as a survival tool. Traditionally, exercise was part of food gathering, not undertaken for amusement or as an end in itself. Rather, inactivity is the preferred leisure-time activity. This is only logical in a culture in which work, physical activity and survival are traditionally tied together. This logic leads ineluctably to a sedentary population when physical activity is no longer required for survival. It still affects many groups in the non-Aboriginal population as well, and has been the target of public health campaigns intended to improve the health of various European populations, in Canada and Europe, through physical activity since the late 19th century.

This combination of socio-economic, cultural and geographic factors that have impacted Aboriginal diet and lifestyle is the main cause of the diabetes epidemic among the Aboriginal population. However, there are other factors that compound the problem.

MENTAL AND SPIRITUAL ISSUES

There are mental and spiritual issues that are significant in increasing vulnerability to diabetes. First, many Aboriginal individuals with diabetes may resist the diagnosis. No one likes being diagnosed with a chronic, life-threatening illness. Even with no other factors present, some diabetes sufferers may refuse to believe they are ill. Given past unpleasant experiences with the health care system and possibly experiences of residential school as well, levels of mistrust felt toward the health care system and health care professionals may be high. Especially when the disease is in its early stages, Aboriginal sufferers may not accept they are ill.

This may also have a gender-based component. There are some indications that the gender disparity in Aboriginal diabetes rates may reflect under-diagnosis of diabetes in the male population. While many Aboriginal women are monitored routinely for diabetes during pregnancy and, especially if they suffered gestational diabetes, afterward, their male counterparts are less likely to submit to testing until they are seriously ill.

ABORIGINAL CULTURE AND CHILDHOOD DIET

Childhood diet is also influenced by Aboriginal culture, which tends to educate through example rather than by prescription. Children are traditionally expected to learn by observing their elders, not by following orders, while their traditional diet is voluntary. This was not a problem when food choices were limited and generally healthy, but is more of one when food choices are broader and include "junk" foods, such as soda pop and potato chips. In addition, families whose older members suffered privations, either growing up on the land or in the residential boarding schools, may not wish to deprive their children of foods they want to eat, and which the families can now afford.

ACCESS TO HEALTH CARE SERVICES

Access to health care services is also a factor in the rise in diabetes rates in the Aboriginal population in Canada. While primary care services may be of good quality, the secondary and tertiary care services needed to both reliably diagnose and treat diabetes are lacking. This is due to a number of factors, including the remote location of many Aboriginal communities, particularly in the North. While primary care is provided by a community health centre, regular physician visits and evacuation for acute illness or injury, many communities are too small and impoverished to afford secondary or tertiary care. These services may also require evacuation to larger centres, something that the patients may resist and which may not be economically or socially feasible for long-term treatment of a chronic illness, because there may be no means to ever successfully return patients to their communities.

This problem affects all remote communities, but it is more significant for the Aboriginal population because more Aboriginal communities are remote and many more Aboriginal individuals with diabetes labour under this burden. Similarly, while poverty is a complicating factor in diabetes rates among all populations, proportionally far more of the Aboriginal peoples live in poverty than is the case for other Canadians, so this factor is consequently much more significant, particularly when it is compounded with the high cost of living in remote communities.

Public health responses to the diabetes epidemic in the Aboriginal population are complicated by divided jurisdictions. Some groups benefit from provincial or territorial health care programs, while others either receive health services provided by the federal government or have their health care devolved to local control. This has led to a lack of clear and consistent policies on controlling and preventing diabetes across the country and has partly masked the extent of the problem from public view. It is reflected by a lack of consistent national data on diabetes rates for the entire Aboriginal population, as data is collected by a patchwork of different organizations, including Statistics Canada, Health Canada, the Canadian Public Health Agency, the First Nations Information Governance Centre and other various provincial and territorial ministries of health. When the data from all different sources is amalgamated it is clear that rates are very high, but enough data to suggest that they may be even higher is not available.

THRIFTY GENE THEORY

There is some scientific evidence to suggest that type 2 diabetes has a genetic component. This is not so say that it is predetermined, but that specific populations have a genetic predisposition to developing diabetes. This is known as the "Thrifty Gene Theory", and hypothesizes that certain populations have a genetic tendency toward storing energy as body fat due to past collective experiences of periodic famine or their traditional lifestyle as hunter-gatherers. With entry into a modern, more sedentary lifestyle and high energy diet, it is thought that this tendency leads to a genetic disposition to develop diabetes. Populations in which this tendency has been identified include Africans, Asians and North American Aboriginals.

This theory has not, so far, been either proved or disproved, and it should be viewed with caution. First, assuming a genetic basis for illness is potentially sensitive and could cause offence, especially when there is no incontrovertible evidence to prove it, either on a population level or at the individual level. Health care professionals should also remember that not all Aboriginal people necessarily share the same genetic makeup—there is as much diversity as there is in the general population. Finally, diabetes is ultimately caused by environmental factors—the absence of diabetes in the Canadian Aboriginal population within living memory is incontrovertible proof of that, as is the sharply rising incidence of diabetes in the general population. The Thrifty Gene Theory is not terribly useful in either treating or predicting diabetes and at worst may distract attention from more important issues, such as diet, exercise and access to health care services.

TREATMENT

The best treatment for diabetes is, of course, preventing it from occurring at all. Little can be done so far about type 1 and gestational diabetes. Both require well-established and effective medical therapies, including insulin, as well as diet and exercise to control symptoms. Type 2 diabetes is another matter. It can be prevented and, with proper treatment, arrested in its progress, leaving the patient free to live a normal, healthy life.

APPROACHES THAT WORK

This being said, there are some approaches that work and others that do not. Most important is for prevention and treatment to be community oriented. That is, they should work with the community, not against it. Most Aboriginal communities have had past experience of well-meaning but invasive and disruptive public health measures. These have ranged from the mass evacuations of individuals to sanatoria for tuberculosis treatment to condescending dietary advice to avoid traditional foods in favour of the grain- and dairy-based diet of the Canada Food Guide (both of these approaches have since been abandoned, and the latter probably contributed to higher diabetes rates). Approaches to prevention and treatment of diabetes that do not involve the community are unlikely to succeed.

CASE STUDY—SANDY LAKE, ONTARIO

We did it for the children. We want to be known, not just as the community with the third highest diabetes rate, but as the community that did something about it.

— Former Deputy Chief Harry Meekis, quoted in *The Toronto Star,*
April 30, 2000.

Community Educaton

Community education is one promising approach to diabetes prevention. Many traditional Aboriginal communities use a consensual approach to decision making. By both educating the community on the risks and consequences of diabetes and involving the community in the process of finding solutions, the problem can be tackled on a community scale. Although in its infancy, this approach has had some impressive successes, particularly in Sandy Lake, in Northwestern Ontario and in Kahnawake, in Southern Québec.

  The community of Sandy Lake in Northern Ontario suffers from very high levels of diabetes. The collapse of the traditional economy has led to widespread dependence on social services since the 1980s, and the cost of living is high due to expensive food prices at the only local grocery store. By the early 1990s, Sandy Lake had the third highest rate of diabetes in the world among the 30- to 65-year-old population. This was driven by increases in all of the risk factors noted for Aboriginal communities: decline in physical activity, a change in diet, and possibly genetic factors (thought to be unique to the Sandy Lake population). The community developed a partnership with diabetes researchers at the University of Toronto and created the Sandy Lake Health and Diabetes Project. The project focused on education through community-wide initiatives and in the schools.

The former included construction of a network of walking trails by community members to permit physical activity without the danger of walking on the main roads, which were unpaved and without sidewalks and thus both dusty and dangerous for pedestrians. The grocery store in the community was encouraged to create a Healthy Food Choice Program, where healthy foods were labelled in both English and Ojibway-Cree Syllabic script, so community members could identify healthy market foods. The community has also organized a yearly round of events designed to encourage community members to improve both their physical activity levels and their diet, including Walk to Work and School Day and Nutrition Awareness Week. A healthy snack program provides children in elementary and high school with a healthy morning snack.

In the schools the grade 3 and 4 curricula provide a culturally appropriate diabetes awareness curriculum, including lessons on how to maintain a healthy diet and appropriate levels of physical activity, and information on diabetes and how to prevent it. The program also includes physical body-fat measurements and feedback on dietary changes that have indicated that the program has seen some success in improving these key risk factors for diabetes.

Sandy Lake still labours under its geographical and economic burdens. The cost of market foods is still much higher than in Southern Canada and the traditional economy is still stagnant, due to the collapse of the fur markets. However, the people are now aware of the dangers of diabetes and are doing their best to overcome these challenges (Cordileone, 2010).

CASE STUDY—KAHNAWAKE SCHOOLS DIABETES PREVENTION PROJECT

The Kahnawake Schools Diabetes Prevention Project (KSDPP) began in 1994, in the Mohawk Nation population of Kahnawake, Québec. Like the program in Sandy Lake, it was created in response to very high levels of diabetes in the Kahnawake population, levels twice those of the Canadian population. These were accompanied by even higher levels of vascular complications (up to 48% of adults had coronary artery disease).

The KSDPP focuses on educating children in the elementary and high schools on the Kahnawake Reserve about the health dangers of diabetes and the importance of diet and exercise in preventing it. According to the Project's mission statement, it "designs and implements intervention activities for schools, families and community to prevent type 2 diabetes through the promotion of healthy eating, physical activity and positive attitude for present and future Kahnawakero:non and for other Aboriginal communities. KSDPP conducts community based research on these activities, trains community intervention workers and academic and community researchers and reports all research results to the community."

The Project has taken a leading role in educating diabetes prevention workers in other Aboriginal communities across Canada and publicizing the results of its educational and treatment programs. Initially the project was funded by the Canadian government through the National Health and Development Research Program, but it has since been supported by the Kahnawake government and various academic and federal grants. The program is unusual in having a tripartite administration of KSDPP staff, Academic advisors and the Community Advisory Board. The Community Advisory Board is identified by the Kahnawake population as the dominant partner with overall direction of the project (Cargo, 2011).

A childhood health education program always takes a long time to affect a population. The prevalence of diabetes is still rising in Kahnawake, since most of the population comprises adults who have never taken part in the program. However, the incidence of new diabetes cases is now dropping in Kahnawake, indicating that the KSDPP is beginning to take effect. Due to Kahnawake's favorable location in Southern Canada, food costs are much more reasonable than they are in Sandy Lake, allowing education to be directly linked to an improved diet, which is a more problematic outcome in remote communities like Sandy Lake.

CASE STUDY—HEALTHY FOOD PARCELS

Education is one approach to lowering diabetes rates. Another is direct subsidies to reduce food costs for remote communities. The Canadian government created the Food Mail Program to provide direct subsidies for market foods that qualify on grounds of nutrient content and popularity. Aboriginal Affairs and Northern Development maintains a monitoring program called the Northern Food Basket, which determines the cost of a range of commonly available and nutritious foods across the Arctic. This is then used to calculate subsidies for the Food Mail Program, which subsidizes the cost to have food delivered to remote communities. The Inuvialuit Settlement Region in the Western Arctic is one of the regions that participates in this program, which has enabled community members to order food from Southern retailers for considerably less than the cost of purchasing food from the local grocery stores.

The program, although popular, has been criticized for excluding traditionally harvested country foods, such as caribou, fish or whale. This, community members feel, has prevented the development of an inter-community trade in country foods. Such a trade might both reduce regional disparities in traditional foods, which have been proven to protect against diabetes and other chronic diseases, and markedly reduce food costs in general. The program has recently been revised, but is now oriented toward providing direct subsidies to the retailers themselves in each community, under the assumption that they will pass on the savings to their customers. Although the Food Mail Program has had mixed results, it has also provided more nutritious market foods, including fruits and vegetables, than would otherwise be available (Nutrition North Canada, 2012).

CRITICAL THINKING EXERCISES

1. Answer the following questions, giving yourself one point for each "yes" and subtracting one point for each "no":
   — Do you eat at least one serving of processed food per day?
   — Do you eat in fast food restaurants more than once a week?
   — Do you sugar your coffee?
   — Do you see yourself as having a sweet tooth?
   — Do you drink sugary soft drinks?
   — Is your favourite leisure-time activity watching TV or using your computer?

   Now answer the following questions, giving yourself one point for each "yes" and subtracting one point for each "no."
   — Do you eat wild game?
   — Do you eat only organic grass-fed meat from domesticated farm animals?
   — Do you prepare all your meals yourself, "from scratch"?
   — Do you avoid sweets?
   — Are you physically active in your spare time?

   Consider your answers to these questions. Compare them with other students; if your total for the second list is higher than the first, then congratulations, you are at low risk of developing diabetes. If your total from the first list is higher, then you are normal. Diabetes is not only increasing in the Aboriginal population, it is increasing throughout the Canadian population. Many students find little time or money to follow the "anti-diabetes" prescriptions in the second list, putting them at risk of type 2 diabetes later in life.

2. Try monitoring your sugar (glucose, fructose and sucrose) consumption over a typical week. How high is it? Most Canadians, irrespective of their ethnic background, consume levels of sugar that put them at risk of type 2 diabetes at some point in their lives.

3. List the community resources available for treatment and support of diabetes in your community? How many of these would be available in communities with less than 500 people?

Discussion Questions

1. What has driven the increased rate of type 2 diabetes in the Aboriginal population?

2. Why is type 2 diabetes increasing in the non-Aboriginal population?

3. How is Sandy Lake coping with its diabetes problems?

4. What are the symptoms of diabetes?

5. What is the cause of type 1 diabetes?

6. Why are high rates of gestational diabetes a concern for the long-term prevalence of diabetes?

7. The prevalence of diabetes in Kahnawake has not declined. Why is the KSDPP still regarded as a success?

8. What chronic conditions are associated with diabetes?

9. How significant is the Thrifty Gene Theory for Aboriginal diabetes rates?

REFERENCES AND FURTHER READING

Cordileone, E. (2010). Inside Sandy Lake's fight with diabetes. *Toronto Star*, http://www.healthzone.ca/health/yourhealth/diabetes/article/788246--inside-sandy-lake-s-fight-with-diabetes.

Cargo, M. D., Delormier, T., Levesque, L., McComber, A. M., & Macaulay, A. C. (2011). Community capacity as an "inside job": Evolution of perceived ownership within a university-Aboriginal community partnership. *American Journal of Health Promotion, 26*, 2.

Ho, L., Gittelsohn, J., Rimal, R., Treuth, M., Sharma, S., Rosecrans, A., & Harris, S. B. (2008). An integrated multi-institutional diabetes prevention program improves knowledge and healthy food acquisition in northwestern Ontario First Nations. *Health Education & Behaviour, 35*(4), 561–573.

Horn, O. K., Jacobs-Whyte, H., Ing, A., Bruegl, A., Paradis, G., & Macaulay, A. C. (2007). Incidence and prevalence of type 2 diabetes in the First Nation community of Kahnawá:ke, Québec, Canada, 1986–2003. *Canadian Journal of Public Health, 98*(6), 438–443.

Martens, P. J, Martin, B. D., O'Neil, J. D., & MacKinnon, M. (2006). Diabetes and adverse outcomes in a First Nations population: Associations with healthcare access, and socioeconomic and geographical factors. *Canadian Journal of Diabetes, 31*(3), 223–232.

Public Health Agency of Canada. (2011). *Diabetes in Canada: Facts and figures from a public health perspective*. Ottawa, ON: Author. www.phac-aspc.gc.ca/cd-mc/diabetes-diabete/index-eng.php.

Salsberg, J., McComber, A. M., Naqshbandi, M., Receveur, O., Harris, S. B., Ann, C., & Macaulay, A. C. (2007). Knowledge, capacity, and readiness: Translating successful experiences in community-based participatory research for health promotion. *Pimisatiwin*, *5*(2), 125–150.

Willows, N. D. (2005). Determinants of healthy eating in Aboriginal peoples in Canada. *Canadian Journal of Public Health*, *96*(Supp. 3), S32–36.

Useful Websites

Aboriginal Diabetes Initiative: www.hc-sc.gc.ca/fniah-spnia/diseases-maladies/diabete/index-eng.php

Canadian Broadcasting Corporation, Foot Amputations Ravage Aboriginal Diabetics: www.cbc.ca/news/canada/manitoba/story/2009/12/08/man-diabetes-shoes.html

Canadian Diabetes Association: www.diabetes.ca

Kahnawake Schools Diabetes Prevention Project: www.ksdpp.org/elder/about_ksdpp.php

National Aboriginal Diabetes Association: www.nada.ca/

Nutrition North Canada. http://nutritionnorthcanada.ca/isr/index-eng.asp

Sandy Lake Health and Diabetes Project: www.sandylakediabetes.com/

Chronic and Infectious Diseases

Chapter Objectives

- The chronic and infectious diseases that particularly affect the Aboriginal population today will be reviewed.
- Their origins as Aboriginal-specific diseases are explained.
- Culturally appropriate approaches to Aboriginal clients are recommended.

Key Concepts

Chronic Disease

Infectious Disease

Genetic Inheritance

Primary Risk Factors

Secondary Risk Factors

Community Risk Factors

Behavioral Risk
Factors

Etiology

Obesity

Sexually Transmitted
Diseases

Key Terms

Cancer

Arthritis

Rheumatism

Renal Disease

Renal Vascular Disease

Digestive Disorders

Respiratory Infections

Chronic Obstructive
Pulmonary Disease
(COPD)

Emphysema/Chronic
Bronchitis

Human immunodeficiency
virus (HIV)

Acquired Immune
Deficiency Syndrome
(AIDS)

Tuberculosis (TB)

Chlamydia

Syphilis

Herpes Simplex

Gonorrhea

Otitis Media

Hypertension/High Blood
Pressure

Glomerulonephritis

WHAT ARE CHRONIC DISEASES?

Chronic diseases are noncontagious diseases of long duration and generally slow progression. According to the Public Health Agency of Canada, chronic diseases have an uncertain etiology, multiple risk factors, long latency, prolonged affliction, a non-infectious origin, and can be associated with impairments or functional disability. Chronic diseases are among the most preventable diseases, since their origins lie in environmental factors and their onset is usually prolonged enough that they can be identified and treated before their effects become irreversible.

These diseases are also among the most difficult to treat as successful treatment requires more than a "magic bullet" (a pill or injection)—it requires treatment of the underlying conditions that led to the disease. Thus, even more than infectious diseases, chronic diseases are linked to the determinants of health. However, addressing the determinants of health requires attention to the social, economic, cultural and environmental conditions that people live in. This is a tall order for a health care system that traditionally has focused on disease and injury, not public health.

Chronic disease is increasing rapidly in the Canadian population in general. This is both a function of the increasing age of the population and environmental factors, including air quality, diet and living conditions. The Aboriginal population experiences the same challenges and is experiencing a similar, but much greater increase in chronic disease rates. Chronic disease rates in Aboriginal children in particular are markedly higher than in the general population, and this is of particular concern for the future health of the Aboriginal population as the children grow up (Figure 7.1).

The top five chronic diseases in Canada are: cardiovascular disease, obesity, cancer, chronic respiratory disease (COPD), arthritis and diabetes. Indeed, most Canadians die of chronic diseases (207,000 of 231,000 deaths recorded in 2005). Among the Aboriginal population the chronic disease pattern is slightly different. Diabetes rates are serious enough that Aboriginal diabetes has been considered separately from other chronic diseases. It also is the major contributor to high rates of Aboriginal cardiovascular disease and renal disease. However, the Canadian Aboriginal population also has very high rates of otitis media, renal disease (chronic kidney disease) and physical disabilities related to other chronic diseases (Figure 7.2).

PRIMARY RISK FACTORS

Risk factors for chronic diseases can be divided into primary factors and community factors. Primary risk factors are those that are directly linked to individuals and their behaviours. Because risk factors tend to be linked, the existence of one risk factor often predisposes individuals to other risk factors. The significant primary risk factors in the Aboriginal population can be divided into three categories: inherited biological risk factors, behavioral risk factors and intermediate biological conditions.

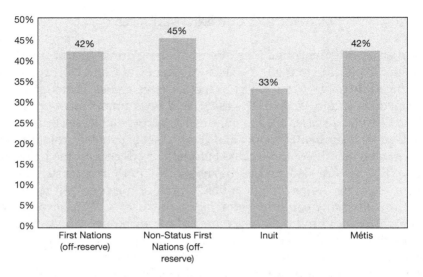

Figure 7.1 *Chronic Disease in Aboriginal Children, Ages 6 to 14*

Note: The Aboriginal Community Survey asked about one or more serious, physician-diagnosed chronic diseases.
Source: Statistics Canada, Aboriginal Community Survey, 2006.

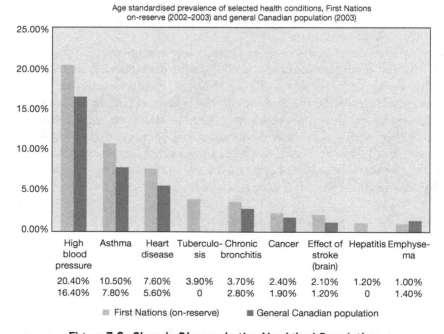

Figure 7.2 *Chronic Disease in the Aboriginal Population*

Source: First Nations Information Governance Committee. First Nations Regional Longitudinal Health Survey 2002–2003; Results for Adults, Youth and Children Living in First Nations Communities. Assembly of First Nations, November 2005; Statistics Canada, Canadian Community Health Survey 2003.

The inherited biological risk factors include:

Genetic inheritance: Some individuals inherit a predisposition to develop certain chronic diseases. Sometimes this disposition can be resisted through managing other risk factors; sometimes it cannot. People with type 1 diabetes can only manage the disease itself, not prevent it. Yet, those who have a predisposition to type 2 diabetes can prevent it by maintaining a healthy diet, normal weight and sufficient exercise.

Age: Chronic diseases are more prevalent in older populations. While individuals may contract a chronic disease in their youth, generally it takes time for the risk factors that lead to the development of chronic diseases to take effect.

Gender: Some chronic disease are either gender specific (e.g., gestational diabetes), or gender weighted (e.g., heart disease is more common in Aboriginal men). This risk factor cannot be changed, but it can be used to create gender-specific prevention strategies.

Behavioural risk factors include:

Tobacco: Smoking has declined in Canada, but remains high in selected demographic groups, including young women and Aboriginal people of both genders.

Alcohol: Alcohol consumption remains high in Canada, although lower than in the past. Among the Aboriginal population, levels of alcohol consumption are unclear. Levels of abstinence are higher than in the non-Aboriginal population, but among those who do drink, binge drinking appears to be a recurring pattern.

Physical inactivity: Physical activity has declined across all sectors of the Canadian population, including the Aboriginal population. Among Aboriginals, even in remote areas such as the Canadian Arctic, the move away from the traditional lifestyle has dramatically impacted physical activity levels.

Unhealthy diet: Both poverty and isolation lead to a poor diet. Grocery stores in remote communities have poor selection and remarkably high prices (it is not unheard of, e.g., for stores to charge $5 for an orange)—a function of both transportation costs and lack of competition. Less expensive food tends to be high in fats and carbohydrates and low in nutrients but it is cheap to bring in, lasts a long time on the shelf and, just as everywhere else, junk food sells well. Traditional diets also require resources—money to buy gas for all-terrain vehicles and snow mobiles, money for ammunition and, for those who have jobs, time to go hunting. Among more urbanized populations, lack of education leads to a poor diet, since informed food choices are a function of education. Also, even in the cities, cheap food tends to be less nutritious.

Left uncorrected these risk factors lead to a number of intermediate biological conditions that, although not chronic diseases, are the precursors to them. They include:

Hypertension or high blood pressure: High blood pressure is caused by a number of factors, including genetics, life stress, sodium (salt) consumption, smoking, lack of exercise, excessive weight gain and high cholesterol.

High cholesterol: Again, changes in lifestyle and diet among Aboriginal peoples have led to changes in diet as a market-based diet replaces traditional food harvested from the land. This has directly impacted cholesterol levels, as saturated and trans-fatty acid levels in market foods are much higher than in traditional foods.

Overweight: Obesity is now considered a chronic disease in its own right. However, overweight (generally classified as a body mass index of 25–30 kg/m^2) individuals also face health problems and the weight of the Aboriginal population is found to be increasing. Lack of physical activity, coupled with dietary change, leads, ineluctably, to weight gain. Socioeconomic factors (poverty) and small isolated communities also restrict the opportunities for physical recreation that most Canadians enjoy. In many remote communities, even walking is a difficult activity to engage in without community action taken to create places to walk, as was done in Sandy Lake.

In addition, acute illness may cause a chronic disease to develop through a depressed immune system. This is compounded by the effects of the other primary risk factors and even more so by the effects of the community risk factors.

COMMUNITY RISK FACTORS

Behind the primary risk factors are those that the individual has less control over because they constitute a factor of the environment—the place where we live. They include social and economic conditions, such as poverty, employment and family composition. These factors are very difficult to modify and often lead to high primary risk factors.

Environment, especially climate and air pollution, is also an important risk factor. In cold climate, people spend much of the year indoors in close proximity to other people. This increases the risk for both chronic and infectious disease directly—through contagion—and indirectly. Thus, for example, if it is −40° outside, how likely are children to gain physical activity through playing outside?

Culture is another risk factor, as cultural practices, norms and values may discourage individuals from engaging in low risk behaviours.

Geographic isolation, which influences housing and access to products and services, is a very important risk factor for chronic diseases. While it is sometimes possible to remedy this by moving to a larger centre, this itself brings other risk factors into play, especially if there is no economic or social benefit to moving that outweighs the cultural displacement.

All of these risk factors are higher in the Aboriginal population and are hard to change as they are intrinsic to the communities in question.

MANAGING RISK

While some risk factors, such as age, sex and genetic make-up, cannot be changed, many behavioural risk factors can be modified, as much as a number

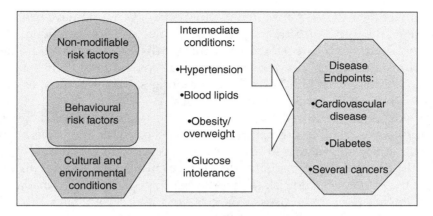

Figure 7.3 *Chronic Diseases Share Common Risk Factors and Conditions*
Source: Public Health Agency of Canada 2012.

of intermediate biological risk factors can be, including hypertension, being overweight, hyperlipidemia and glucose intolerance. With considerably more effort the societal, economic and physical conditions that influence and shape behaviour and indirectly affect other biological factors can also be modified. Recognizing these common risk factors and conditions is the conceptual basis for an integrated approach to chronic disease that treats the causes, not the symptoms. In essence, controlling and preventing chronic disease become a matter of managing risk, by combining medical treatment with the much harder task of improving the behavioural and community risk factors that ultimately are the cause of most chronic diseases (Figure 7.3).

CHRONIC DISEASE IN THE ABORIGINAL POPULATION

Chronic disease rates are generally much higher in the Canadian Aboriginal population than in the general population, although there are exceptions, such as breast cancer, which is much lower. The rise of chronic disease can be linked to rapid social change, including urbanization, the arrival of new media (e.g., television and the internet) and socioeconomic change. This is directly linked to the erosion of traditional Aboriginal culture, which is tied to the residential school experience of deliberate acculturalization, and also the effects of modernization in general. This has also directly influenced changes in diet and activity level as the shift away from traditional lifestyles has dramatically reduced activity levels and has changed diets. These experiences can also lead to chronic stress, which is also linked to the development of chronic diseases and to poverty and other socioeconomic risk factors as well.

Even members of the Aboriginal population too young to have experienced the residential schools directly may have been affected by generational trauma, which contributes to the development of chronic disease. In this syndrome, survivors of residential schools develop chronic diseases due to their experiences there, and, through the effects on their parenting skills, pass them on to their children, who in turn develop chronic diseases.

The effects of chronic diseases on the Aboriginal population are grave. Chronic diseases result in premature death and shorter life span, overall poorer health, disability and increased health care costs. Including diabetes, over one-third of the Aboriginal population suffers from a chronic disease, making chronic diseases the primary health risk in the Aboriginal population in Canada today.

The impact of chronic diseases is profound and reverberates through the Aboriginal population and also into the general Canadian society in two ways: As both an economic burden and a social burden, the economic cost to the health care system is obvious. However, the social burden of having a distinct section of the population chronically ill, and the negative reflection that casts on Canadian society in general, are also significant. Canada generally sees itself, and is seen internationally, as a progressive, developed First World country. The presence of a large section of the population with health indicators more commonly seen in the Third World, and with socioeconomic conditions at a similar level, does not reflect well on the nation.

OBESITY

Obesity rates are rising rapidly in the Canadian population, both in the Aboriginal and non-Aboriginal populations. Obesity leads to other chronic diseases, such as cardiovascular disease, diabetes and renal disease. It is also a chronic disease in itself and it has severe impacts on the life of people suffering from it.

Obesity is firmly rooted in the determinants of health—education, income level, social environment and, to some degree, biology, which all play a role in the growth of obesity. Among the Aboriginal population, obesity is linked to rapid social change caused by modernization. Movement into settlements, loss of the traditional diet and consumption of unhealthy market foods are all linked to the growth of obesity. As of 2001, among on-reserve First Nations 31.8% of adult men, 41.1% of adult women, 14.0% of youth and 36.2% of children were considered obese. This is roughly twice as high as the rates in the general population (Figure 7.4).

Similar factors, somewhat less pronounced, also drive the growth of obesity among the general population. Certainly the Canadian diet has changed dramatically in the last 50 years, as have activity levels as Canadians have become more urbanized and more dependent on processed foods high in fat, sugar and salt. By identifying and successfully treating Aboriginal obesity, the tools for improving rapidly worsening obesity rates in the general population may also be identified.

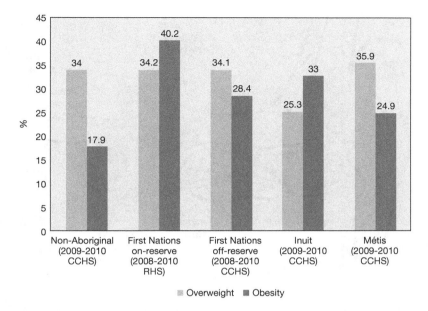

Figure 7.4 *Overweight and Obese Aboriginal and Non-Aboriginal Adults*

Note: Overweight is based on a BMI greater than or equal to 25.0 kg/m² but less than 30.0 kg/m²;
obesity is based on a BMI greater than or equal to 30.0 kg/m².
Source: Public Health Agency of Canada (2011), using data from the 2009–2010 Canadian Community Health
Survey (Statistics Canada) and the 2006 Aboriginal Peoples Survey (Statistics Canada); First Nations Information
Governance Center (2011) using data from the 2008–2010 First Nations Regional Longitudinal Health Survey
(Phase 2) (First Nations Information Governance Center).

Associated Health Conditions

A variety of health conditions and chronic diseases are associated with obesity. These include: diabetes, cardiovascular disease, cancer and respiratory disease. Obesity interacts with these diseases, acting as a factor in their development and, as people reduce activity levels and induce low self-esteem, contributes to increases disease severity.

OTITIS MEDIA

Otitis media, or chronic middle ear infections, occur as a result of repeated infections or blockage of the Eustachian tube that connects the middle ear to the back of the throat (Figure 7.5). This condition usually develops in childhood but has lingering effects in adulthood, which can include ongoing ear infections, hearing damage and delayed language development.

The World Health Organization (WHO) describes a prevalence of 4% as a massive public health problem that is often found in developing countries and is described as a disease of poverty. In Northern regions of Canada and in Aboriginal communities, the prevalence is more than 10 times the WHO cut-off of 4%. In

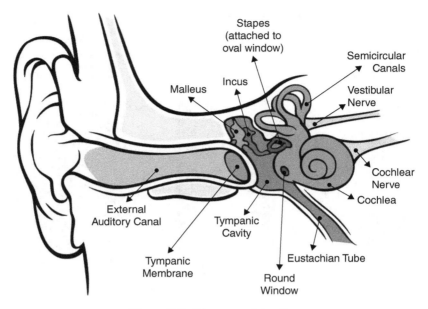

Figure 7.5 *Diagram of the Ear*

Source: The Hearing Foundation of Canada, How the Ear Works: http://www.thfc.ca/cms/en/
HearingLoss/HowHearingWorks.aspx?menuid=70.

mixed Aboriginal and non-Aboriginal communities the rates of Aboriginal otitis media reach as high as 40 times the non-Aboriginal rates. This indicates that this condition is specific to the Aboriginal community, not to specific geographic regions. The high prevalence of otitis media leads to hearing loss, language development problems and other health and developmental conditions.

Although there is some controversy over the causes of otitis media, it is clear that the single most significant means of preventing it is breastfeeding infants, preferably for a year or more. This may be due to stimulation of the immune system from nutrients and antibodies in the mother's breast milk. The mechanical action of breastfeeding, which acts to clear the Eustachian tubes and the middle ears of fluid, is another possible reason for this protective effect. Even psychological stimulation of the infant immune system from extended intimacy with the mother during breastfeeding may also play a role. Irrespective of the exact mechanism, breastfeeding has been connected with five-fold lower rates of otitis media in children, both Aboriginal and non-Aboriginal. The protective effects of breastfeeding also seem to continue throughout individuals' lives, as rates of otitis media remain low even after breastfeeding ceases (Thomson, 1994).

CHRONIC OBSTRUCTIVE PULMONARY DISEASE

Chronic obstructive pulmonary disease (COPD), also referred to as emphysema or chronic bronchitis, is a condition where the airways and air sacs in the lungs lose shape and elasticity. The walls between many of the air sacs are destroyed

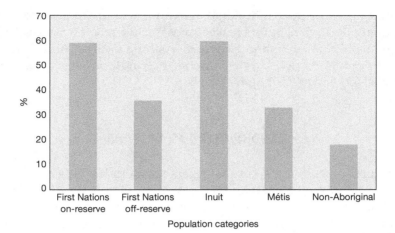

Figure 7.6 *Prevalence of Smoking in Aboriginal and Non-Aboriginal Populations*
Sources: 2006 Aboriginal Peoples Survey; 2007 Canadian Community Health Survey, cycle 4.1;
First Nations Regional Health Longitudinal Survey 2002/2003.

and the walls of the airways become thick and swollen. Cells in the airways also make more mucus than usual, which blocks the airways. This results in short-ness of breath, coughing, hyperventilation and sputum production, which are symptoms characteristic of COPD.

COPD is primarily caused by smoking, although it can also be caused by long-term exposure to air pollution, particularly fine particulate emissions, and it is very common in older smokers and those exposed to significant amounts of second-hand smoke over a long period of time (usually persons who are fam-ily members of smokers). Due to the very high rate of smoking in Canadian Aboriginal communities, COPD is up to 60% more common than in the general population (Figure 7.6). Due to its debilitating effects, COPD sufferers are also more likely to become obese, and to develop cardiovascular disease and diabetes. Since it is usually the result of long-term smoking, it is also associated with high rates of lung cancer.

CHRONIC RESPIRATORY DISEASE (ASTHMA)

Chronic respiratory disease, better known as asthma, is noncontagious and pri-marily affects children, although it often lingers throughout the individual's lifespan. It is not COPD, although the symptoms may be similar. In asthma, environmental triggers cause tightening and irritation of the airways. This may include spasms, resulting in difficulty in breathing.

The causes of asthma include a family history of the disease (genetic trigger), environmental triggers (an attack is often caused by environmental allergies—such as pollen or animal fur) or second-hand smoke, which may also trigger an asthma attack in vulnerable individuals. Asthma rates are increasing throughout the Canadian population, but increased rates in children and rapidly rising rates in Aboriginal children are of more concern. Asthma rates are higher in the urban Aboriginal population, while rates among the rural, on-reserve and Northern populations were lower (Crighton et al., 2010).

CARDIOVASCULAR DISEASE

Cardiovascular disease is a term that refers to multiple diseases of the circulatory system including the heart and blood vessels, whether the blood vessels are affecting the lungs, the brain, kidneys or other parts of the body. Cardiovascular disease includes coronary heart disease, peripheral vascular disease, inflammatory heart disease, stroke, myocardial infarction (heart attack) and valvular heart disease. All forms of cardiovascular disease have common roots in atherosclerosis and high blood pressure and may also be direct side-effects of other chronic diseases, especially diabetes. These in turn are caused by lifestyle factors, including obesity, smoking, diet, sedentary lifestyle, high blood pressure, diabetes and stress.

Cardiovascular disease is the leading cause of death in adult Canadian men and women, followed by cancer and respiratory diseases. Injuries rank fourth. By contrast, for Aboriginal peoples, injuries are the leading cause of death, followed by cardiovascular disease and cancer. However, these statistics are starting to change as lifestyle changes impact the health of the Aboriginal population. Diet is a particularly significant risk factor due to decreased consumption of country food or market fruits and vegetables and increased consumption of processed foods high in saturated and trans-saturated fats.

Historically, cardiovascular disease was almost nonexistent in the Aboriginal population in Canada. Diet and lifestyle provided ample protection against it. Even among the Inuit, whose diet consisted almost entirely of fat and meat, environmental conditions and the high levels of marine mammal fats (extremely high in omega-3 fatty acids) contributed to an almost zero rate of cardiovascular disease. Rates were low enough that some authorities thought that Aboriginals had an innate resistance to cardiovascular disease. Even today, the Inuit, who still consume significant quantities of traditional food, have rates of cardiovascular disease below that of the general population.

However, dietary and lifestyle changes have altered this picture. Cardiovascular disease is now a visible problem in the Inuit and First Nations population, especially in those who have adopted a wholly Southern diet, and is the second most common cause of death in First Nations. It can be expected that this condition will increase in significance over time as the behavioural risk factors for cardiovascular disease increase among all Aboriginal groups.

Fresh fruits and vegetables can protect the heart and blood vessels. They provide fibre and contain antioxidants, substances which work against the development of blockage in the arteries. A traditional Aboriginal diet also acts to protect the heart and blood vessels, sometimes for different reasons. Unfortunately, a traditional diet is not usually replaced with a healthy European diet, but with an unhealthy one. In addition, socioeconomic factors are predictors of risk factors related to cardiovascular disease. The Aboriginal population, as noted, is highly at risk due to lower-than-average incomes, limited educational opportunities and remote and under-serviced communities. All of these are obstacles to accessing the health services that provide support in both preventing and treating cardiovascular disease.

CANCER

Cancer rates were historically lower in the Aboriginal population than in the general Canadian population. However, this picture is slowly changing. The leading causes of cancer deaths in Canada are lung, prostate, breast and colorectal cancer, with lung cancer (overwhelmingly due to cigarette smoking) still the leading cause of death from cancer for the entire population, Aboriginal and non-Aboriginal (Figure 7.7).

The Aboriginal population still has lower cancer rates for all varieties except prostate cancer, but numbers are climbing as risk factors increase in the Aboriginal population and decrease in the general population. The risk factors for cancer include: smoking, diet, physical activity, alcohol consumption, family history, personal health practices and environmental exposure. Cancer is the third leading cause of death in Aboriginals, while it is the second leading cause of death in the general population.

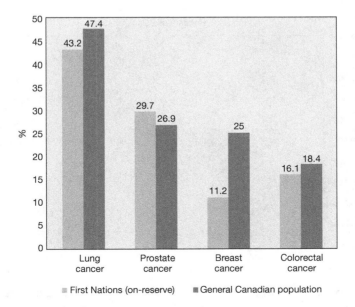

Figure 7.7 *Selected Mortality Rates*

Source: Statistics Canada, 2001. Canadian Vital Statistics, Birth and Death Databases.

At least 20% of cancer deaths are linked to a poor diet—including consumption of alcohol. Fruit and vegetable consumption is protective for a variety of cancers, whereas a diet high in red meat, processed meat and saturated fat has been linked to an increased risk of several cancers. However, traditional Aboriginal diets and lifestyles, despite being high in red meat and often quite low in fruit and vegetable consumption, have also led to very low cancer rates.

For all forms of cancer in the Aboriginal population, there are lower rates of screening, which means that patients are more likely to be diagnosed at a later stage of the disease. This leads to higher mortality rates for those diagnosed, even though the disease rates still remain lower than in the general population.

DISABILITIES

Physical disabilities are linked to limited mobility and activity, increased personal isolation and increased burden on the family to care for the disabled. The lack of services in many remote communities also leads to an increased risk for complications, including the development of other chronic diseases such as diabetes, cardiovascular disease and COPD through the lack of exercise and dependence on an unhealthy market food diet that disabilities tend to lead to. In severe cases, families may be forced to move to urban areas to find appropriate levels of care of a disabled member. Levels of disabilities among the Aboriginal population are high, with as many as 31% of First Nations and 29% of Inuit carrying some form of physical disability (Figure 7.8).

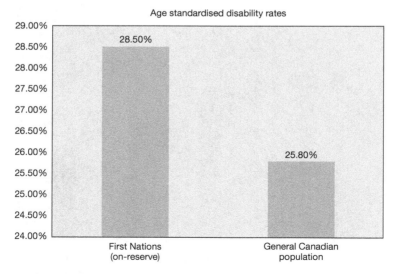

Figure 7.8 *Disability Rates in the First Nations and non-Aboriginal Population*

Source: First Nations Information Governance Committee, First Nations Regional Longitudinal Health Survey 2002–03; Results for Adults, Youth and Children Living in First Nations Communities. Assembly of First Nations, November 2005; Statistics Canada, Canadian Community Health Survey 2003.

ARTHRITIS

Arthritis is inflammation of the joints. It may take the form of osteoarthritis, which is caused by wear and tear on the cartilage of the joints, or rheumatism, which is an inflammatory autoimmune disorder. Both varieties may strike at any age, but are more common in older populations and in women. The average age of diagnosis in the Aboriginal population is 35 years of age. In British Columbia, for which reliable Aboriginal statistics exist, the incidence of arthritis is 17% in the First Nations community, which compares to only 5% in the non-Aboriginal population. Rates of arthritis increase with age, and it affects women more than men among both the Aboriginal and non-Aboriginal populations, but Aboriginal women over the age of 65 have an extremely high incidence of arthritis when compared with their non-Aboriginal counterparts (Figure 7.9). This may be due to diet, to stress levels, or to life history. Data are lacking on the discrepancy between Aboriginal and non-Aboriginal prevalence of arthritis.

RENAL DISEASE

Renal disease is also known as kidney disease and is caused by the kidneys losing their ability to filter blood. It is characterized by progressive deterioration of kidney function, but because the kidneys are very efficient often symptoms are not displayed until 70% of kidney function is compromised. Eventually, it progresses to end-stage renal disease (ESRD), where dialysis or kidney transplant is required for survival.

The three leading causes of renal disease are diabetes, renal vascular disease (i.e., renovascular hypertension) and glomerulonephritis (inflammation of the kidneys). Although Aboriginal rates of chronic kidney disease are lower than that of the general population, the disease progresses much more quickly.

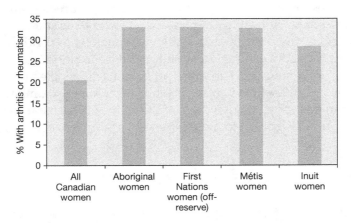

Figure 7.9 *Arthritis or Rheumatism Rates in Aboriginal Women*

Source: Statistics Canada, Aboriginal Peoples Survey, 2006, and Canadian Community Health Survey, 2007.

As a result, Aboriginal ESRD mortality rates are about twice that of the general population. This is often attributed to high diabetes rates, but research has found that even among nondiabetic Aboriginal ESRD patients, mortality rates are 70% higher. Aboriginal patients with ESRD tend to be younger, female, and more likely to have diabetes mellitus, chronic heart failure and peripheral vascular disease than non-Aboriginal patients with ESRD.

DIGESTIVE DISORDERS

Digestive disorders are another chronic health issue in the Aboriginal population. These are disorders of the mouth, esophagus, stomach and intestines. They may be caused by infection or by exposure to drugs. Digestive disorders prevalent in the Aboriginal population include dehydration, constipation, diarrhea, nausea and vomiting, gallbladder disease, gastroesophageal reflux disease, ulcers, hernia and irritable bowel syndrome. Hospitalization rates of infants and toddlers with gastroenteritis are also high, possibly due to socioeconomic factors. Contributing factors to high rates of digestive disorders can include drug and alcohol use, inadequate diet, lack of education and infection with pathogens that cause the condition. For example, very high rates of digestive disorders in Canadian Arctic communities have been linked with contamination of their water supplies by *Helicobacter pylori* bacteria (Goodman et al., 2008). Contributing factors to high rates of digestive disorders can include drug and alcohol use, inadequate diet, poverty and lack of knowledge of preventative measures.

WHAT ARE INFECTIOUS DISEASES?

Chronic diseases are largely caused by environmental stressors and inherited tendencies. Respiratory diseases are spread by pathogens, either by bacteria or viruses, from person to person. Although infectious diseases are directly caused by pathogens, the determinants of health still play a key role in their spread, by either permitting or blocking the conditions that allow contagions to continue. In general, there is a direct link between socioeconomic status, education and infectious disease rates. The better educated and more prosperous all people are, the less likely any of them are to get sick. When society harbours a large number of members whose determinants of health are very poor, their misery also harbours infectious diseases that can easily spread to more prosperous members of the population.

RESPIRATORY DISEASES

Respiratory diseases affect the upper and lower respiratory systems. They can be infectious, but are not necessarily always so. Asthma and COPD both affect the respiratory tract, but both are noninfectious chronic diseases. Even though respiratory diseases, such as influenza, pneumonia, the common cold and tuberculosis are all infectious, environment also plays a major role in their spread. Smoking, or inhaling second hand smoke, by weakening the immune system, also increases susceptibility to infectious respiratory diseases. Overcrowded housing is also a major risk factor, as is ambient air pollution (indoors or outdoors). Otherwise, personal health practices, such as hand washing, are the major means of preventing the spread of infectious respiratory tract infections.

Respiratory Diseases in Canada

Respiratory diseases are on the rise in the Canadian population. Most of them are chronic, such as COPD, asthma, lung cancer and cystic fibrosis. However, these conditions in turn increase the incidence of respiratory tract infections by weakening the immune system, while also increasing their severity. Even the common cold can be dangerous to an individual with a weakened immune system.

Respiratory Diseases and Aboriginal Health

The Aboriginal population has higher rates of respiratory diseases, particularly in children, who primarily contract infectious respiratory diseases. A study conducted by the University of Alberta found that Aboriginal children were twice as likely to be seen in emergency rooms for asthma but were less likely to receive a referral to a specialist (Rosychuk, 2010). Among the Aboriginal comunity, respiratory disease accounts for 85% of hospital admissions of infants and children. Even though some communities have gained greater affluence, the incidence of infectious respiratory tract infections has increased. Among Aboriginal children, pneumonia, croup, streptococcus, influenza and the common cold are all serious health issues.

Acute infections have the potential to develop into chronic conditions through weakening of the pulmonary system causing permanent lung damage. As children with repeated acute lung infections grow older, their conditions often do become chronic. More than 19% of Aboriginals over the age of 15 have a chronic lung health problem. As an ongoing condition, this will often lead to COPD with age.

TUBERCULOSIS

Tuberculosis (TB) is caused by a bacterial infection caused by *Mycobacterium tuberculosis*, usually of the lungs, although it was also spread through the consumption of infected milk and meat until recently. It has historically been considered a chronic disease because infection was permanent until the development of antibiotic treatment regimes after the Second World War. Historically, it was one of

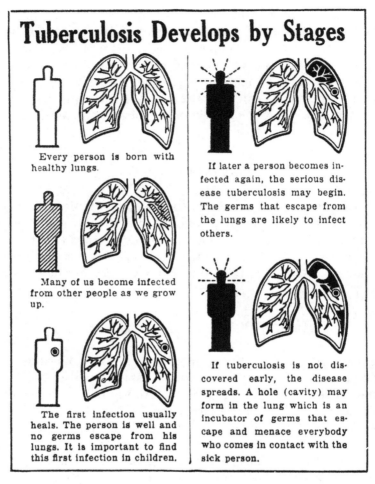

The Stages of Tuberculosis

Source: Canadian Lung Association.

the most lethal epidemic diseases to afflict the Aboriginal population of Canada. As late as the 1930s, the death rate from TB in the First Nations population was 10 times higher than in the rest of the population. Even today TB is a treatable condition that still leads to over 2 million deaths per year globally. Within Canada TB remains a public health risk as it still infects both the Aboriginal population and immigrants from regions where it is still endemic.

In 2005, the TB rate was 27 active cases per 100,000 in Aboriginal peoples. There were only 5 active cases per 100,000 in the Canadian population overall. Of the 1,600 active TB cases reported in Canada in 2005, 19% of the patients were Aboriginal peoples, 13% were non-Aboriginal Canadian-born and 63% were foreign-born. To put these numbers in perspective, Aboriginal Canadians make up only 4% of the population, but make up almost 20% of all TB cases. TB is also the leading cause of death in HIV/AIDS-infected individuals.

TB in the Aboriginal Population

Since the Aboriginal population had no resistance to TB when it arrived in North America, it tended to be correspondingly more virulent. TB among the Aboriginal population was more active and killed more people faster than among contemporary Europeans. In a major epidemic documented among the Copper Inuit in the 1920s, victims were literally consumed by the disease—it dissolved the tissue surrounding the lungs, exposing their body cavities to the air. Death could, and often did, proceed in a matter of a few weeks, rather than years.

TB was endemic to many of the residential schools, leaving the students to infect their families when they returned home on a visit. Concerted anti-TB measures by public health authorities finally brought the disease under control, but it remains far higher in the Aboriginal population—a function of their remote communities, lack of health services, crowded dwellings, and the lingering reservoir of TB carriers from the period when the disease was even more common.

20th-Century TB Control

Prior to the 20th century, TB was probably endemic in the European population. Most people carried the TB bacillus, even though many did not present symptoms for years, if ever. After initial infection, the body's immune system encloses the infected tissue in a cyst in the lungs. It may remain dormant (and non-contagious) there indefinitely. Only if the immune system is weakened can the pathogens erupt from the cyst and begin actively infecting the body. At this point the disease is contagious and the infected person has the symptoms typical of TB. This includes coughing, sputum production and increasing debilitation.

The Sanatorium Approach

Sanatoria were the preferred method of treating TB right up until the 1970s. By secluding patients and controlling their environments it was felt that the disease could be both controlled and eliminated more effectively. The sanatorium movement began in the 19th century and reached its peak after the Second World War, when there were almost 20,000 beds available for TB patients across Canada.

The typical sanatorium emphasized rest, sunlight, surgery for the worst cases, and eventually drug therapy. Tens of thousands of Canadians passed through the sanatoria in the effort to eradicate the disease, an effort that was ultimately only partly successful, because the disease remained dormant in the Aboriginal population, especially in remote communities.

Mountain Sanatorium in Hamilton

Mountain Sanatorium in Hamilton, Ontario. This sanatorium was the destination for many Inuit
evacuated from the Central and Eastern Arctic in the 1950s. Some spent years here.
Source: Canadian Lung Association.

Before the development of antibiotics, the only effective treatments for TB were
seclusion in a special hospital, known as a sanatorium, which involved a regime
of vitamin D suplementation, usually through exposure to sunlight (although,
failing that, cod liver oil supplements were also fed to patients) and a variety of
surgical techniques, including collapsing one lung to "rest" it. Antibiotic treatment was initially used in conjunction with sanatorium care, until the decline of
the disease under a series of massive public health campaigns permitted the last
Canadian tuberculosis "san" to close in 1973.

Aboriginal Resistance

Initially TB in the Aboriginal population was largely neglected. This was partly
due to ignorance and partly due to general parsimony with funding for health
care of the Aboriginal population. Recent research has suggested that TB infected
the Aboriginal population in Northern Canada in the early fur trade period, but
remained largely dormant until socioeconomic and cultural change allowed it to
become active. The creation of reserves with the sedentary and crowded lifestyle
they fostered weakened the population and allowed TB to become a serious epidemic (Pepperell, 2011). When the extent of Aboriginal TB became apparent, special sanatoria were eventually built, but they treated the more accessible southern
Aboriginal populations first. This allowed TB to remain endemic in more remote
populations, where it has remained endemic even today. Treatment at the sanatoria was controversial, as patients were often kept apart from their families for
years, thus severely disrupting communities already damaged by the impact of
residential schools.

After the Second World War, more attention was paid to the incidence of TB
in the Aboriginal population, if only because the high prevalence of TB in the
Aboriginal population increased the likelihood that it would act as a reservoir

Inuit Tuberculosis Patient

Inuit TB patient Anthony Amauyak from Chesterfield Inlet in Clearwater Sanatorium, March 1956.
Source: Gar Lunney/National Film Board of Canada. Photothèque/Library and Archives Canada/PA-189645.

for the disease. This would allow it to re-establish itself in the general population after it had been eradicated there. As a consequence intensive campaigns to reduce Aboriginal TB were started. These were increased after the severity of TB among the Canadian Inuit in the Canadian Arctic became public and the willingness of American military medical staff to treat it themselves became apparent and also a sovereignty issue.

This led to mass evacuations of Inuit TB patients to southern sanatoria, often with little explanation given to individuals (and their families) of the fate in store for them. They often remained in the hospital for years, as even with antibiotic therapy TB can take a very long time to resolve.

Alternative Treatments

Although TB sanatoria provided the standard treatment for TB for everyone, Aboriginal or non-Aboriginal, there were other options for treatment. Once drug treatment was available, community-based treatment was feasible. In addition, smaller more numerous sanatoria, closer to families and able to accommodate entire family units as one, would have been far less disruptive to Aboriginal culture and families. Yet, although the acute phase of the Aboriginal TB epidemic passed, it still remains endemic in the population.

Quote: Dr. Stuart Carey, Clearwater Sanitorium, 1965

In northern Manitoba, tuberculosis still smoulders slowly like muskeg fires. If outbreaks are not tracked down and stamped out one by one, a major problem could arise.

This is because the cost and effort required for sanatorium treatment often meant that only Aboriginal people with active TB were treated. Those with latent TB were often overlooked, a function of both geographic isolation and a lack of medical services. As a result, the people infected with latent TB provide a reservoir of TB for their communities, and with modern transportation system and mobility, for the entire country.

A Recurring Health Issue

TB remains very much a current health issue. Although extremely rare in the general population, strains of drug-resistant TB are now emerging, including both multiple drug resistant TB (MDR-TB) and extremely drug resistant TB (XDR-TB), which are difficult to treat with existing antibiotics. Treatment of these strains requires different and more potent cocktails of drugs which need to be taken for much longer perioda of time. This in turn increases the risk of noncompliance and the chance that even more drug resistant strains of TB might emerge.

Very high latent infection rates of TB in the Aboriginal population are directly due to the anti-TB campaigns of the past neglecting the rural and northern population, especially the Aboriginal population of the Boreal North, where the sovereignty concerns that drove the Inuit TB campaigns and evacuations were not present. While it seems likely that TB has been latent in these populations for up to 300 years, in today's highly mobile society it can easily spread and pose a grave public health hazard.

The disease remains latent in the Aboriginal population today due to inadequate health services, poverty, overcrowded dwellings and the geographical isolation of many communities. Since respiratory tract infections are common in the Aboriginal population anyway, the early signs of TB may be ignored or misdiagnosed, allowing the infection time to spread. While primary care is often good, secondary and tertiary care is often poor, making follow-up and monitoring of treatment problematic.

Finally, the presence of TB in the Canadian Aboriginal population should be placed in perspective. Eradication will require more than drug treatment. As long as the socioeconomic conditions, especially overcrowding, in many Aboriginal communities remain poor, TB can always re-establish itself. After all, most TB cases in Canada are among immigrants from countries where the disease is still endemic, providing a constant reservoir of contagion that the right conditions can always allow to take root and flourish.

SEXUALLY TRANSMITTED DISEASES

Sexually transmitted diseases (STDs), also known as sexually transmitted infections, are the subject of considerable social phobia. They comprise a spectrum of infectious diseases that are transmitted through the exchange of body fluids, either through sexual contact, by sharing intravenous syringes, or rarely, through blood transfusions. They include: HIV/AIDS, chlamydia, hepatitis C, herpes simplex, syphilis, gonorrhoea and human papillomavirus. Some STDs are treatable with antibiotics and some with vaccines, while some are incurable. The most deadly STDs have complications that can include impaired sexual function, infertility, brain damage or death.

HIV/AIDS

The most serious STD, and the only one for which adequate national statistics is available in Canada, is the HIV. This is a retro-virus which, by attacking the immune system, eventually leads to AIDS. HIV is contracted through either sexual intercourse, particularly intercourse involving trauma and direct contact of raw flesh with infected body fluids, or through the exchange of body fluids via intravenous needle.

Once contracted, HIV infection may remain latent for up to 10 years before it develops into AIDS. AIDS gradually destroys the immune system and leads to infection by opportunistic diseases (e.g., TB or cancer) and eventually death. If a patient with HIV is treated with antiretroviral drugs the progress of the disease can be retarded. There is, however, no cure and no vaccine yet available for HIV infection or AIDS.

HIV/AIDS in the Aboriginal Population

Although they represent only 3.3% of the Canadian population, Aboriginal persons comprised 5% to 8% of prevalent HIV infections (persons currently living with HIV infection in Canada) and 6% to 12% of new HIV infections in Canada in 2002. Injection drug use continues to be a key mode of HIV transmission in the Aboriginal community (Figure 7.10). Due to the participation in the sex trade and exposure to both IV drug use and infected clients, HIV/AIDS also has a significant impact on Aboriginal women. From 1998 to 2005, women made up 47% of all new HIV diagnoses among Aboriginal people, compared with 21% among

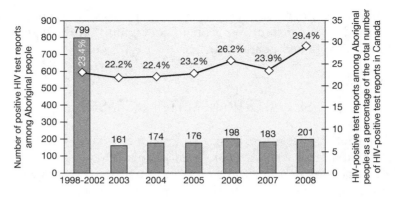

Figure 7.10 *Aboriginal HIV*

Source: Public Health Agency of Canada. (2010) Population-Specific HIV/AIDS Status Report: Aboriginal Peoples.

non-Aboriginal people. Moreover, Aboriginal people receive a diagnosis of HIV at a younger age than non-Aboriginal people—one out of three Aboriginal persons newly diagnosed with HIV is under 30 years of age. By contrast, one out of five non-Aboriginal persons newly diagnosed is under 30. This has disturbing implications for the future trajectory of AIDS rates among Aboriginal persons, and ultimately the general population.

Although the incidence of HIV has gone down in the Canadian population, it appears that HIV rates have been steadily increasing in First Nations and Inuit populations. They are at increased risk for HIV infections for several reasons. Social, economic and behavioural factors such as poverty, substance use (including injection drug use), STDs and limited access to health services, have increased their vulnerability.

Although Aboriginal AIDS rates are currently comparable to the general population, HIV rates are much higher, as much as twice that of the general population, and growing. This is an indication that this will become a major public health issue in the future.

Chlamydia

Chlamydia is caused by the bacteria *Chlamydia trachomatis*. It is one of the most common STDs, but as it is seldom fatal, its incidence is not fully understood. Symptoms of chlamydia include a burning sensation during intercourse, genital discharge, painful intercourse, and if it spreads through the body, occasionally conjunctivitis (inflammation of the eye). Untreated, chlamydia may lead to chronic pain, infertility, pelvic inflammatory disease and/or ectopic pregnancy. Although currently treatable with antibiotics, chlamydia is rapidly developing antibiotic resistance.

Chlamydia is highly prevalent in the Canadian Aboriginal population. Incidence in Nunavut is thought to be up to 18 times the national average, and incidence in the Northwestern Territories is thought to be seven times the national average. However, chlamydia is also increasing rapidly in the general population. Its incidence in the Aboriginal population is compounded by late diagnosis, inadequate medical treatment and failure to follow medication schedules. These factors are leading to ongoing infection, transmission and increased antibiotic resistance. Since chlamydia is a bacterial infection, re-infection after treatment is both possible and common. Like other STDs, prevalence of chlamydia in the Aboriginal population is exacerbated by high risk factors and the underlying problems with the determinants of health, including personal health practices (especially unsafe sex).

Hepatitis C

Hepatitis C is a viral infection of the liver. Its effects are similar to hepatitis A and B, but it is transmitted only through blood transmission, sometimes through sexual intercourse but more often through shared IV needles. Hepatitis C has a slow onset and patients typically live for years after diagnosis, unless a confounding factor, such as another infectious or chronic disease (e.g., diabetes or AIDS) increases vulnerability. Hepatitis C leads to scarring and cirrhosis of the liver and eventually to liver failure and death. There is currently no cure and no vaccine available for hepatitis C.

Herpes Simplex

Herpes simplex is caused by a close relative of the cold sore virus. It is a very common STD, but seldom monitored as its consequences are relatively mild. Infection is lifelong as the virus remains latent in the body, emerging regularly as sores on the genital region. When the disease is active (there are open sores), it is highly infectious; however, it is not infectious when dormant. The complications of herpes simplex infection include irritation, social exclusion and possible fertility issues.

Syphilis

Historically syphilis, caused by a spirochete bacterium, was the most feared STD. Untreated, syphilis kills the infected person over a period ranging from months to years, although by the 20th century the disease usually took decades to run its course.

Historical treatments included mercury (which did retard the progress of the disease, but also slowly killed the patient) and malaria treatment (the high fevers caused by malaria killed the syphilis spirochete, but also often killed the patient). Current treatment is through the use of antibiotics, which are capable of arresting the disease at any point in its progress.

Syphilis follows three stages: primary syphilis leads to the formation of an open sore (chancre) on the infected person (usually in the genital region, but sometimes on the tongue). After the chancre heals, secondary infection sets in with symptoms of fever, sore throat, severe rash, extensive wart-like skin lesions, weight loss and hair loss. Finally, 3 to 5 years after initial infection, tertiary syphilis begins. This can affect the cardiovascular or neural system. Historically it also infects other parts of the body, leading to extensive inflammation and degeneration of the infected areas. Unchecked tertiary syphilis leads to heart failure, aneurysm or dementia, and death. With timely antibiotic treatment, this outcome is now extremely rare.

Syphilis rates in the Canadian Aboriginal population are 5 cases per 100,000 as of 2009, and have increased by almost 10-fold since 1993. Data on syphilis rates in the Aboriginal population are lacking as no national statistics are kept. However, Health Canada has identified 22.8% of syphilis cases in its database as Aboriginal. In Alberta, syphilis rates among young Aboriginal women were 18.6 times higher, and among Aboriginal men they were 2.8 times higher than in the non-Aboriginal population (Office of the Chief Medical Officer of Health, 2010).

While the proximate cause of syphilis is infection by the spirochete bacterium, underlying causes of both the disease and its persistence in populations include the same risk factors that inform the prevalence of other STDs. Participation in the sex trade is an important risk factor, and is the reason for the very high levels of syphilis in Aboriginal women (which, in turn, contribute to high levels in Aboriginal men); but it is in turn linked to poverty, low self-esteem and generational trauma. Lack of health services allows the disease to spread unchecked through the population and is the primary cause of congenital syphilis, which is otherwise preventable.

Gonorrhea

Gonorrhea is caused by the *Neisseria gonorrhoeae* bacteria. It is spread through any variety of sexual intercourse and can be contracted by contact with the mouth, penis, anus and vagina. Symptoms include a burning sensation upon urination, discharge from the urethra, sore throat and painful intercourse. If the infection spreads through the body it may lead to intense pain in the lower abdomen, fever and arthritic pain. Gonorrhea may lead to pelvic inflammatory disease, infertility and ectopic pregnancy. Untreated, it may infect a fetus in the womb, or lead to joint infections, heart valve infection or meningitis.

Gonorrhea is often contracted in conjunction with chlamydia or other STDs. It responds well to antibiotic treatment in its early stages, although antibiotic-resistant strains are now beginning to appear. Unfortunately, epidemiological data on rates of gonorrhea in both the Aboriginal and general population are lacking. The limited datasets available to Health Canada (Health Canada, 2009) indicate that the rate of gonorrhea in the Aboriginal population is higher than in the general population. Its prevalence is driven by the same socioeconomic and cultural factors that contribute to higher rates of other STDs.

Human Papilloma Virus

The human papilloma virus (HPV) is responsible for warts, but some specific strains also infect the genitalia and are spread through sexual contact. This condition is also known as genital warts. Most varieties of HPV do not cause visible symptoms (warts), but some are known to cause cancer. They may lead to cancers of the cervix, vulva, vagina and anus in women and cancers of the anus and penis in men. More rarely, these varieties of HPV can also cause cancers of the head and neck (tongue, tonsils and throat). Vaccines to protect against the most common cancerous varieties are available and are increasingly provided through the public health system in Canada.

HPV is one of the most common STDs in Canada. Due to inadequate data its prevalence within the Aboriginal population is not well understood, but thought to be considerably higher than within the general population as its spread tends to be closely associated with transmission of other highly contagious STDs, such as chlamydia or gonorrhea.

CRITICAL THINKING EXERCISES

1. How could the individual in the first case study following be helped, in a culturally safe way, to resolve his problems? (There are multiple correct answers to this, and many poor ones as well.)

2. List the risk factors that the individual in the second case study presented. Which of them may have been significant for her particular case? (Hint: Consider her career.) Was there any way the hospital staff could have approached the patient differently?

3. Compare the two case studies. Why was the individual in the first case study diagnosed, while the individual in the second case study was not? What does this say about health care in these two contexts in Canada?

4. What do the outcomes of these case studies say about health care in rural and urban Canada?

CASE STUDY ONE

Charles is a middle-aged man from a small fly-in community in the Northwest Territories. He is married to Marie and has five children, whom he supports by doing odd jobs around the community, through social assistance, and by hunting, trapping and fishing to provide traditional food.

He was diagnosed with infectious TB 2 years ago, but has probably lived with the disease in dormant form since his childhood when he was exposed to it at a residential school. Marie was hospitalized with complications of infectious TB on her brain a year ago, and is now permanently disabled.

Charles was prescribed medication to eradicate his TB and instructed to wear a surgical mask at home in order to avoid infecting his children. He has arrived at the community health centre complaining of a persistent cough and is worried that the TB has become infectious again. On being interviewed by the community health nurse, he admitted that he discontinued his medication and does not wear the surgical mask. He explains that he did not do so because he could not keep up his daily activities and provide for his family due to the nausea caused by the medications. He could not bring himself to see the nurse previously because of his fear, dating from his childhood in the school, of government officials, teachers and doctors. He is terrified that he has infected his children with TB, that he will die, and that he will leave with no one to care for his family.

CASE STUDY TWO

A middle-aged Aboriginal woman comes into the clinic at her small city's main hospital. She is well known to the staff, since she is a prominent and well-respected social worker, also the mother of three young children. Her complaint is of an ongoing cough and a general feeling of malaise. She is examined, found to have only a slightly raised temperature and is diagnosed with a cold. The attending physician sends her home with instructions to drink plenty of fluids and get bed rest. Some weeks her health takes a sudden turn for the worse. She collapses and is rushed to the hospital, where she dies of an acute TB infection.

Her case was reviewed, but she presented none of the risk factors that the hospital staff had been trained to look for. She lived in an urban area, she was affluent, well educated and had stable family life. To all appearances she had contracted nothing more serious than a severe cold. Only a specific test for TB could have indicated otherwise, but it did not seem indicated in her case.

Discussion Questions

1. What factors contributed toward the epidemics among Aboriginal people during the 20th century?

2. Why are renal disease rates high among the Aboriginal population?

3. Cancer rates are lower overall among the Aboriginal population than in the non-Aboriginal population, but mortality rates are higher. Why would this be so?

4. The Inuit have much lower rates of heart disease than either the First Nations or the general Canadian population. Why?

5. What is the primary cause of COPD?

6. What are the causes of high levels of otitis media in Aboriginal children?

7. Why have chronic diseases increased in frequency in the Aboriginal population since the 1940s?

8. Why are high levels of both infectious and non-infectious TB among the Canadian Aboriginal population a matter of public health for everyone?

9. Is obesity only a public health concern among the Aboriginal population? Why would identifying its causes among Aboriginal people help everyone?

10. How can modifying risk factors help prevent chronic diseases?

11. What role can the determinants of health play in preventing the growth of both chronic and infectious diseases?

REFERENCES AND FURTHER READING

Crighton, E. J., Wilson, K., & Senécal, S. (2010). Relationship of socioeconomic and geographic factors on asthma among Canada's Aboriginal population: an analysis of the 2001 Aboriginal People's Survey. *International Journal of Circumpolar Health, 69*(2), 138–150.

Goodman, K. J., Jacobson, K., & Veldhuyzen van Zanten, S. J. (2008). Helicobacter pylori infection in Canadian and related Arctic Aboriginal populations. *Canadian Journal of Gastroenterology, 22,* 289–295.

Health Canada. (2009). *A statistical profile on the health of First Nations in Canada: Self-rated health and selected conditions, 2002 to 2005.* Ottawa, ON: Health Canada.

Office of the Chief Medical Officer of Health. (2010). *The syphilis outbreak in Alberta.* Edmonton, AB: Alberta Health and Wellness.

Pepperell, C. S., Granka, J. M., Alexander, D. C., Behr, M. A., Chui, L., Gordon, J., . . . Feldman, M. (2011). Dispersal of mycobacterium tuberculosis via the Canadian fur trade. *Proceedings of the National Academy of Sciences of the United States, 108*(16), 6526–6531.

Public Health Agency of Canada. (2010). *Population-specific HIV/AIDS status report: Aboriginal peoples.* Ottawa, ON: Public Health Agency of Canada. http://www.phac-aspc.gc.ca/aids-sida/publication/ps-pd/aboriginal-autochtones/index-eng.php.

Reading, J. (2009). *The crisis of chronic disease among Aboriginal Peoples: A challenge for public health, population health and social policy.* Victoria, BC: Center for Aboriginal Health Research at the University of Victoria. http://cahr.uvic.ca/docs/ChronicDisease%20 Final.pdf

Rosychuk, R. J., Voaklander, D. C., Klassen, T. P. et al. (2010). Asthma presentations by children to emergency departments in a Canadian province: a population-based study. *Pediatric Pulmonology, 45*(10), 985–992.

Smylie, J. (2001). A guide for health professionals working with Aboriginal peoples. Health issues affecting Aboriginal peoples. Ottawa, ON: Society of Obstetricians and Gynaecologists of Canada.

Thomson, M. (1994). Otitis Media: How are First Nations children affected? *Canadian Family Physician, 40,* 1943–1950.

Wynne, A., Currie, C. (2011). Social exclusion as an underlying determinant of sexually transmitted infections among Canadian Aboriginals. *Pimatisiwin, 9*(1), 113–127.

Useful Websites

Canadian Lung Association: www.lung.ca

CBC Archives: Former TB Patients revisit Fort San: www.cbc.ca/archives/categories/ health/disease/tuberculosis-old-disease-continuing-threat/former-tb-patients-revisit-fort-san.html

CBC Radio: Old Disease – Continuing Threat: The Science of Tuberculosis: www.cbc.ca/ archives/categories/health/disease/tuberculosis-old-disease-continuing-threat/the-science-of-tuberculosis.html

CBC Technology: Voyageurs' TB thrives among First Nations: www.cbc.ca/news/tech-nology/story/2011/04/04/science-tb-Aboriginal-french-canadian.html

Public Health Agency of Canada, Sexually Transmitted Infections Surveillance and Epidemiology: www.phac-aspc.gc.ca/sti-its-surv-epi/surveillance-eng.php

The Hearing Foundation of Canada, How the Ear Works: www.thfc.ca/cms/en/ HearingLoss/HowHearingWorks.aspx?menuid=70

Tuberculosis: The forgotten disease: www.winnipegfreepress.com/tb/

Women's and Children's Health

Chapter Objectives

- To educate practitioners on the particular issues that affect women's and children's health and their historical origins.

- To examine both the appropriate and inappropriate approaches to Aboriginal clients.

- To explain the importance of both cultural and gender understanding.

Key Concepts

Status of Women

Fertility

Domestic Sphere

Prescriptive Education

Caregivers

Healing

Gender Norms

Traditional Education

Nurturing

Key Terms

Healers

Matriarch

Midwives

Residential Schools

Shamans

WOMEN'S HEALTH

The health of women and children are closely linked across every population as poor health indicators for women lead directly to poor health indicators for infants and children. Beyond this, 50% of children are female. Their health is both a child health issue and, ultimately, a women's health issue as their childhood experiences inform their role as mothers and partners.

Aboriginal women have a life expectancy higher than that of Aboriginal men, but significantly lower than that of the general population (Figure 8.1). Current health issues include domestic violence, sexually transmitted diseases, depression, culturally appropriate childbirth and diabetes. Aboriginal women occupy an important place in Aboriginal culture and society, both historically and in contemporary society. Their role makes their health and well-being a key means of improving the health of the entire population.

Fertility rates remain higher for Aboriginal women compared to non-Aboriginal women. In the 1996 to 2001 period, the fertility rate of Aboriginal women was 2.6 children, that is, they could expect to have that many children, on average, over the course of their lifetime; this compared with a figure of 1.5 among all Canadian women. In the same period, the fertility rate for Inuit women was estimated to be 3.4 children, compared with rates of 2.9 children for First Nations women and 2.2 for Métis women. In 2006, the median age of Aboriginal females was 27.7 years, compared with 40.5 years for non-Aboriginal females, a gap of almost 13 years. (The median age is the point where exactly one-half of the population is older, and the other half is younger.) Of the three Aboriginal groups, Inuit are the youngest. The median age of Inuit women and girls was 22.3 years, compared to 26.4 years for First Nations females, and 29.9 years for Métis females (Figure 8.2).

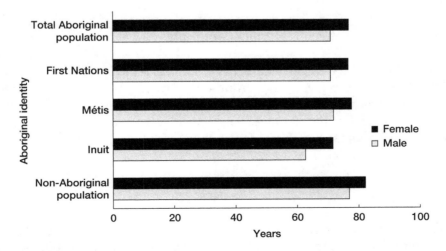

Figure 8.1 *Aboriginal Life Expectancy at Birth, 2001*

Source: Statistics Canada. Census of Population 2001.

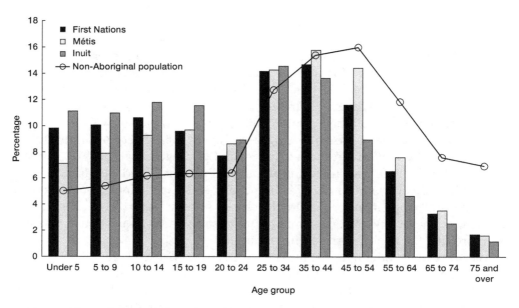

Figure 8.2 *Age of the Female Aboriginal Population in Canada, 2006*

HISTORY AND CHANGE

Women's Role in Traditional Aboriginal Society

In traditional Aboriginal society women played a role as family caregivers, healers and midwives, and they had a strong spiritual and religious role. A few Aboriginal groups, such as the Six Nations, codified the gender roles of women and men, but most often these roles were intrinsic to Aboriginal society and traditions.

Family Caregivers

These traditional roles were not necessarily as limited as modern conceptions would indicate. As family caregivers, women raised children, participated in harvesting traditional food, processed the harvest (cleaning fish, preserving meat and fish) and prepared the food for their families. They participated actively in the traditional economy, which ultimately was focused on the needs of the family and community.

Healers

As healers, women dominated traditional medicine in most Aboriginal societies. Healing physical ailments was the province of female healers, who possessed most of the knowledge of traditional medicinal plants, as well as physically gathering most of them. The focus of women in healing was on nurturing and promoting health.

The combative role of defending against attacks from the spirit world was dominated by shamans, however, who were usually, but not always, male. Shamans seldom intervened in purely physical ailments, unless spiritual interference was suspected. In biomedical terms, their role approximated that of psychiatrists or psychologists.

Midwives

A particularly important role in healing and health promotion was childbirth. Given personal experience with pregnancy and childbirth, Aboriginal women were the vast majority of traditional midwives. While the degree of involvement depended on religious taboos around childbirth, Aboriginal midwifery usually included some physical assistance with the birth. In addition, they gave advice and assistance with pregnancy and postnatal care, especially for inexperienced young mothers.

This being said, it is important to remember that traditional Aboriginal society was not professionalized. With the exception of shamans, most Aboriginal people were prepared to take on different roles in society. Although some women might have more experience or expertise in midwifery or in the use of traditional medicinal plants, all women were expected to have some familiarity with these skills—just as all men possessed some skills at hunting or fishing.

Spiritual and Religious Role

These roles in traditional society made women the bearers of culture in Aboriginal society and led to strongly female-oriented societies, even when the leaders were ostensibly male. This is also true of many traditional societies elsewhere in the world.

Women's Role in Early European–Aboriginal Contact and Trade

The role of bearers of culture gave Aboriginal women an important place in early contact with Europeans. As the arrival of Europeans led to social and economic interaction with explorers, fur traders and eventually colonists, women played a key role. In addition to working in the new economies formed by Europeans, they formed relationships with them, especially with the early explorers and fur traders. Sometimes these did not last, due to traders moving out of the region without their Aboriginal partners, but often they were explicit marriage alliances, especially with the fur traders. This strengthened their people's ability to bend trade to their advantage, while assuring the traders of friendly relations with their in-laws. While some fur traders abandoned their Aboriginal spouses when they left the country, others did not. They either settled permanently in the country or brought their wives with them back to Europe (Van Kirk, 1980).

Founders of the Métis Nation

The Métis Nation was, by definition, founded by Aboriginal women who married European men, placing themselves between the two worlds. Their children were raised with both European and Aboriginal culture, and could choose one of three routes: to become Aboriginal, to become European or to embrace both their natal cultures. Métis women have played an important role in Métis society, economically, socially and culturally. They were full participants in the traditional Métis economy, oriented around farming, hunting and the fur trade, while they also bore the responsibility for raising and educating children. Through their

---

Changing Times and the Douglas Family

Amelia, Lady Douglas (1812–1890) was a Cree, born to a Hudson's Bay Company fur trader and his Cree wife. She married James Douglas, a Creole fur trader working for the Company in Ft. St. James, British Columbia, when she was 16. She saved his life on at least one occasion and went on to promote his career in the Hudson's Bay Company, not least through the influence of her father, a former Chief Factor.

Lady Douglas gave birth to 13 children, five of whom survived, and in the course of her lifetime became the matriarch of the most powerful family in colonial British Columbia. After her death, a large part of her Cree folklore was collected and published by her daughter, Martha, in 1901.

Lady Douglas's husband, Sir James Douglas (1803–1877) was born in the Caribbean of a Scottish father and Creole mother (of mixed African and English descent). He married Amelia in a traditional Cree ceremony ("country marriage"), but held a Christian marriage ceremony a decade later. James Douglas rose to become the first governor of British Columbia when it became a unified colony in 1858. He was instrumental in keeping the region from becoming an American territory and he set the precedent of signing treaties to transfer land from First Nations to settlers, a precedent that was not followed for another century and a half. In early British Columbia, respectability was not founded on race, but on culture and accomplishments.

By the late 19th century, most of the eminent families in British Columbia were of First Nations descent, many of them through Amelia Douglas and other "country brides" of former fur traders. Race did not become an important issue until American racial theories and prejudices began to influence British Columbia and Canada in the late 19th century. As a sign of the changing times, in 1886, American historian Hubert Bancroft visited Victoria, where he socialized with the leading families of the town. After his return to the United States he denounced them all in his writing as racially degenerate (Adams, 2001; Van Kirk, 1997/8).

influence in councils, they often exerted a considerable diplomatic force, usually directed toward ensuring peaceful resolution of disputes. Although seldom public figures, their voices have always been strong within their families and communities and they have been identified as the bearers of culture for their people.

European Gender Norms

When Aboriginal peoples encountered Europeans, they also encountered European gender norms. This is a difficult topic, as the status of women varied widely across Europe and over time, depending on respective national legal codes and their evolution. The usual interpretation of European gender norms assumes that the social status of women is based on their place in English common law prior to the 20th century.

In England, the rights of women were restricted. They were not recognized as persons under the law and their fathers and husbands had financial authority over them, including automatic control of property. This could only be elided through financial stratagems that were seldom available to anyone but the

Amelia, Lady Douglas Near the End of Her Life
Source: Library and Archives Canada / C-005051 / MIKAN 2267337.

wealthy. Otherwise, only widows with underage sons might control their property. Of course, in England before 1900, most women were too poor for this to be even an issue.

However, England was an anomaly in Europe. France and other continental countries had many more legal rights for women, including control of their inherited property after divorce or separation.

Law and Tradition

Laws are only part of the story. The status of women in Europe depended on their traditional role as well. Women were usually the head of the household, often controlled domestic finances, and had a strong role in guiding children from birth through marriage. In effect, women dominated the domestic sphere. Men dominated the public sphere of government, the professions and business. Although there were many exceptions where male family members used the legal codes to abuse traditional roles, these were nonetheless still powerful up to the 20th century, and still influence European gender relationships today.

Tradition, Women and Health

Prior to 1900, most European women below the stratum of the elites also practised some degree of traditional medicine and midwifery. Given that most Europeans lived in poverty, or at best in a traditional cash-poor economy (if they were rural), few could afford to pay physicians until late in the 19th century. Only the middle class and wealthy went to the (male) doctor for help with illness or childbirth before 1900.

European Law and Aboriginal Women

The application of English Common Law in Canada changed the status of Aboriginal women, placing them in a legally inferior position. Taken out of its English context and applied to Aboriginal society and culture, which had different customs and rules, the Common Law did have an adverse effect on Aboriginal women. The Common Law's legal discrimination against women justified social discrimination, and was used to suppress traditional roles, particularly in the education of children and the female voice in councils.

However, more important than the effect of the Common Law, invidious as it was, was the social disruption that disease, settlement and increasing racism eventually brought to Aboriginal society as a whole. These changes severely weakened the role of Aboriginal women within their society by stigmatizing them as inferior and morally dissolute for not conforming to European middle-class norms, yet refusing to accept them on racial grounds when they did attempt to integrate.

Social Change and the Status of Aboriginal Women

The epidemics that swept North America after contact left Aboriginal society in turmoil and led to a re-negotiation of traditional hierarchies and social relationships. This was also a period of extended conflict as groups depleted with disease were displaced by others who remained more vigourous. Even while demographic and social disruption wrought by disease was underway, traditional economies were also undermined by European settlement and efforts to assimilate the Aboriginal population to European social and economic norms. These influences, far more than legal niceties, damaged the role of Aboriginal women in their societies.

Social Change

These changes to economy and society affected all women to some degree. Even European women found their situation changed when they immigrated, and not always for the better. In Europe, economic changes also altered the traditional economies that had sustained women's traditional roles there. However, these economic

---

E. Pauline Johnson

Emily Pauline Johnson (1861–1913) was the daughter of George Johnson, a leader of the Mohawk Nation and his English wife, Emily. Raised on the Six Nations Reserve near Brantsford, Ontario, her family was considered part of the Canadian upper middle class, with visitors to the family home including the Marquess of Lorne and his wife, Princess Louise and Lord Dufferin (both Governor-Generals), and numerous other colonial and British notables. Already a successful poet, she was driven to a career in public recitation after her father's death left the family destitute.

Johnson explicitly identified herself as Mohawk and First Nations, as well as Canadian in both her poetry and her prose. She opposed European stereotypes of Aboriginal women and attracted widespread praise in Canada, Britain and the United States for her poetry. She appeared in public performances of her poetry in traditional dress, as well as more conventional European clothing, and supported efforts by British Columbian First Nations to appeal restrictions on their traditional rights. Having moved to Vancouver, she succumbed to breast cancer in 1913. Her funeral was held in Christ Church Cathedral in Vancouver and she was buried in Stanley Park. The Canadian Women's Club raised a monument to mark her resting place there. Johnson is now considered both as an example of a successful Aboriginal woman and as a feminist (Strong-Boag and Gerson, 2000).

Photograph of E. Pauline Johnson

E. Pauline Johnson, also known as Tekahionwake, in traditional dress.
Source: Library and Archives Canada / MIKAN 3215023.

changes affected Aboriginal women more quickly and more thoroughly altogether as their societies were disrupted on many levels, all at roughly the same time. Their old roles as community leaders, healers and midwives were disrupted, but new roles were hard to find. Moreover, Aboriginal women also confronted the male half of European culture—through government and business. This was the public sphere of European society and Canadian society. There were roles for Aboriginal men in this milieu, but seldom for Aboriginal women. Those Aboriginal women who did succeed usually lived on the fringes of the European world, or did so by inventing roles for themselves that exploited European romanticism, as E. Pauline Johnson, popularly known as the Mohawk Princess, managed to do in the 19th century.

Professionalization of Health Care

Despite a few successes by exceptional women like Pauline Johnson, most avenues for Aboriginal women to practise their traditional roles disappeared as the 19th and 20th centuries wore on. This was particularly noticeable in traditional medicine.

By the 19th century, the medical profession was growing in Europe and Canada and eager to expand its client base. Physicians began actively discouraging competitors everywhere, not just in Canada. While competitors in Europe included chiropractors, phrenologists, and a variety of other aspiring professional groups, the largest, but most vulnerable competitors to medical practices were traditional medicine practitioners (mostly women) in Europe and North America. Aboriginal healers, although not the primary targets of these campaigns, were affected too.

The Slow Death of Aboriginal Midwifery

Aboriginal midwifery is a particularly good example. Midwifery was the most common and popular way to deliver babies almost everywhere before 1900, among the Aboriginal and non-Aboriginal populations. Women, whether in Europe or Canada, had always dominated assistance with childbirth for the eminently logical reason that they had the most experience of it.

However, the growing professionalization of medicine and the formalization of medical education led physicians to claim that they possessed better, more systematic, more logical and more effective skills in delivering children than did midwives, whose knowledge was largely experiential and cumulative. This was hard for even European midwives to counter, since physicians were, until the late 19th century, all men. Nurses in Britain, with Florence Nightingale as their powerful public spokeswoman, retained a role in midwifery, but not in Canada. Here, male physicians dominated the public sphere of discourse on childbirth, and used that dominance to convince the public and Canadian governments to make delivering babies a (male) medical specialty and to legally discourage all midwifery. Only now is that beginning to change, as both Aboriginal and non-Aboriginal midwifery re-emerge from the shadows and margins they have been pushed into.

Aboriginal Women's Role Today

Today, Aboriginal women appear to take on a much wider range of roles than they have previously. Their public role has become much more prominent, as has their economic role. To some extent, this is an extension of traditional leadership roles in Aboriginal society, which non-Aboriginal society is only now recognizing. However, it is also real change, driven by changes in both Aboriginal society and Canadian society and the economy in general, and has implications for women's health and the health of Aboriginal society overall.

Family Leaders

Leadership within the domestic sphere was both traditional in Aboriginal culture, and accepted by many Europeans—which has allowed it to be passed down without the disruption caused to the economic life of the Aboriginal community. Aboriginal women today have often kept their roles within the family and strong female role models are also common in Canadian Aboriginal groups. The leaders of the Inuit Tapiriit Kanatami are often women, and Aboriginal women's associations (such as the Native Women's Association of Canada) play an important advocacy role in social issues. In many ways, the public role many Aboriginal women play today is an extension of their role within the family, especially given that the Aboriginal definition of family is often quite different than non-Aboriginal meanings of the term.

Extended Family

Aboriginal families are still extended families in the sense that most Canadians have abandoned. Families include a network of relatives that extends through the community and often to other communities through marriage ties as well. While men are important members of these extended families, it is usually the women who maintain the social network that sustains them. This role within a domestic sphere, which is much larger than the non-Aboriginal nuclear family, gives Aboriginal women significant power behind the scenes, and often forms the basis of support for their political careers as well.

Spiritual and Cultural Leaders

Women bear and transmit cultural values in Aboriginal society. This gives them a key role in their families and communities, as their participation in traditional culture provides a means to keep it alive. Sometimes this is publicly apparent and many of the powerful Aboriginal politicians of recent years, such as Mary Simon of the Inuit Tapiriit Kanatami, have been women. However, even when Aboriginal communities appear to be male dominated, often Aboriginal women play a more important role than outwardly apparent.

Material Providers

Perhaps the greatest change to Aboriginal women's roles has been their tendency to become the breadwinners for their families. Aboriginal women have often occupied clerical and other white-collar work, but this was often regarded as ancillary to the male role as hunters and trappers. It was a supplementary income, rather than the primary means of support for the family. The collapse of the fur trade has often made these clerical jobs the only income in Aboriginal families. Thus, Aboriginal women are often transformed into their family's source of support, displacing the men from that position.

Changing Gender Roles and Violence

These changing gender roles are also a source of violence. Aboriginal men, and often boys as well, are raised to believe that they are both the public face of their families and communities, and their economic support as well. Most are also socialized to engage in physical labour, rather than white-collar work—which is why Aboriginal trades certifications are actually higher than in the general population. With the fur industry declining and few economic roles available to replace it in remote communities, many men find their gender roles under attack, while their wives, sisters and daughters become the economic providers. The resulting sense of social, cultural and economic insecurity is a powerful factor in domestic violence and community violence.

Women's Health Issues Today

Today Aboriginal women experience a wide range of health issues, often quite distinct from both Aboriginal men, and non-Aboriginal women. This is partly connected to their age profile, which is distinctly different from non-Aboriginal women in Canada (see Figure 8.2). This is partly connected to higher fertility rates and partly to lower life expectancy. As well, chronic conditions are much more prevalent among Aboriginal women than among either non-Aboriginal women or Aboriginal men, reflecting the decline in traditional lifestyles and concomitant increase in obesity and related health issues (Figure 8.3). Just as importantly, the disappearance of the traditional economy has led to social disruption, domestic violence and related challenges to the health of Aboriginal women.

Violence

Violence is a major health issue for Aboriginal women. Although statistical data are based on very small samples of the population, it appears that rates of spousal abuse are approximately twice those of the non-Aboriginal population, and are often more serious (i.e., life threatening). Violence is closely linked to both the determinants of health and the historical circumstances of Aboriginal peoples in Canada, particularly the residential schools. While not every woman attended a residential school or is descended from someone who attended one, at least 21% of Aboriginal women living off-reserve are descendants of residential school survivors. On-reserve, numbers are probably higher, and the limited social circles inherent in small communities magnify the impact of dysfunctions in the community. This is not, in other words, a minor fraction of the female Aboriginal population.

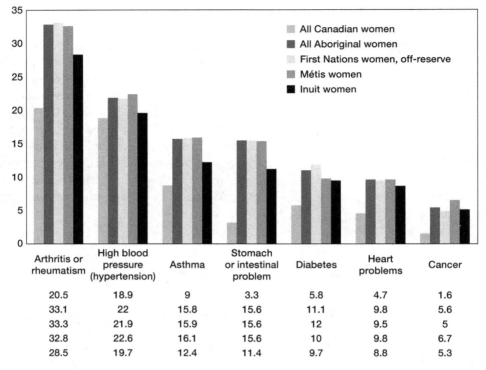

	Arthritis or rheumatism	High blood pressure (hypertension)	Asthma	Stomach or intestinal problem	Diabetes	Heart problems	Cancer
	20.5	18.9	9	3.3	5.8	4.7	1.6
	33.1	22	15.8	15.6	11.1	9.8	5.6
	33.3	21.9	15.9	15.6	12	9.5	5
	32.8	22.6	16.1	15.6	10	9.8	6.7
	28.5	19.7	12.4	11.4	9.7	8.8	5.3

Note: Total Aboriginal women include First Nations women living off-reserve, Métis women and Inuit women.

Figure 8.3 *Chronic Conditions in Aboriginal Women*

Udadjusted and age-standardised prevalence of diagnosed chronic conditions for women aged 20 years and over, by Aboriginal identity, Canada, 2006/2007.
Sources: Statistics Canada, Aboriginal Peoples Survey, 2006, and Canadian Community Health Survey, 2007.

Violence also has a generational impact. Children in an abusive family can absorb the message that this is "normal" behaviour. They may then in turn enter into abusive relationships, or become abusive themselves (Table 8.1).

Sexually Transmitted Diseases (STDs)

As noted in the previous chapter, chlamydia and human papilloma virus (HPV) appear to be highly prevalent among Aboriginal women, although these conditions are also increasing rapidly in the non-Aboriginal population, and accurate national statistics are lacking for both populations. Rates of syphilis and other life-threatening STDs also appear to be much higher than in the non-Aboriginal female population, based on regional studies. The only STD for which accurate national evidence is available is HIV/AIDS. HIV infection rates among Aboriginal women are significantly higher than those among the non-Aboriginal general population.

Table 8.1 *Self-Reported Spousal Violence for Aboriginal and Non-Aboriginal Populations, Aged 15 and Over, Canada, 2009*

Victims of Spousal Violence	Aboriginal	Non-Aboriginal
Percentage who reported being physically or sexually victimized by a spouse in the previous 5 years	15	6
Of those who had been physically or sexually victimized by a spouse in the previous 5 years, percentage who reported that they:		
Had been sexually assaulted, beaten, choked and threatened with a gun or knife	48	32
Sustained an injury	58	41
Feared for their life	52	31

Source: Statistics Canada, General Social Survey, 2009

Among Aboriginal women, as among non-Aboriginal women, both identification and treatment of STDs are obstructed by the social stigma they bear. Poor self-esteem, early sexual activity, lack of education and participation in the sex trade, either directly or through a partner, are risk factors that contribute to the prevalence of STDs among Aboriginal women.

However, the determinants of health offer a more nuanced view of these STD rates. Not only do many Aboriginal women live in poverty without access to adequate health services, they also may live in small and remote communities, where the social stigma of an STD is greater, the social pressure to forego condom usage is higher and the facilities to support long-term treatment for STDs are limited. Many Aboriginal women also suffer from Post-Traumatic Stress Disorder, either from their own experiences of residential school abuse or from abuse perpetuated by community members who are themselves survivors of residential school abuse. Women with experiences of childhood abuse are at much higher risk for STDs due to substance abuse as well as prostitution (Figure 8.4).

Depression and Low Self-Esteem

Depression and low self-esteem are severe problems among Aboriginal women. This is a product of racism, marginal socioeconomic status and lack of health services. Women are responsible for their families' well-being in traditional society. Modern stresses, including low income, unemployment and the collapse of traditional lifestyles, have put considerable pressure on Aboriginal women to improve their communities and families. When they are unable to do this, unable to ameliorate the social problems that plague their communities, their sense of self-worth suffers. This leads to higher suicide rates, substance abuse and often contributes to, or perpetuates, abusive relationships (Figure 8.5).

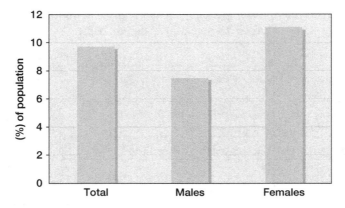

Figure 8.4 *Sexually Transmitted Diseases and the Aboriginal Population*

Source: Statistics Canada, 2003 Canadian Community Health Survey.

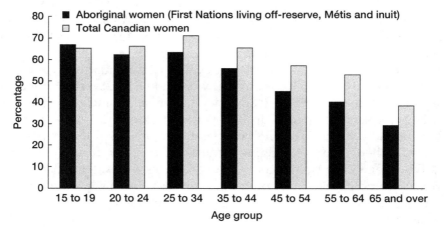

Figure 8.5 *The Opposite of Depression: Aboriginal Women Reporting Good Health*

Percentage of women reporting excellent or very good health, by age group,Canada, 2006/2007.

Childbirth

Since the advent of almost complete medicalization of childbirth in Aboriginal communities, most women give birth in a hospital's obstetric ward. This is slowly changing as Aboriginal birthing centres and Aboriginal midwifery services are re-established. The lack of secondary health services, poor diet, remote locations and smoking during pregnancy are all elevated risk factors in pregnancy and childbirth. Medical services for the birth itself are usually adequate, but also usually involve extended time away from the family in hospital, itself a source of stress on both the mother and the rest of the family. Neither prenatal nor postnatal care is adequate for most Aboriginal women, victims of the lack of secondary and tertiary care in most Aboriginal communities. This contributes to an unacceptably high level of postnatal infant mortality and morbidity in many Aboriginal communities, although concrete statistics remain difficult to access on this subject (Smylie, Fell, Ohlsson & the Joint Working Group on First Nations, Indian, Inuit and Métis Infant Mortality of the Canadian Perinatal Surveillance System, 2010). The leading cause of death of Aboriginal infants between the age of 1 month and 1 year (the postneonatal period) is sudden infant death syndrome (SIDS). This is also the leading cause of death in infants in the non-Aboriginal population, but SIDS rates are much higher in the Aboriginal population for reasons that are poorly established.

The ongoing high levels of infant mortality in the Aboriginal population are particularly significant given high levels of fertility among Aboriginal women. Childbirth occurs earlier and more often than it does in the non-Aboriginal population, making maternal and child health a particularly urgent priority, given continued poor outcomes in this area (Figure 8.6).

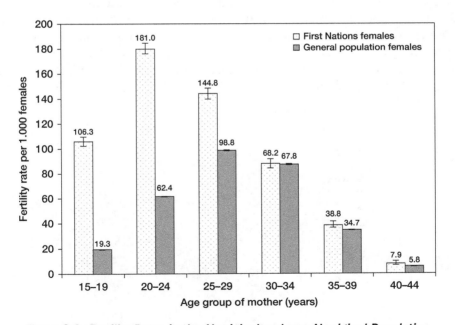

Figure **8.6** *Fertility Rates in the Aboriginal and non-Aboriginal Population*

Age-specific fertility rates per 1,000 population, by age group of motherregistered First Nations and general population, Atlantic and Western Canada,2001–2002 (average).
Source: Health Canada: A Statistical Profile on the Health of First Nations in Canada: Vital Statistics for Atlantic and Western Canada, 2001/2002. Data from: Health Canada, First Nations and Inuit Health Branch in-house statistics, Health Canada, 2003; Canadian Vital Statistics Birth Database, Statistics Canada, 2010.

Diabetes

As noted in Chapter 6, "Diabetes, Diet and Nutrition", diabetes is an increasing problem among Aboriginal women. Although it now appears that the difference between male and female diabetes rates were either due to measurement errors or are declining, diabetes is still an increasing problem among Aboriginal women. It is driven by lifestyle changes and dietary changes that have led to increasing obesity in the population, which in turn puts increased stress on the pancreas. As traditional economies have collapsed, so too have activity levels, since the seasonal round of harvesting traditional foods was very labour intensive. It has been replaced with much more sedentary lifestyles. The result is high levels of type 2 diabetes among Aboriginal women. The susceptibility to diabetes is often passed on to children through gestational diabetes, which is much higher among the Aboriginal population than in the non-Aboriginal population, and shared lifestyle choices that Aboriginal women may pass on to their children (Figure 8.7).

Interaction of Different Health Issues

All the health issues that Aboriginal women face are interactive with each other and with the determinants of health. Aboriginal women are often seen as dysfunctional, without much understanding or interest in the social context of their purported dysfunctionality. For example, low-self-esteem may be the product of an abusive childhood, but it also correlates with unemployment, lack of education, poverty and a willingness to participate in high-risk sexual activities and

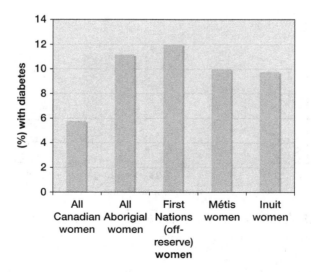

Figure 8.7 *Diabetes Rates in Aboriginal Women*

Sources: Statistics Canada. Aboriginal Peoples Survey, 2006, and Canadian Community Health Survey.

The Fur Trade and Women's Health

The fur trade remained a major economic activity in remote Aboriginal communities until recent anti-fur campaigns disrupted the market for furs. Participation in the fur trade was largely a male preserve, but its decline is also an issue for women's health. Why?

The fur trade provided a source of family income and employment. It also supported traditional harvesting, as many fur-bearing animals are also eaten as well, and was part of both community and, crucially, male identity. The decline in the fur trade has left many Aboriginal men underemployed, on social assistance, and unable to afford to harvest traditional food for their families. This affects their self-esteem and increases their stress levels, as well as leaving them with little to occupy their time. These communities, which have suffered economically from the loss of the fur trade, have experienced increased levels of domestic violence, degraded diets (with more junk food available from the stores), obesity and related chronic and infectious diseases.

---

with acceptance of domestic violence. As this suggests, the inter-relationship of different risk factors and the underlying influence of the determinants of health in shaping the social, economic and cultural context of women's health leads to a multigenerational cycle of dysfunctionality, which is difficult to break without addressing the causes of ill health as well as the ill health itself. This is something that both governments and the health care system are seldom prepared to commit to addressing.

CHILDREN'S HEALTH

Children in Aboriginal Society

As noted, the Canadian Aboriginal population is young, with the median age being 27, while the median age of the general population is 40. This is, quite simply, due to a higher birth rate. Roughly 21% of Aboriginal households have four or more children, compared with only 8% of non-Aboriginal households. In Aboriginal society, women are expected to bear several children and raise them. These numbers may drop as the determinants of health in the Aboriginal population approach those of the non-Aboriginal population, but they may not. Child-bearing is considered a cultural duty for women in Aboriginal society and may remain more prevalent than it is in non-Aboriginal society (Figure 8.8).

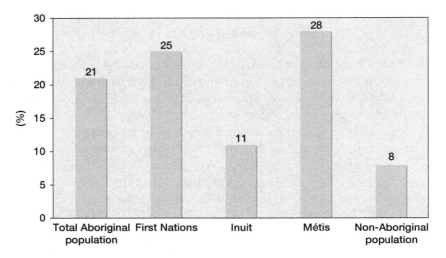

Figure 8.8 *Aboriginal Family Size*

Proportion of children under 6 years of age, living in a family of four or morechildren,
by Aboriginal identity, 2006.
Source: Statistics Canada. 2006 Census of Population.

An Inuit Family

Community Drumming: Children learn traditional skills through emulating their elders.
Source: V. K. Douglas.

Social Role

Children traditionally had a special place in Aboriginal society and culture. Education was through example and experience, rather than being prescriptive. Discipline was often exercised through the same path. Adults assumed that children would learn proper behaviour through observing their parents and other adults, and by making their own mistakes. Those mistakes served as informal discipline. Adults seldom exercised explicit discipline on children through telling them what they must do. Instead, children were told what they should do and were then encouraged to do it.

This being said, the learning path for children in every premodern society is radically different from that of modern educational systems. Even where physical punishment was used, education was largely based on knowledge of the natural world. This was gained through personal experience, with the wisdom of elders to clarify and interpret that experience. Formal education was limited or non-existent (although shamans, most notably, might train apprentices).

Problems in the Modern World

Entry into the modern world has proved difficult for Aboriginal children since modern educational methods often prove disruptive of traditional education. Most modern methods depend on rote memorization of facts, often abstracted from their physical context. Schools can also undermine traditional society and social relationships. For example, many Aboriginal children may be computer literate, but may also be unable to speak to their grandparents, or even skin a moose. This increases the gulf that separates generations in Aboriginal communities and raises issues about cultural survival and sometimes physical survival.

The loss of such traditional skills such as moose skinning may not be an insurmountable problem for survival in large cities. In remote communities, however, it is an issue for both food security and cultural security. Computer literacy, although useful, is unlikely to put food on the table in a remote community. However, the act of skinning a moose in a remote community may not only provide food for the family, but it also represents participation in traditional harvesting practices. This enactment of the skill provides a link between older generations and youth. It reassures the community that its values and traditions are being passed on and it also acknowledges that the skills needed to ensure a supply of food are not lost.

Child Health Issues

While some pediatric health problems are global in scope, the major issues specific to Aboriginal children are poverty, violence, otitis media and diabetes. All have their origins in the determinants of health and their effects are played out on Aboriginal society. These effects are perpetuated through children, who internalize the condition of their communities and their own treatment as normal, and in turn pass them on to their own families and children after they reach adulthood.

Poverty

Poverty is one of the most urgent health issues facing Aboriginal children. Poverty generally leaves children to suffer from a poor diet, overcrowded living quarters, a lack of education, a lack of access to health services, and often an unhealthy physical environment. The stressors that are related to poverty may also lead to domestic violence. All children in poverty suffer under these burdens, but proportionally far more Aboriginal children do so because far more Aboriginal children live in poverty. Not only are these conditions caused by poverty, they are also causes of poverty, indicating how deficits in the determinants of health are passed down through generations.

Childhood diets have suffered due to multiple factors. Low income levels in Aboriginal communities leave few resources to purchase food from the stores. The food that is purchased is often high energy, low nutrient "junk" foods—indeed, soda pop is the epitome of this aspect of the diet. Traditional foods previously made up for the nutritional deficit in Aboriginal children, and may in fact have given them a substantially healthier diet than their non-Aboriginal counterparts, judging from the very low chronic disease levels of the past. However, traditional diets are under attack on economic and social grounds. With hunting, fishing and harvesting in decline, the balance of many Aboriginal children's diets has shifted to market foods. In addition, Aboriginal children in even the most remote communities are now influenced by the same media and the same cultural pressures that their urban counterparts are. This leads to increased demand for market foods, especially unhealthy ones, demands that their elders often find hard to refuse.

Overcrowding affects Aboriginal children's health as much, if not more, than it affects the health of adults. Overcrowded homes are an artefact of larger families and of lower incomes. It is coupled with less physical activity and less time spent out on the land, because the active traditional lifestyle that their parents have lost means that there is less activity for the children and more time spent at home as well. It is integrally tied into the state of the physical environment as well, as overcrowding tends to put strain on waste disposal, sanitation and water supply, which all contribute to an unhealthy environment.

Lack of education is both a cause and a result of poverty among all populations. However, among the Aboriginal population there are further complicating factors. In many remote communities, the value of more academic education is often unclear to both children and their families. Unemployment is usually systemic and unless people are willing to leave the community, and to at least partly give up that aspect of their identity, the question that is raised is what is the value of more school-based education? Most Aboriginal people do want more traditional education, however, which, with the decline of the traditional economy, has become part of the schools curricula in many communities. Yet, expanding the schools curricula takes resources that may be in short supply in lower-income communities.

Lower-income communities also tend to have poor access to health care, which is compounded by low levels of education that may leave parents unaware of problematic health conditions, allowing them to develop into life-threatening chronic diseases. Remote communities find this further compounded by their distance from the secondary and tertiary services available in urban centres. Although primary health services are usually quite good in remote communities, secondary and tertiary care is not, as neither the population nor the number of health care professionals is large enough to provide these services (Figure 8.9).

Violence

Aboriginal children suffered from both disease and misguided attempts at forced assimilation. These included the effects of the residential schools on generations of Aboriginal children. In British Columbia it also included the so-called, 60s scoop. Beginning in the 1960s the government instituted a policy of removing children from what were considered dysfunctional families and placing them with foster families or putting them up for adoption without parental consent.

Children of single parent families, children of parents on social assistance and children of parents with legal issues were judged to be at risk. All these

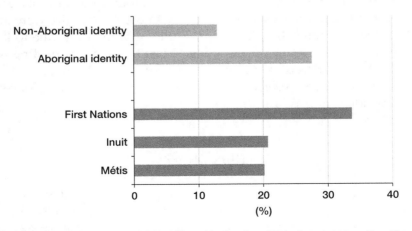

Figure 8.9 *Percentage of Canadians Under Age 15 in Low-Income Families, by Aboriginal Identity, 2005*

Source: Statistics Canada, 2006 Census of Population.

groups were over represented among the British Columbia's First Nations population. At the time, even when First Nations children were born to a single parent, the mother's family usually provided some or all assistance with child-rearing. This was disregarded and many Aboriginal children were removed from their own families and placed with non-Aboriginal families, further tearing the fabric of First Nations communities, and further weakening the roles and self-esteem of many First Nations women.

Although some children were, inevitably, abused, most foster and adoptive parents were well-meaning. However, many of these children grew up between two worlds, neither belonging to the Aboriginal communities they had been born into, but not becoming fully part of the non-Aboriginal communities and families they were adopted into either. Some succeeded in forging new, hybrid identities for themselves, whereas others melted into Canadian society, but most faced a lifetime of insecurity and social problems traceable to this experience.

For those children who remained in their communities, social disruption has also taken its inevitable toll as traditional family and community safeguards have been eroded by loss of community self-worth and self-esteem. This has increased the risk of child abuse and neglect.

Erosion of Traditional Social Roles and Violence Against Children

Traditional culture may also be taken advantage of by outsiders. A case in point is traditional Inuit society, which values consensus and avoids conflict and confrontation. In the 1970s and 1980s a school teacher from Southern Canada teaching in Cape Dorset (now in Nunavut) sexually abused many of the children in the community. He used his status as an outsider and prestige as a school teacher, both of which granted him immunity to traditional Inuit values and social restrictions, to perpetuate his crimes although many in the community were aware of his actions. None of the children would mention it at the time, due to the deep shame they felt, but the scars remain today. Cape Dorset is now dealing with the emotional scars it suffered as a community, facing the aftermath of its effects, including ongoing social problems, high levels of substance abuse, domestic violence and suicide.

Otitis Media

As noted, Aboriginal children have a very high prevalence of chronic middle ear infections, or otitis media. Even if the medical causes are unclear, as noted, breastfeeding infants for at least a year seems to be the most effective preventative measure. However, the determinants of health obviously play an important role as well. Children with poor housing, poor nutrition and high levels of stress due to family issues are obviously at higher risk for ill health. The stress these conditions place them under, whether knowingly or unknowingly, can also upset the balance between the flora and the fauna of the middle ear, leading to more infections.

Diabetes

Diabetes is a specific health concern of Aboriginal children, much more so than among non-Aboriginal children. Aboriginal children are diagnosed with type 2 diabetes far more often than other children and at a much younger age. This is partly due to much higher rates of gestational pregnancy leading to a biological predisposition to diabetes in affected children.

It is also partly the product of social change leading to dietary change. More consumption of purchased high-energy, low-nutrient "junk" foods is a serious issue in the diet of many Aboriginal children. Activity levels have also dropped dramatically, as traditional lifestyles of spending considerable amount of time on the land with the family hunting, trapping or fishing are replaced with life in the community, often playing video games or watching television. This latter development is also, of course, a problem in non-Aboriginal children as well and is having similar if less dramatic effects.

Eating Traditional Food
Some Aboriginal children still eat traditional food.
Source: V. K. Douglas

CRITICAL THINKING EXERCISE

1. Use the case study below and the Safety and Health Enhancement (SHE) Framework from Cory and Dechief (2009) to formulate an approach to supporting women in abusive/violent situations.

   — Answer the following question: "What is the basic philosophy behind health care providers' approach to women's safety and health?"
   — Divide a piece of paper/blackboard/whiteboard into two columns. Give one the title "What Do I Need?" and give the other the title "What Can I Offer/Do Differently?"
   — Place the components of your approach under the appropriate heading.
   — Compare your results to your fellow students' and the resources available to support women in abusive/violent situations in your jurisdiction.
      How do your results differ from the resources available?
      How do your conclusions differ from those others reached?

Case Study: Grace

A young Aboriginal woman entered the waiting room in a woman's centre in Toronto. She was dressed in ragged, dirty clothing and looked like a street person. She refused eye contact, keeping her head down and arms wrapped around her. When staff members approached her, she fled, without speaking.

A staff member approached the nurse in charge of the day shift at the centre, and asked her for advice. The head nurse told the staff member to leave the young woman alone and placed a cardboard box full of clothing on the bench next to her. The young woman left the box alone for 2 hours, then suddenly seized a handful of clothing and ran out the door. She appeared the next day, dressed in some of the clothing. Staff members were concerned and disturbed by this behaviour, but the head nurse again told them to leave the woman alone, but if they had any second-hand clothing, to leave it beside her in a cardboard box.

This continued for 2 weeks, with no communication between the young woman and the staff, but gradually the aura of tension and fear around her subsided and she began sitting more normally. Finally, one day the head nurse sat down beside her and asked the young woman her name and her story. The young woman, whose name was Grace, had been raped by a family member at a young age. She had been thrown out of the house shortly afterward, and put to work as a prostitute. Her experiences on the street had included repeated physical and sexual abuse by other street people and the johns. She had become addicted to heroin and was very close to suicide when she began coming into the woman's centre, to try to find some place warm and quiet to sit. She had come to believe that she was completely without value, worth less than an animal.

The head nurse found safe accommodation in a woman's shelter for her and arranged for her to enter a drug and alcohol rehabilitation program. Grace graduated from the program, went on to undertake training as an addictions counsellor and is now recognized as one of the greatest success stories the centre has ever had.

Discussion Questions

1. What is the leading cause of death in Aboriginal children aged between 1 month and 1 year?

2. Why have traditional healing roles declined for Aboriginal women?

3. How do Aboriginal families differ from the Canadian nuclear norm?

4. How does traditional education differ from the form of education used in the school system today?

5. How does the treatment of children perpetuate socioeconomic problems in Aboriginal communities?

6. How does male unemployment affect women's and children's health?

7. What was the role of women in the development of European–Aboriginal relations after Contact?

8. How does poverty influence the diet of Aboriginal children?

9. What is the major cause of otitis media?

10. What connects the historical role of Aboriginal women with their role today?

REFERENCES AND FURTHER READING

Adams, J. (2001). *Old square-toes and his lady: The life of James and Amelia Douglas.* Victoria, BC: Horsdal & Schubart.

Bourassa, C., McKay-McNabb, K., & Hampton, M. (2004). Racism, sexism and colonialism: The impact on the health of Aboriginal women in Canada. *Canadian Woman Studies, 24*(1), 23–39.

Collin, C., & Jensen, H. (2009). *A statistical profile of poverty in Canada.* Ottawa, ON: Library of Parliament, Social Affairs Division. www.parl.gc.ca/Content/LOP/ResearchPublications/prb0917-e.htm#a9

Cory, J., & Dechief, L. (2009). *SHE framework: Safety and health enhancement for women experiencing abuse.* Vancouver, BC: BC Women's Hospital. www.bcwomens.ca/NR/rdonlyres/8D65CADE-8541–4398-B264–7C28CED7D208/37000/SHE_Framework_May20091.pdf

Health Canada. (2011). *A statistical profile on the health of First Nations in Canada: Vital statistics for Atlantic and Western Canada, 2001/2002.* Ottawa, ON: Health Canada.

Smylie, J., Fell, D., Ohlsson, A., & the Joint Working Group on First Nations, Indian, Inuit, and Métis Infant Mortality of the Canadian Perinatal Surveillance System. (2010).

A review of Aboriginal infant mortality rates in Canada: Striking and persistent Aboriginal/non-Aboriginal inequities. *Canadian Journal of Public Health, 101*(2); 143–8.

Strong-Boag, V. J., & Gerson, C. (2000). *Paddling her own canoe: The times and texts of E. Pauline Johnson (Tekahionwake).* Toronto, ON: University of Toronto Press.

Van Kirk, S. (1980). *Many tender ties, women in fur-trade society, 1670–1870.* Winnipeg, MB: Watson & Dwyer.

Van Kirk, S. (1997/8). Tracing the fortunes of five founding families of Victoria. *BC Studies, 115/116,* 149–80.

Useful Websites

Native Women's Association of Canada: www.nwac.ca

Public Health Agency of Canada, Aboriginal Head Start: www.phac-aspc.gc.ca/hp-ps/ dca-dea/prog-ini/ahsunc-papacun/index-eng.php

Researched to Death: Literature Review on Violence and Aboriginal Women. Ending Violence Association of BC: www.endingviolence.org/node/305

Mental Health

Chapter Objectives

- To examine the dominant influences that affect Aboriginal health and place them in their socioeconomical and historical context.

- To help students gain awareness of the distinctiveness of Aboriginal mental health issues.

- To explain how resolution of Aboriginal mental health issues may require a different clinical approach than the general population.

Key Concepts

Mental Health
Mental Illness
Self-Destructive Behaviour
Developmental Delay
Depression
Acculturation

Indoctrination
Traditional Healing
Dysfunction
Abuse (Physical, Emotional, Mental, Sexual)

Key Terms

Residential School Syndrome
Post-Traumatic Stress Disorder (PTSD)
Fetal Alcohol Spectrum Disorder (FASD)
Binge Drinking
Abstinence
Alcoholism
Violence

Substance Abuse
Dyscalculia
Dysgraphia
Dyslexia
Addiction
Accident
Injury
Suicide

DSM 5 CLASSIFICATION OF MENTAL ILLNESS AND ABORIGINAL PEOPLES

There are two major international systems for classifying mental disorders. These are the *Diagnostic and Statistical Manual of Mental Disorders*, now in its fifth revision (*DSM 5*), and the mental health section of the *International Classification of Diseases (ICD)*.

The first was created and is maintained within the United States, although it is used internationally. *DSM 5* carefully classifies mental disorders as behavioural or psychological syndromes of the individual. While admitting that it can be caused by behavioural, psychological or biological dysfunctions within the individual, it rigorously excludes conflicts between the individual and society and behavioural patterns that are culturally sanctioned. Deviant behaviour alone is not symptomatic of mental disorder unless it is due to a dysfunction in the individual.

The *ICD* is sponsored by the World Health Organization and provides a numerically coded list of diseases and conditions for epidemiological reporting purposes. Mental disorders are classified by their symptoms and causes (where identified). Other systems exist for particular cultures with different definitions of mental disorder. For instance, China has its own system of classification for mental disorders. As this suggests, it is important to remember that "mental disorder" is a (partly) culturally based term. There have been many attempts to force Aboriginal peoples into biomedical mental disease classification and treatment systems. These have had and continue to have mixed results, as they tend to isolate mental health from its historical, socio-economic and cultural contexts.

Behaviours that have a firm basis in Aboriginal culture may seem to reflect mental illness to health professionals unaware of the cultural context. Conversely, some normal behaviour of non-Aboriginal Canadians may seem odd and deviant to Aboriginal people, for reasons that are rational in their context (see the case studies at the end of this chapter for two examples).

Poor mental health, as measured by deviancy from internal cultural norms, is present in the Aboriginal population and may have a number of causes, environmental, biological and psychological. These causes have common symptoms, which may include: Post-Traumatic Stress Disorder, sexual abuse, children/spousal abuse, high suicide rate, substance abuse, dysfunctional families, high school drop-out rate and physical illness. Mental illness tends to have economic consequences as well, as those who suffer from it have difficulty functioning in society and tend to be marginalized. In small, remote communities, mental illness can affect the whole community, as the resources for treating it are limited. The problems the biomedical system faces in providing adequate mental health services for the Aboriginal population have led many mentally ill Aboriginal people to be neglected, or if their problems lead to violence, to be incarcerated in the criminal justice system. These failures have led to the development of culturally based treatment programs. Most of these treat either substance abuse or Residential School Syndrome, when other treatment routes have failed. Some Canadian prisons have also started cultural healing programs to attempt to rehabilitate Aboriginal inmates.

However, mental health treatment regimes, whether traditional or biomedical, have to contend with growing rates of biologically based mental disorders tied to ongoing substance abuse issues in the Aboriginal population, particularly alcohol abuse.

MENTAL HEALTH AND ABORIGINAL PEOPLES

Fetal Alcohol Spectrum Disorder

Fetal Alcohol Spectrum Disorder (FASD) is an umbrella term encompassing the serious physiological and cognitive impacts of fetal alcohol syndrome and the more subtle symptoms of fetal alcohol effects. Fetal alcohol syndrome (FAS) is a medical diagnosis referring to a specific cluster of anomalies associated with the use of alcohol during pregnancy. It includes cognitive, behavioural, physical, and growth dysfunctions. Fetal alcohol effects (FAE) is a term used to describe the presence of some cognitive and behavioural characteristics of FAS.

As the name suggests, FASD is entirely due to the effects on the fetus of excessive consumption of alcohol by women while pregnant and its cognitive effects are due to changes in brain function caused by the teratogenic effects of alcohol on brain development in the fetus. Binge drinking during pregnancy appears to be a particular risk factor for FASD, but it is unknown what, if any, level of alcohol consumption is safe. Too often FASD and the risk of FASD are used to stigmatize at-risk women, when the mechanism that causes it is poorly understood. Though FASD is recognized as being completely preventable through abstinence, understanding the pressures caused by problems with the determinants of health on at-risk women is necessary to develop prevention strategies that are effective and nonjudgmental and that will have an intergenerational impact. Once damage to the fetus is done, it can only be treated through understanding the etiology of FASD and how to best accommodate people with this often invisible physical disability.

This condition is a leading cause of developmental delays in infants/children. Children with FASD may experience any or all of the following primary challenges:

- Face difficulty in planning, prioritizing and setting goals
- Have difficulty with memory and are often unable to learn from past mistakes
- Suffer from impaired judgment and are unable to distinguish safe from dangerous situations and relationships
- Are socially, emotionally and cognitively delayed in their development
- Face communication problems, often including learning disabilities, such as dyscalculia, dysgraphia and dyslexia

▓ Have slow physical response time to stimuli

▓ Have language problems

The primary characteristics of FASD often lead to the development of secondary behaviours that pose further challenges to the child, the family and the educational and health care systems:

▓ Fatigued, irritable, resistant, argumentative

▓ Anxious, fearful, chronically overwhelmed

▓ Frustrated, angry, aggressive, destructive

▓ Poor self-image, often masked by unrealistic goals

▓ Isolated, few friends, picked on

▓ Family or school problems including fighting, suspension, or expulsion

▓ May run away, have other forms of avoidance

▓ Trouble with the law, addictions

▓ Depressed, may be self-destructive, suicidal

FASD AND CULTURE

Studies on FAS and FAE are very limited in Canada, but evidence suggests a very high incidence among Canadian Aboriginal children. Research in British Columbia and the Yukon suggests that the rate in some First Nations communities is one in five children. Overall, FASD/FAS/FAE among First Nations is estimated to be 25 to 30 times the national average. FASD can be treated through education and therapy, but it is a challenging and time-consuming process that requires understanding the biological foundation of FASD and how this influences the superficial symptoms of this condition. Special education programs have been designed for children who have been diagnosed with FASD and

---

Quote from Wemigwans and Cunningham (2005)

The underlying factors contributing to FASD are related primarily to social background, including: untreated or under-treated mental health issues; social isolation; histories of abuse (including severe childhood sexual abuse); lower education levels; lower socioeconomic status; inadequate nutrition; a poor developmental environment; and reduced access to prenatal and postnatal care and services. All of these factors can aggravate prenatal exposure to alcohol, drug use and smoking.

some of them have shown some promise, but there are no fast and easy answers. Effectively, FASD is a completely preventable disability that has a lifelong effect. However, with well-designed strategies and awareness on the part of health care professionals and educators of approaches to accommodation, individuals with FASD can experience healthy, safe and fulfilling lives (Malbin, 2011, Canadian Paediatric Society, 2002).

FASD Neuro-Cognitive Characteristics, Expectations, Secondary Behaviors and Examples of Accommodations

Resolving values clashes:
Primary neurobehavioral symptoms, values clashes, and accommodations

FA/NB is a brain-based condition, and that is not really the problem. The problem is the lens through which behaviors are usually viewed, and the fit between behavioral symptoms and interpretations of the meaning of behaviors. These are determined by cultural values and beliefs. As a result, behavioral symptoms of FA/NB are often interpreted as being at odds with the values of the dominant culture. The chart on the following page provides a visual of how primary symptoms of FA/NB are typically viewed, and how accommodations could prevent problems by recognizing behaviors as symptoms of a neurobehavioral disorder. This is intended to normalize common reactions, clarify interventions based on these reactions, and expand options.

Column 1: "Primary symptoms" are common neurobehavioral symptoms of FA/NB. For example, "slow auditory pace" is a symptom of changes in the brain that means the person "listens slowly" and needs time to understand or process language.

Column 2: "'Fit' with values and expectations" outlines the expectations for "normal" behaviors. Listen fast, understand what is being said.

Column 3: "Interpretation of behaviors: Feelings" refers to the meaning assigned to the behavioral symptom: "He's ignoring me," "She's not paying attention." The *meaning* we give to behaviors dictates our feelings about those behaviors. These range from mild discomfort to significant irritation, and these beliefs and feelings generate interventions shown in the fourth column.

Column 4: "Interventions" outlines what happens when behaviors are seen as intentional. Behavioral interventions target the behaviors for change. Techniques are typically not based on understanding of brain dysfunction and FA/NB.

Column 5: "Secondary behaviors" often develop when interventions attempt to change behavioral symptoms of brain dysfunction. These secondary behavioral symptoms are what would be seen if a blind child were punished for "refusing" to read the blackboard, or if they were punished for not being able to think fast: Anxiety, frustration or anger.

Column 6: The last column, "Accommodations build on strengths," shows how recognizing primary behaviors and providing simple, appropriate accommodations contributes to preventing frustration and deterioration.

The goal is to prevent frustration in children and adults and prevent the need for punishment by identifying primary behavioral symptoms and providing appropriate accommodations.

(*continued*)

FASD Neuro-Cognitive Characteristics, Expectations, Secondary Behaviors and Examples of Accommodations   (continued)

1 Primary Symptoms	2 "Fit" with Values and Expectations	3 Interpretation of Behaviors: *Feelings*	4 Interventions	5 Secondary Behaviors	6 Accommodations Build on Strengths
Slow auditory pace, goes blank	Think fast, pay attention, stay on task	He/she is ignoring me, being resistant: *Personalized, angry, frustrated*	Talk fast Therapy Punish	Anxiety Frustration Shut down	Slow down Give time Adjust workload
Slow cognitive pace, doesn't answer	Think fast, timed tests, finish work within time allotted in schedule	He/she is controlling, avoidant, not trying: *Angry, frustrated*	Take away privileges Shame Ridicule	Anxiety Frustration Tantrums	Give time Slow down Reduce work load Accept slow pace
Difficulty generalizing -- gets the piece, not the picture	Follow the rules, learn inferentially, "get it" by watching	He/she is being willful, behaviors are intentional; he *knew* what the rule was! *Frustrated*	Punish	Fear Frustration Anger	Accept need to reteach a concept in different settings
Dysmaturity: Developmentally younger than their age: 7.5 more like a 3-year old, 16 more like a 10-year-old	Act your age Be responsible Be appropriate	He/she is socially inappropriate, acting like a baby: *Irritated, frustrated, angry*	Teach age-based skills Punish "inappropriate" behaviors	Lonely Isolation Depression	Think younger Establish *developmentally appropriate* expectations
Memory problems, "on days and off days"	Learn the first time and remember from day to day	He/she doesn't care, is lazy, needs to try harder: *Angry*	Punish Ground Shame	Anxiety/Fear No confidence Eroded self-esteem	Recognize and allow for variability, prevent anxiety
Sensory issues: Overstimulated, overwhelmed, distractible	Pay attention, sit still, ignore distractions	He/she is not trying, undisciplined, off task, ADD: *Irritated, angry*	Punish More work Medicate No recess	Agitation Overactive Avoidance Anger / anxiety Tantrums	Evaluate the environment, adjust accordingly, provide breaks
Easily fatigued	Keep up, try harder	He/she is not trying, is lazy, work-avoidant, unmotivated: *Angry*	Punish More work	Anger Tantrums	Adjust work load Provide breaks and snacks
Impulsive, inability to predict outcomes, acts fast but thinks slowly	Think ahead, plan, set goals, rein in impulses	He/she is willful, disobedient, inappropriate, doesn't care: Angry	Punish	Avoidance Defiance	Prevent problems, build on strengths Use visual cues
Concrete thinker, learns by doing	Abstract, sit still, pay attention, listen and learn	He/she is lazy, unmotivated or it is due to poor parenting: *Frustrated*	More hours on homework No recess Therapy	Burnout Shut down Give up	Provide kinesthetic, experiential, relational options for learning
Rigid, perseverative, difficulty stopping or changing activities	Stop what you're doing when you're told, transition easily, don't resist	He/she is controlling, bossy, oppositional: *Angry*	Interrupt Assert control Require transitions	Resistance Anger Big Tantrums	Adjust workload to achieve closure Provide adequate time

Source: (Malbin, 2011). FASD, Fetal Alcohol Spectrum Disorder.

RESIDENTIAL SCHOOL SYNDROME

Residential schools are a major contributor to Aboriginal mental health issues, even now, years after the last one was closed in 1996. This is because many Aboriginal adults who attended the schools are still alive. They experienced either abuse or simply the trauma of being removed from their families at a young age and sent into an alien and sterile environment. Their experiences often shape their ability to function personally and within their families.

The schools were much more common than is generally recognized. There were 16 in British Columbia alone, while over 100 existed at one time or another across Canada. Most were administered by various religious denominations on behalf of the Canadian government. Approximately 60% were operated by the Roman Catholic Church, and 30% by the Anglican Church and various Protestant denominations. The remaining 10% were directly operated by the Canadian government.

Some schools were run humanely, while others, notoriously, were not. All constituted a sustained and determined attempt to acculturate the Canadian Aboriginal peoples through direct indoctrination of their most vulnerable members, their children. Even humanely run schools required children as young as 7 to be removed from their families and culture, leaving them without their emotional support at a critical stage in their development.

The most significant outcome of the residential schools process has been Residential School Syndrome. This is considered a variety of Post-Traumatic Stress Disorder (PTSD), but is considerably more profound than most varieties of PTSD, due to its impact on children and the significant cultural component involved. Survivors and their descendants experience a range of effects caused both by physical and sexual abuse and the emotional trauma of separation from family, community and culture.

Diagnostic Criteria for Residential School Syndrome

- The person has attended an Indian residential school or is closely involved with a person who has attended such a school.

- The school attendance was experienced as intrusive, alien and frightening.

- The person's response to the school attendance involved fear, helplessness, passivity and expressed or unexpressed anger.

  The effects of attendance at the Indian residential school persist following cessation of school attendance in one (or more) of the following ways:

- Recurrent and distressing recollections, including images, thoughts, perceptions or dreams of the Indian residential schools.

(continued)

Diagnostic Criteria for Residential School Syndrome   (continued)

▓ Acting or feeling as if the events of Indian residential school attendance were recurring (includes a sense of reliving the experience, illusions, hallucinations, and dissociative flashback episodes, including those that occur on awakening or those that occur when intoxicated).

▓ Intense psychological distress at exposure to internal or external cues that symbolize or resemble an aspect of Indian residential school attendance.

▓ Physiological reactivity on exposure to internal or external clues that symbolize or resemble an aspect of the Indian residential school attendance.

Persistent avoidance of stimuli associated with the Indian residential school and numbing of general responsiveness (not present before attendance) as indicated by three (or more) of the following:

— Efforts to avoid thoughts, feelings or conversations associated with the Indian residential schools.

— Efforts to avoid activities, places or people that arouse recollections of Indian residential school attendance.

— Inability to recall one or more important aspects of Indian residential school attendance.

— Markedly diminished interest or participation in significant cultural activities.

— Feelings of detachment or estrangement from others.

— Restricted range of affect (e.g., apparently high levels of interpersonal passivity).

Persistent symptoms of increased arousal (not present before Indian residential school attendance), as indicated by two (or more) of the following:

— Difficulty falling or staying asleep.

— Irritability or outbursts of anger, particularly when intoxicated with alcohol.

— Difficulty concentrating, particularly in a school setting.

— Hypervigilance, particularly with regard to non-First Nations social environments.

— Exaggerated startle response.

Symptoms may also include:

▓ Markedly deficient knowledge of own First Nations culture and traditional skills.

▓ Markedly deficient parenting skills, despite genuine fondness for offspring.

▓ A persistent tendency to abuse alcohol or sedative medications/drugs, often starting at a very young age.

(Brasfield (2001), pp. 80–81)

DEPRESSION

Clinically depressed individuals are often undiagnosed and simply considered "lazy" and unmotivated. Untreated, depression may lead to suicide, substance abuse, alcoholism, violence and high risk sexual activity. Depression has a strong tie to suicide in the Aboriginal population. Aboriginal individuals who commit suicide younger than 34 years old are more likely than non-Aboriginals to have grown-up in families with a history of alcohol abuse, suicide, and/or childhood sexual abuse or physical abuse. While medical treatment regimes may include antidepressants and other drug therapies, traditional healing techniques, including talking circles, sweat lodges and smudging have also had some success, particularly within the context of the traditional healing centres established to treat addictions and residential school syndrome.

VIOLENCE

Violence is both a significant manifestation of impaired mental health and a major cause of it, as the aftereffects of violence reverberate through families and communities. Within the family, violence is usually directed against children, women and the elderly. It is often alcohol and drug related. Some studies suggest 1 in 10 non-Aboriginal women are abused but 1 in 3 Aboriginal women are abused. Most Aboriginal women do not initially report abuse and often have been abused at least 10 times before coming forward. Convicted offenders are returned to their communities, which are often small and offer little opportunity to avoid a former partner. Many Aboriginal women feel little support from the Canadian justice system or from Aboriginal leaders.

The other form of serious, family violence in Aboriginal communities is child abuse. This may be emotional, spiritual, physical, sexual or a combination of all forms of abuse. Child abuse usually involves multiple abuses by multiple perpetrators, mostly by family members. It is often related to alcohol and drug abuse (i.e., it is committed while intoxicated). To address this, children can be removed to custody, but this is also problematic, as this too has involved abuse, especially historically. Eventually, children are often returned to abusive families, or may be removed but abusers still have access, particularly in small communities where removal may not create enough of a barrier between abusers and abused.

Violence outside the family tends to be between males and is associated with drug and alcohol use. Rates of assault are greater in the First Nations on-reserve population than other, off-reserve populations and firearms are the most common weapon used. Levels of assault are greater within the Aboriginal population than those involving non-Aboriginals, but this may simply reflect the more homogeneous populations on most reserves.

SUICIDE

Suicide accounts for up to a quarter of all injury deaths in First Nations people, but given that some suicides may be identified as accidents, numbers may be even higher. It can occur in clusters or as isolated cases. Hanging and firearms are the most common methods of suicide in Aboriginal males, while hanging and drug overdose are more common in Aboriginal females. Overall, as in the non-Aboriginal population, males are more likely to be successful and to choose more violent forms of suicide.

Beyond this there are both parallels and differences between Aboriginal and non-Aboriginal suicides. For reasons that are not clearly understood just over one third of the Aboriginal suicides occurred in the period between October and December, and almost half occurred on a Saturday or Sunday

---

Patterns of Aboriginal Versus Non-Aboriginal Suicide

TYPES OF SUICIDE

Aboriginal	Non-Aboriginal
Acute intoxication	Not intoxicated
Autumn weekends after midnight	No timing pattern
Home or relative's home	Home
Impulsive	Planned
Shooting/hanging	Shooting

STRESSORS

Aboriginal	Non-Aboriginal
Relationship problems	Mental illness
Depression	Relationship problems
Criminal behaviour	Physical illness
Physical illness	Employment problems
Employment problems	Physical illness
Alcohol abuse in family	Suicide in family
Suicide in family	
Child sexual/physical abuse in family	

between 2400 and 0600 hours. There is no similar seasonal or chronological pattern to suicide rates in the non-Aboriginal population. On the other hand, suicide in the Aboriginal population, like suicide in the non-Aboriginal population, tends to occur in a familiar place, usually the home. Both Aboriginal and non-Aboriginal suicides tend to occur in families with a history of suicide, but Aboriginal suicides also tend to occur against a background of alcohol, criminal behaviour, and/or sexual or physical abuse. Most non-Aboriginal suicides are planned, whereas Aboriginal suicides are impulsive acts, often committed while intoxicated.

Aboriginal communities with low suicide rates rely on strong traditions and customs, religious ceremonies and traditional healing methods to provide youth with a feeling of security and a sense of belonging. Strong, culturally, socially and economically secure children seldom commit suicide.

Aboriginal Suicide in British Columbia

Complete statistics have been compiled for Aboriginal and non-Aboriginal suicides in British Columbia and reflect the special circumstances of suicide rates, both there and in the Aboriginal population across Canada.

Overall, estimates of suicide in First Nations communities average three to five times the estimates for Canadian non-Aboriginal population's suicide rates. In British Columbia, Aboriginal males accounted for 79% of suicides between 1987 and 1993 and 41% of Status Indian male suicides were under 25 years of age, compared with only 16% in the general population. Status Indian female suicide rates were over three times higher than the average for all British Columbian females and numbers of suicides also peaked in the under 25 years of age group, but above this age group suicide rates for Aboriginal women gradually decreased.

As significantly, the on-reserve suicide rate in British Columbia was 37 per 100,000, while the off-reserve rate was only 16 per 100,000. Suicide rates also showed distinct geographic patterns, with rates highest in central British Columbia and lower in the northwest and southwest. However, Aboriginal suicide rates in major urban centers (Vancouver, Victoria, Prince George, etc.) were comparable to the general provincial population in urban areas.

On average, people in British Columbia, Aboriginal and non-Aboriginal, living in areas with high suicide rates had the following issues with the determinants of health:

- Had lower levels of education
- Lived in households with a large number of occupants
- Had more children living at home
- Included more single parents and fewer elders
- Had lower incomes, generated by a smaller proportion of the population

The Aboriginal suicide rate in British Columbia reflects these trends. High Aboriginal suicide rates occurred in the reserve population profile when at least four of the following occurred:

- Average of more than 4.3 persons per dwelling
- More than 10% of households have six or more occupants
- Average of more than two children at home per family
- Less than 25% of families have no children at home
- More than 20% of families headed by a single parent
- More than 30% of the population aged 15, with highest education being grade 9 or less
- Less than 8% of population are aged 65
- Aboriginals represent more than 5% of the population in the surrounding off-reserve area as well

Reserves that share these characteristics are concentrated in central British Columbia, whereas the northwest and southwest Aboriginal populations have historically better employment rates, higher incomes and thus overall better determinants of health. This is a major reason why their suicide rates are significantly lower.

Causes of Aboriginal Suicide

Aboriginal suicide rates have a variety of underlying causes, rooted in the determinants of health. Treating these systematic issues for population health is difficult, and requires both strong community will and considerable support from beyond the community. However, suicide rates can be reduced through counselling and mental health services, thus helping to break the chain of despair that leads to more suicides.

The problem is that suicide rates can vary widely from one First Nations community to another and the impact of suicide outbreaks can be devastating on others in the community, thus encouraging more suicides, leading to suicide clusters. Public reaction to high Aboriginal suicide rates also tends to be fragmentary and shortsighted. As the case of the Innu of Davis Inlet demonstrates, resources tend to go to communities best able to command attention. They are not allocated based on more valid measures of need nor are they applied equitably.

Crisis interventions do not appear to be driven by community mental health needs, but by perceived emergencies. Part of the problem is that there is no national mandate for Aboriginal mental health. Policy is complicated by federal/provincial and federal/territorial jurisdictional issues, the lack of a coordinated national plan, the lack of strategies for identifying problems at an early stage and the lack of support and remuneration for appropriate mental health services. Basically, it is hard to find some level of government willing to take overall responsibility for mental health, because responsibility entails being willing to pay the bills. While it is true that, as the Royal Commission on Aboriginal Peoples (RCAP) noted: "Any program which improves the community and helps the people who live in it feel worthwhile, will serve as a suicide prevention program" (RCAP, 1995, p. 64). The problem is that altogether too many programs do not do so.

CASE STUDY: INNU OF DAVIS INLET

The Mushuau Innu, a boreal First Nations people, live in Davis Inlet on the coast of Labrador. They are usual among Canada's boreal First Nations in never having signed treaties surrendering their traditional lands, something that is partly an artefact of Newfoundland's late entrance into the Confederation in 1948 and partly due to lack of interest in the region for settlement and development until recently.

The Innu were moved from their original community on Davis Inlet in 1967 to the eastern side of the island of Iluikoyak, off the coast, in order to allow the government to provide services more efficiently. Unfortunately, the new location is too remote from traditional hunting grounds for the Innu to continue hunting caribou. It was also located on basically solid rock and the government constructed houses that lacked both water and sewage systems. Overcrowding quickly became a problem, as did contamination of the water supply. Diseases such as tuberculosis became active in the community and the new market food diet from the stores proved unhealthy. The community became notorious for very high levels of addiction, suicide and violence. This came to national and international attention when, in 1993, a group of children were videotaped and featured on national television discussing suicide, while sniffing gasoline close to a bonfire, in an attempt to become high.

The community requested a fresh start at a new location. The federal government relocated them to a new townsite in Davis Inlet called Natuashish during the winter of 2002/2003. Construction of the new community and relocation of the Innu population cost an estimated $152 million.

The Mushuau Innu Band Council managed the delivery of the project through a professional project manager. Every contractor involved in the project included a component for Innu employment and training. This led to significant employment in the community. At the peak of construction some 70 to 80 Innu were employed along with the other 225 non-Innu workers. Innu workers learned and practised trades during construction that included labourer, heavy equipment operator, housekeeper, carpenter, electrician, mechanic and masoner. When completed, the new community had 175 houses, sewage and water systems, streets and service roads, a wharf and an airstrip. Community buildings included a school, the band council office, fire hall, police station, community garage and nursing station. The community is also constructing a store, hotel and recreation centre.

However, the new community, although an improvement on the old one, did not solve the underlying causes of Innu addictions, suicide and other mental health problems. While the population has a better place to live, unemployment rates are still very high and access to education and health services are still problematic because even the new community is still remote. Perhaps most important, the Innu of Davis Inlet have lost much of their traditional lifestyle and culture. They no longer follow a seasonal round of subsistence activities, and it appears that there is little to take its place in their modern community.

ACCIDENTS AND INJURIES

Accidents and injuries are not obviously related to mental health in most people's minds. However, they comprise one of the leading causes of death and disability for Aboriginal populations across the country. More importantly, while many are indeed accidents, others are caused by underlying mental health issues, including depression and substance abuse, and may be either veiled suicides or reflect reckless behaviour that verges on suicidal, which often has the same outcome. It is also worth remembering that one of the disabilities associated with FASD is impaired coordination and impulse control. Although no definitive studies have been done, there is a strong potential for FASD to contribute to higher accident and injury rates in the Aboriginal population.

Unsurprisingly, given their role outside the home, rates of accidents and injuries are higher in men than in women. Accidents are the leading cause of death for First Nations people under the age of 45. The most common causes of accidents are motor vehicle accidents, drowning, accidental poisoning, accidental falls and fire. High accident rates make death by injury roughly twice as likely in the Aboriginal population as in the non-Aboriginal population. Consequences of accidents include: hospitalization, long-term disability, increased health care costs and the social, emotional, physical, spiritual costs to individuals, families and communities. Accidents are commonly caused by unsafe storage and misuse of firearms, drug and alcohol use, poverty and substandard housing (which raises the risk of fires and household accidents). Emotional and social causes of accidents, indicating the links to suicide rates, are reckless and potentially self-destructive behaviour caused in turn by cultural and material loss (of possessions, of identity), and adverse psycho-social and economic factors (family problems, anger, unemployment). All of these lead to less concern for self-preservation and suggest the links between high Aboriginal suicide rates and high accident rates.

INTERCONNECTIONS BETWEEN CAUSES

Mental illness is caused by many different factors, stemming directly from the determinants of health and also sometimes from factors that are difficult to localize. It can also have many different manifestations, ranging from substance abuse to violence, self-destructive behaviour and biological damage to children before birth. These causes and symptoms are related by their tendency to feed one another. Even communities with generally strong determinants of health can be torn apart by the damage mental illness can cause in the community and to future generations, causing a cycle of dysfunction that must be broken to generate both individual and community health.

WHY SHOULD NON-ABORIGINALS CARE?

Poor mental health can be identified in Aboriginal communities through high levels of substance abuse, frequent injuries and accidents, high rates of violence and suicides and the prevalence of FASD. Its impacts affect individuals, their families and their communities. However, it also affects the health care system, the penal system (as more mentally ill people are in prison than are in mental institutions) and society in general. Nor is this a problem that Canadian society can continue to ignore, as it has for so long. Chronic Aboriginal mental health issues affecting a large sector of the population are problems that reduce resources for Canadians and ultimately the quality of life everywhere in the country. Furthermore, the presence of untreated chronic mental illness in a distinct population within the country embarrasses Canada internationally.

CRITICAL THINKING EXERCISES

1. The two case studies that follow reflect the cultural basis of definitions of mental health and mental illness. Behaviours that seem to reflect mental instability when examined out of context are normal within their context.
   a. Consider the two Southern, non-Aboriginal individuals and their reactions. How does their behaviour reflect their cultural biases?
   b. How might the Inuit in each community regard these two non-Inuit individuals?

2. Divide the different symptoms of Residential School Syndrome into three categories: Dysfunctional, Functional and Marginal, depending on how well an individual could function normally in day to day life in non-Aboriginal society.
   a. How well would an individual who manifested only the Functional symptoms of Residential School Syndrome fit into non-Aboriginal Canadian society? How well do you think they would fit into Aboriginal society?
   b. How well would an individual who manifested the Marginal symptoms of Residential School Syndrome function in Aboriginal society?
   c. What do your answers to these questions say about the differences between Aboriginal and non-Aboriginal social relations? What are the implications for Aboriginal mental health services?

3. List ways you could improve mental health among the Innu of Davis Inlet. Would these be applicable to other Aboriginal communities? Would they be applicable to non-Aboriginal communities?

CASE STUDY ONE

A regular visitor from Southern Canada is walking through a small Inuit village one day. He sees a casual acquaintance, a local hunter, behaving in an uncharacteristic way. The Inuit man was moving swiftly and excitedly, gesturing broadly and obviously upset. On being asked what the problem was, he responded angrily, "I just can't get him to understand that I can't go to Church every week. He just won't understand it!"

The visitor asked the Inuit man who he was referring to. He answered. "God! I can't get God to understand that I can't go to Church every week!" The visitor thought that this was amusing and said that he himself often spoke to God. Jokingly, he asked, "Does God answer back?"

The Inuit man was surprised and responded. "Of course He does. But I can't get Him to understand that I can't go to Church. He doesn't believe me!"

This response, with the implication that this Inuit man believed he could conduct a two-way conversation with God, severely disturbed the visitor, who thought that it represented a mental illness. However, the Inuit traditionally do believe that they can both speak to and be spoken to by spirits. This belief has sometimes been transferred to the present day, leading Inuit to conduct conversations with God. Although irrational by non-Aboriginal standards, it does not represent mental illness, because it is normal within its cultural context.

CASE STUDY TWO

A new resident from a city in Southern Canada was walking through the village in the Arctic he had recently moved to for the summer. He moved at the pace he was used to, in order to maximize his cardiovascular workout. One of the Aboriginal residents stopped him and asked him what was wrong. The Southerner was surprised, for he was just out to get some exercise, and explained that there was nothing wrong.

He was told that people were worried about him. His behaviour was considered strange and indicated a disregard for his personal safety. No one in the village walked quickly or ran, as he did, unless there was an emergency. The natural hazards of hunting and fishing, far from assistance and health care, meant that everyone in the village learned at an early age to move carefully and watch for potential danger.

Discussion Questions

1. What are the causes of the primary characteristics associated with FASD?

2. How do these cause the secondary behaviours associated with FASD?

3. What is the most common drinking pattern in the Aboriginal population: sustained heavy drinking or binge drinking?

4. How do Aboriginal suicide patterns differ from non-Aboriginal suicide patterns?

5. When do Aboriginal suicide victims tend to attempt suicide? Why do you think this might be so?

6. What is the major cause of Aboriginal mental health issues?

7. Who are the most common victims of violence within the Aboriginal community?

8. What is the most common preventable cause of death among Aboriginals?

9. Why were children removed from their families and sent to residential schools?

10. Why does the relocation of the Innu appear to have failed in its goal of reducing social issues and addictions in Davis Inlet?

REFERENCES AND FURTHER READING

American Psychological Association. (2013) *Diagnostic and statistical manual of mental disorders, fifth edition (DSM-5)*. Arlington, VA: American Psychological Association.

Brasfield, J. R. (2001). Residential School Syndrome. *BC Medical Journal, 43*(2), 80–81.

Browne, A. J., Smye, V. L., & Varcoe, C. (2005). The relevance of postcolonial theoretical perspectives to research in Aboriginal health. *CJNR (Canadian Journal of Nursing Research), 37*(4), 16–37.

Canadian Paediatric Society, First Nations and Inuit Health Committee. (2002) Position statement: Fetal Alcohol Syndrome. *Paediatrics & Child Health. 7*(3) 161–174.

Kirmayer, L. J., Brass, G. M. & Tait, C. L. (2000). The mental health of Aboriginal peoples: transformations of identity and community. *The Canadian Journal of Psychiatry/La Revue canadienne de psychiatrie,* 607–616.

McCormick, R. M. (2007). Aboriginal traditions in the treatment of substance abuse. *Canadian Journal of Counselling and Psychotherapy/Revue canadienne de counseling et de psychothérapie, 34*(1), 25–32.

MacMillan, H. L., MacMillan, A. B., Offord, D. R. & Dingle, J. L. (1996). Aboriginal health. *CMAJ: Canadian Medical Association Journal, 155*(11), 1569.

Malbin, D. (2011). *Fetal alcohol/neurobehavioral conditions: Understanding and application of a brain-based approach – A collection of information for parents and professionals* (3rd ed.). Portland. OR: Fetal Alcohol Syndrome Consultation, Education and Training Services, Inc. www.fascets.org

Mussell, B., Cardiff, K., & White, J. (2004). *The mental health and well-being of Aboriginal children and youth: Guidance for new approaches and services.* Chilliwack, BC: Sal'i'shan Institute.

Provincial Outreach Program For Fetal Alcohol Spectrum Disorder. (2012). *LEIC planning tool.* Prince George, BC: POPFASD.

Tookenay, V. F. (1996). Improving the health status of Aboriginal people in Canada: new directions, new responsibilities. *CMAJ: Canadian Medical Association Journal, 155*(11), 1581.

Waldram, J. B. (2004). *Revenge of the Windigo: The construction of the mind and mental health of North American Aboriginal peoples.* Toronto, ON: University of Toronto Press.

Wemigwans, J., & Cunningham, M. (2005). *FASD tool kit for Aboriginal families.* Toronto: Ontario Federation of Indian Friendship Centres.

Useful Websites

British Columbia Ministry of Health, Aboriginal Youth Suicide Fact Sheet: www.health. gov.bc.ca/mhd/pdf/fact_sheets/ab_youth_suicide.pdf

CBC Digital Archives: Davis Inlet: *'I'll never stop sniffing gas'.* www.cbc.ca/archives/categories/society/poverty/davis-inlet-innu-community-in-crisis/ill-never-stop-sniffing-gas.html

Provincial Forum on First Nations Youth Suicide "Courage, Strength and Identity", February 21–23, 2007: http://www.fnhc.ca/index.php/initiatives/mental_wellness/

Provincial Outreach Program For Fetal Alcohol Spectrum Disorder: www.fasdoutreach.ca

Hybridization of Health Care and the Way Forward for Aboriginal Health

Chapter Objectives

- To summarize the issues regarding Aboriginal health.
- To indicate how epistemological accommodation can create a secure space for both professionals and Aboriginals within the health care system.
- Using a case-study-based approach to offer a sense of what a hybrid health care system would look like.

Key Concepts

Epistemology
Epistemological
  Accommodation
World View
Ways of Knowing

Hybrid Health
Code of Ethics
Traditional Healing
Hybrid

Key Terms

Biomedicine
Cultural Competency
Cultural Safety
Professional Standards

Religious Belief
Resistance
Compromise

THE HYBRIDIZATION OF HEALTH CARE

Epistemological accommodation is what we are engaging in when we practise cultural safety. We create an environment that is culturally "safe" for the patient, but do so without compromising our own code of practice or ethics. Ultimately this process will create a hybrid health care system in which the techniques, technology and ethics of biomedicine are integrated with the holistic epistemology of health that exists within the Aboriginal world view and is implicit in the naturalistic physical planetary model of the Gaia Theory. This will lead to a healthier, more involved, more empowered Aboriginal population.

Nurses have an important role to play in the health care system; they act as the interface between biomedicine and the population which, Aboriginal or not, does not necessarily share the values and world-view of biomedicine. Nurses must provide an environment in which patients can feel both physically and culturally safe in receiving health care and become involved in providing feedback on the effectiveness and safety of their care. In doing so nurses will participate in building a better health care system and a healthier populace, both Aboriginal and non-Aboriginal.

Describing such a hybrid health care system is a challenge, because it has not been built yet. However, by combining theory and case studies with an example of a hybrid system, some sense of the way forward can be discerned.

MAKING NATIVE SPACE WITHOUT ELIMINATING PROFESSIONAL SPACE

Better health for Aboriginal people means making space for their ways of knowing and thinking about health, but it is important to do so intelligently, as not everyone is the same. Some Aboriginal individuals may be very traditional, others not at all. This also applies to members of cultural groups and visible minorities throughout the population.

However, everyone deserves respect for his or her way of knowing and thinking about health, including the health care professional. While it is important to "make space" for Aboriginal beliefs, it is also important to keep a space for professional practice. For nurses, as for other professionals, culturally safe care does **not** mean engaging in practices that contravene the professional code of ethics. Epistemological accommodation means accommodating others' practices, not giving up one's own.

The diagram of Aboriginal health in Figure 10.1 indicates the two ways of knowing about the world. Nursing epistemology draws on biomedicine, but it also draws on the tradition of caring about both patients and about the population at large, that has been central to the profession since Nightingale founded it in the 19th century (Nightingale, 1992).

INUULITSIVIK MATERNITIES

The Inuulitsivik Maternities, which was briefly surveyed earlier, is worth a closer look in this context. The Maternities in many ways stand as testament to the

Figure 10.1 *Diagram of a Hybrid System*

Source: V. K. Douglas.

possibility of creating a hybrid health care system that is founded on the principle of epistemological accommodation. They were created in 1986 when the Inuit community of Puvurnituq refused an obstetric ward in their new hospital in favour of a birthing centre. The community was determined to assert control over childbirth and to end the policy of evacuating women to Southern hospitals for birth, something that had been medical policy for at least a decade before (Douglas, 2006).

Puvurnituq, located in Arctic Québec, was a community with a long tradition of political activism in housing, land claims and health. When a new hospital was planned for the community in the late 1980s the government planned to install an obstetric ward. The women in the community refused and demanded a birthing centre within the hospital that would incorporate community (Inuit) midwives and Southern midwives and be community directed.

This last feature is reflected in the communal decision-making process. High-risk pregnancies are still evacuated to Southern hospitals, but the decision to evacuate is made by a community board, with representation from the Inuit midwives, Southern midwives, community members and medical staff. The board's decision is final and attempts by physicians in the hospital to overrule the board and order evacuations have led to official reprimands. Evacuation is decided on only if the health risk to the mother is felt to outweigh the risk to the family and community from having her absent for a considerable length of time.

The first birthing centre was very successful and led the other communities in the region to request that branches open in their own health centres. The Inuulitsivik Maternities now has three branches and there are proposals to expand further by replacing the obstetric ward in the regional capital, Kujjuaq, with a birthing centre. This growth has been driven by several converging factors. First, it is very popular with the Inuit. They prefer to give birth in their communities, where the mother can oversee her existing family and be overseen herself by members of the community. Then, too, the Inuit midwives at the

Maternities provide complete prenatal and postnatal care, ensuring that women and their children receive seamless support throughout and not just the primary care that evacuation provided. Finally, although the communal risk evaluation method may be unorthodox from the medical perspective, it has been very successful. Outcomes are comparable to any Southern hospital, rates of complications (especially caesarian sections) are much lower than the national average, and the costsaving to the health care system from reduced evacuations is substantial. All of these aspects are important as the Inuit are well aware of the benefits of

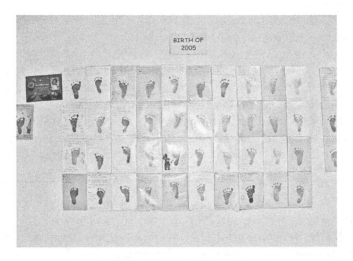

Outcomes at the Maternities

The record of 2005 births at the Inuulitsivik Maternities.
Source: V. K. Douglas.

Reviewing Cases at the Maternities

Inuit and Southern midwives reviewing impending births at the Inuulitsivik Maternities.
Source: V. K. Douglas.

Case Study 1

A young Aboriginal woman is shown into an examining room. The attending physician enters and immediately suggests that a "medicine man" or an elder attend to provide traditional health care.

Is this good practice?

No, it is not.

The young woman becomes extremely angry and informs the physician that she is a doctoral student and that her health has nothing to do with shamans or medicine men. She accuses the physician of patronizing and stereotyping her.

What did the physician do wrong? Why?

The physician provided care according to the principles of cultural competency. Upon seeing a person of Aboriginal ancestry the physician immediately offered to provide culturally relevant care. However, a culturally safe approach would have required the physician to make some general enquiries first—to determine if the patient was interested in culturally specific care, and if so to what degree.

---

modern medical care and also of its potential costs. They want effective health care, economically delivered, but they want it to be integrated into their own epistemology of health. The Inuulitsivik Maternities has done this in the field of childbirth (Douglas, 2007).

PROFESSIONAL DEVELOPMENT FOR HEALTH CARE PERSONNEL

Most health care professionals, nurses included, are not educated in culturally safe care. For a nurse who has received this training, the workplace is a site for further professional development and education of colleagues who may not be aware of the opportunities and limitations of culturally safe care.

CULTURAL SENSITIVITY, EPISTEMOLOGICAL ACCOMMODATION AND ABORIGINAL HEALTH

Nurses are expected to maintain the standards of their profession, but must also consider the feelings and worldviews (epistemology) of both their colleagues and patients. Cultural sensitivity provides the basic tool to maintain awareness of others' differences and the social and cultural background that informs them. Some health care professionals may themselves come from Aboriginal or other non-Western backgrounds, and may experience first hand issues of cultural safety in the health care environment. Other professionals may find that working in an Aboriginal community as a community health nurse leaves them with their own cultural safety issues. They may feel under pressure to allow their cultural sensitivity to impinge upon their professional standards. Ultimately, this will not only compromise their professional identity, it can also lead to unsafe practice, something that Aboriginal patients and communities are as eager to avoid as nurses and other professionals.

THE LIMITS OF ACCOMODATION—FROM BOTH SIDES

This leads to the recognition that there are limits to epistemological accommodation on both sides. Just as Aboriginal patients should never be required to compromise their identity to receive quality health care, nurses should never compromise their professional standards to provide culturally safe care. Professional standards are the bedrock on which the quality of health care rests and culturally safe care should NEVER breach professional standards. On the other hand, professional standards are no excuse for engaging in insensitive, emotionally

---

Case Study 2

An immigrant family from the Horn of Africa approaches a physician practising in Toronto. Their cultural practices include female circumcision and infibulation (sewing up most of the vaginal opening until marriage—also known as Pharaonic circumcision) upon their daughter reaching menarche. They ask the physician to perform the surgery on the grounds that it is a culturally normal and required act. Their daughter will not be a respected member of their community unless she has the surgery.

Should the physician agree?

Female genital mutilation is a common cultural practice among certain ethnic groups in Northern Africa, but female genital mutilation falls under Criminal Code Sections 267 (assault causing bodily harm) and 268 (aggravated assault, including wounding, maiming, disfiguring). It is illegal to perform female genital mutilation in Canada or anywhere in the world on a Canadian citizen.

A physician performing the surgery would be charged and imprisoned. Anyone else who assisted or was aware of the surgery beforehand and did not report it would likely also face criminal charges. The parents would also face criminal charges. It is the physician's responsibility and that of any other health care professional who becomes aware of it both to refuse to perform this surgery, and to report it to the authorities.

damaging behaviour either. Epistemological accommodation lies in the middle-ground between these two extremes. Even where explicit rules forbid action to comply with a patient's request for culturally safe care, the nurse can engage in advocacy to support the patient, and by extension future patients, in achieving their goals within the framework of the health care system, whether the patients are Aboriginal or not.

RECONCILING ABORIGINAL STANDARDS
WITH PROFESSIONAL STANDARDS

It is possible to reconcile Aboriginal traditions with professional standards, but this requires tact and willingness to compromise by both groups. In Saskatchewan, due to the initiative of a junior RN, All Nations Healing Hospital installed a smudging room for Aboriginal families to conduct traditional ceremonies. A room was selected and renovated to meet all fire and public health codes, and as such it satisfies professional standards and also allows Aboriginal patients to participate in traditional healing practices.

MAINTAINING QUALITY OF CARE

Just like other patients, Aboriginal patients want high quality health care and have the right to expect it. The problem for health care professionals is recognizing that Aboriginal definitions of health may or may not exactly match their own. For instance, in most hospitals in Canada resuscitation is automatically practised on any terminal patient until death intervenes, and is considered a basic part of the role of the health care system. Many professionals consider it part of their ethical duty to sustain life. However, some families and individuals may oppose full code resuscitation on cultural grounds (to permit a "good death"). They may wish care to be exactly the same quality as other patients, but only up to a point. It is the responsibility of the health care team, and especially of the nurses who often act as the interface among patients, patient's families and the health care system, to find a compromise that satisfies everyone's ethical and cultural needs, both professional and patient.

RECOGNIZING THAT ABORIGINAL PRIORITIES INCLUDE GOOD HEALTH

Another problem is that Aboriginal priorities in the health care system may seem to clash with those of professionals. Professional ethics focus on the individual patient, but Aboriginal health practices may be focused on families and communities. Pregnant women in remote Aboriginal communities may risk miscarriage rather than accept evacuation for birth. This seems to deliberately neglect the health of both the mother and the fetus according to professional ethics.

However, most Aboriginal women have existing families to raise and protect. Extended evacuation for birth may leave older children without proper care, and the mother's responsibility is to the health of the entire family. The unborn baby, and even her own health, may be secondary to existing children in the mother's calculation of risks and benefits.

Balancing risks such as these lies at the heart of Aboriginal epistemology of health, but has become alien to the modern health care system. Health care professionals have to realize that other ways of measuring health are as valid as those used in biomedical riskscoring. Aboriginal people may have as acute a concern for health as their nurses or doctors, but their definition of health may extend far beyond the walls of the hospital or clinic.

YUKON HOSPITAL FIRST NATIONS HEALTH PROGRAM

The Whitehorse General Hospital created the First Nations Health Program when control over health care was devolved to the Territory in 1992. The program offers inpatient services at the Hospital, as well as follow-up care in the community for patients who require it. An Elders Working Group developed the program during a series of consultations held between 1995 and 1998. The Program's purpose was to advocate for Aboriginal people at Whitehorse General Hospital to ensure quality and culturally sensitive holistic health care. The Elders were involved in all aspects of the development of the program and services, from designing the healing room and gathering traditional medicines, to developing operating policies and job descriptions.

The First Nations Health Program at the Whitehorse General Hospital offers seven programs, including a traditional medicine program. Patients can choose to receive the services of a traditional healer, including traditional medicines. The traditional medicine program coordinator consults with physicians on traditional medicines and practices to be used, and the program is increasingly accepted by the health care professionals at the hospital.

> The medicine people would deal with all parts of a person: emotional, spiritual, mental and physical. This is what a traditional medicine person would deal with. Families still use traditional medicines.
> (Clara Schinkel, First Nations Health Program, Whitehorse General Hospital. Pamphlet, n.d.)

Patients may also access a healing room, which was opened in 1999, for ceremonies, funerals, talking circles, preparation of medicines, or for some quiet time with family. Other services include staff to provide support for Aboriginal children staying at the hospital, a community liaison planner, an internship program in Aboriginal dietetics and a selection of items from a traditional food menu offered through the hospital cafeteria.

It is important to note that this program is integrated into the hospital. Aboriginal patients who elect to receive its services (they are not mandatory) receive biomedical care as well. The two services work in parallel to offer superior care to Aboriginal patients by offering them the best of both worlds, rather than leaving them stranded between them, as has often been the case in the past.

LESSONS FROM OTHER EPISTEMOLOGICAL ENCOUNTERS

Religion and Health Care

Epistemological accommodation is already thriving within health care and has been doing so for centuries, without anyone noticing—in the form of religion. There is a long tradition of religious involvement in health care. Originally nurses in Canada were members of Christian nursing orders (both Catholic and Anglican) and some hospitals were founded by religious nursing orders (e.g., St. Paul's Hospital in Vancouver or the Grey Nuns Hospital in Edmonton). Some hospitals continue to be church administered. For instance, Wrinch Memorial Hospital in New Hazelton, British Columbia, is operated by the United Church of Canada.

As this suggests, nurses seldom think about the accommodations made for patients with strong religious beliefs. Only when they directly conflict with biomedical codes, such as refusal to accept a blood transfusion on religious grounds, do such patients become noticeable. Then ethical, moral and legal questions begin to rise. Some of them have simple answers, as in the case study. Some actions are not acceptable under Canadian law. Others lie in a grey area, and must be handled carefully.

Case Study 3

A young Aboriginal woman has just given birth and she asks the nurse attending her to give her the placenta, so she can bury it in a traditional ceremony. The hospital has no policy permitting this or explicitly forbidding it.

What should the nurse do? Why?

The nurse should decline. In most jurisdictions, placentas are normally disposed of according to hospital public health guidelines as biohazards. Hospitals may change these policies, but individuals cannot unilaterally do so. The consequences could include loss of licence and possibly criminal charges for endangering public health.

What CAN the nurse do?

The nurse SHOULD encourage the mother and family to petition the hospital to change the policy and could facilitate this. It would also be appropriate to express sympathy and explain why the patient's request could not be accommodated.

There are religious accommodations made to practise in a religious context—such as a church-run hospital—or in the presence of a hospital chaplain. These are already ingrained in the Western cultural matrix, as is the understanding that not all people are religious—some want a chaplain's services, some do not. Few would force religious services on a patient who didn't want them, nor would many withhold them from a patient who did. Aboriginal patients deserve the same accommodations.

Cultural Accommodation

The cultural and epistemological accommodation to religion is largely automatic. Most health care professionals have internalized this to the point where it does not matter what the specific religious beliefs are—they accommodate them—as long as they do not breach professional practice. Acquiring similarly culturally safe practices for the Aboriginal population is more a matter of finding ways to accommodate to new beliefs, and overcoming professional resistance to new practices and new ways of knowing.

OVERCOMING RESISTANCE

This is the greatest obstacle to developing a culturally safe practice. Biomedical ethics assume a mechanistic, biologically based health care system in which the body of the patient is a machine to be repaired. Recognizing that some people, Aboriginal and non-Aboriginal, do not look at health this way is often difficult for professionals, including nurses, to accept. This is complicated by the need to consider the geographic and socioeconomic context of the patient encounter. A patient from a remote community may not find advice for secondary treatment helpful, because the treatment may not be available in the community, and may

---

Case Study 4

A middle-aged, full-time employed Aboriginal man approached a physician at the health clinic in a Northern community. He had taken part in a workshop on residential school experiences that was broadcast live over community radio that day. He had felt impelled to speak about his own experiences, which included being raped by one of his teachers as a child. Upon realizing that his private pain was now public in the community, he asked the physician for a note excusing him from work for a time. The physician refused as there was nothing medically wrong with the patient and the trauma in question had happened long ago.

(*continued*)

Case Study 4   (continued)

The nurse on duty noticed the patient leaving the examining room in great distress and she asked him what had occurred and, upon learning of the situation, intervened. After a conversation with the physician, he did sign the form but commented that it was unjustified, as the patient "had been paid" for his revelations already, through an honorarium provided by the workshop organizers.

What was the issue?

The patient in question lived in a relatively small community. Whatever impulse led him to make his revelation, once made it became community knowledge. Thus, all his friends, his coworkers, and family were aware of an incident that he considered as deeply shameful. He needed the time to come to terms with this, something that the nurse recognized and which the other health care professional did not.

Case Study 5

A young Inuit woman in a community in Nunavut sought care for her young son, injured in a physical accident, by bringing him to the local community health centre. The nurse on duty recognized the signs of domestic abuse (black eyes and damaged mouth). The young woman confirmed that the injuries were indeed due to domestic abuse. The nurse then forcefully told the woman that she could not properly care for her son unless she left her domestic situation.

Was this the right thing to do?

No it was NOT. Why?

This was the wrong thing to do on several levels: First, the patient was the child, NOT the mother. The nurse's focus should have been on the injured child, not her mother. Second, the approach used placed a strong burden of guilt on the mother, without the circumstances of the abuse being properly examined or understood. This placed enormous psychological pressure on the Inuit mother, in a culture that places great emphasis on care of and affection for children. Finally, where was the mother to go? This is a small Arctic community where everyone is related to everyone else. There is no battered woman's shelter for hundreds of miles and leaving the home (in winter? in extreme weather?) is seldom an option.

While the abuse was undoubtedly a health concern, the approach was inappropriate. It had the effect of discouraging the woman in question from seeking future care, both for herself and her children and counselling for her spouse.

require frequent travel to get it, which may not be possible. Similarly, diabetic patients with limited economic means may not have the option of changing their diet to one high in vegetables and fibre, especially if their communities have very high food costs. Their economic priorities may also lie with their family, rather than with their own personal well-being. These physical, emotional and spiritual factors need to be considered and the patient's medical treatment needs balanced against them.

BUILDING A HYBRID HEALTH CARE SYSTEM

The precediing case studies illustrated some of the pitfalls in providing culturally safe care. As nurses we have a responsibility to provide appropriate care for all our patients, but we must still retain our professional standards, the core of our profession, and safeguard our own identity as nurses.

The solution is to build a health care system that recognizes that effective health care is a hybrid of the patient's beliefs and values, and those of nursing itself. That means both recognizing different ways of knowing and respecting them. Nursing practice must interact with these ways of knowing, Aboriginal and otherwise, without losing its own integrity.

There is no set formula for doing this. To do so means approaching each patient as an individual human being and in turn respecting individual beliefs and values, but also never losing sight of the nurse's own. This will make nursing culturally safe. It will also make better nurses.

CRITICAL THINKING EXERCISES

Think about what a hybrid health care system would look like from your perspective as a nurse, using the case studies in this chapter to determine what would and would not work.

1. What would be your role as a nurse?
2. What would be the limits of your practice?
3. How would your behaviour with patients reflect culturally safe practice?
4. What does this system look like from an Aboriginal perspective?
5. How would Aboriginal patients interact with the nursing staff, with other health care professionals?

Discussion Questions

1. How do locally produced and culturally appropriate health knowledge systems contribute to equity in health?

2. How can nurses mediate between Aboriginal patients and the health care system?

3. What role does religion play in modern health care?

4. What is unusual about the Inuulitsivik Maternities' risk-calculation model?

5. Why has this model proved to be successful?

6. How does the First Nations Health Program at the Whitehorse General Hospital contribute to building a hybrid health care system?

7. How does cultural safety contribute to a hybrid health care system?

8. What would a hybrid health care system look like? What could nurses' roles be in it?

REFERENCES AND FURTHER READING

Douglas, V. K. (2006). Childbirth among the Canadian Inuit: a review of the clinical and cultural literature. *International Journal of Circumpolar Health*, *65*(2), 117–32.

Douglas, V. K. (2007). Converging epistemologies: critical issues in Canadian Inuit childbirth and pregnancy. *Alaska Medicine*, *49*(Supp. 2), 209–14.

Latour, B. (1992). *We have never been modern*. Cambridge: Harvard University Press.

Nightingale, F. (1992). *Notes on Nursing: What it is and what it is not*. Philadelphia, PA: Lippincott, Williams and Wilkins. (Reprint with introduction and contributions).

Useful Websites

Aboriginal Nurses Association of Canada: www.anac.on.ca/

First Nations Health Program at the Whitehorse General Hospital: http://yukonhospitals.ca/firstnationhealthprogram/

Nunavik Regional Board of Health and Social Services (Inuulitsivik Maternities): www.rrsss17.gouv.qc.ca/index.php?option=com_content&view=article&id=74&Itemid=91&lang=en

Society of Obstetricians and Gynaecologists of Canada, Aboriginal Clinical Practice Guidelines (8 reports, one in Inuktitut): www.sogc.org/guidelines/index_e.asp#ICM

Index

Note: Page numbers followed by *"f"* and *"t"* refer to figures and tables in that page.

CPSIA information can be obtained
at www.ICGtesting.com
Printed in the USA
LVHW061300120619
620989LV00007B/186/P